AF487195

JOAN DEMAKIS

GAZING at my FEET

How I fell in love with Greece

For my grandparents,
Euthymios Demakes and Yannoula Koutsogeorgi
Demakes, and Gregory Jenis and Fotini (Fannie)
Kakkava Jenis.
You left behind your families and the world that you knew,
impoverished as it was, to set out for the unknown.
You risked everything to build a better life and a more
hopeful future for your children.
For the courage that you had and the sacrifices
that you made, thank you.

For magnificent and beautiful Greece and for the
exuberant and irrepressible Greeks.
You welcomed me with open arms and embraced me.
I adopted you and you adopted me.
I am proud to be "one of yours".
Thank you.

For the United States of America and for the values that
you instilled in me.
Thank you for always saying "Welcome home, Ma'am"
as I go through passport control whenever I make a trip
back to the States.

*"There's basically an element of fiction
in everything you remember."*

Isabel Allende

CONTENTS

Introduction

On November 24, 1972, the Friday after Thanksgiving, my husband, Elias, and I flew to Paris. This would be the beginning of our life in Greece, together. In Paris, we picked up a car that we had ordered and then drove through Europe, arriving in Athens on the day after Christmas.

We arrived late in the day and, because I was much too tired to absorb anything else for the remainder of the day, I began my official assimilation on the next day into a culture that was thoroughly foreign to me. I had been under the impression that I would be able to take my Greek-American culture and transplant it into Greece. That did not happen.

What happened instead was a slow re-alignment of myself and my behavior and habits into the Greek culture. The re-alignment would take years with a number of reversals and setbacks, but with a greater number of steps, and sometimes even leaps, forward. I re-conditioned myself. I learned to live far away from my parents, brothers, family and friends. I gradually understood that Greece was not the United States and that this was okay. Finally, I acknowledged that I was not going back to the States to live and that Greece was now my home. That was the biggest step of all.

I learned to accept that wherever I was, whether it was in Athens, or in a village in the Peloponnese, or in Lynn, the suburb north of Boston where I was born and grew up, people would view me through their own prisms. I was, for a very long time, a curiosity to everyone.

In Greece, I dressed "like an American". In Lynn or Boston, people told me that I looked very European.

"My clothes are from Talbots", I would say.

The Greeks always made a point of commenting on my American accent and could not understand why I did not speak perfect Greek.

The Americans could not understand my eventual tolerance for Greek politics, calling me a Socialist or a Communist whenever I was in Lynn.

And, when they visited me in Greece and I cooked for them or we went out to eat, they always said, "This is not like my mother's or my grandmother's or like home."

The Greek women, on the other hand, wanted to know, in detail, how I cooked each Greek dish and where the recipe came from because their mothers, who were the *best* cooks, cooked every dish this way or that and why wasn't I cooking my dish the same way. And then I would remind them that I, too, had a mother who was the *best* cook and who had taught me how to cook and there the discussion would stop.

I was in the middle. What was I? Where did I want to be? And who did I want to be?

Re-alignment. Re-adjustment. Assimilation. These are big words and although they partially describe what I experienced, the actual process was more than assimilation or re-alignment. My experience was a journey, a long journey, one with that repetitive and unforgiving pattern of two steps forward and one step back.

It took time to appreciate the differences that I came across every day and to tolerate them. It took time to understand that the Greeks were expressing their affection for me and their interest in me whenever they commented on my dress or my cooking or even my poor Greek. These topics sometimes were the only ones where we could all have a discussion and still be on the same page. It took time to feel that this was home.

This is the story of my journey, one that continues even today, fifty years after Elias and I moved to Greece. That is approximately two thirds of my life. I know who I am now. I have assimilated into the Greek culture but have also maintained my ties to my family and friends in the United States.

I have re-aligned a lot of my behaviors. I certainly do not assume or compare anything anymore. I observe and I listen. But more than that, I am comfortable enough now to enjoy each and every day in this beautiful country.

- 1 -

Identity Crises

"It was as if you could have it both ways, identity and assimilation, without having to think about it very much."

Adrienne Rich[i]

When I was in the ninth grade in junior high school in Lynn, my Civics teacher, Mr. Ross, did an unexpected exercise in class. Mr. Ross began with the first student in the first row, asking a seemingly innocent and simple question.

"What nationality are you?"

"I'm Italian," the first student answered.

"And you?" Mr. Ross asked, pointing to the second student who answered, "I'm French".

---

[i] Adrienne Rich, Split at the Root. An Essay on Jewish Identity. Philip Lopate, *The Art of the Personal Essay, Anthology from the Classical Era to the Present,* New York, Anchor Books / Doubleday, 1994.

The third student said that he was Polish.

I was the fourth student. I waited nervously for Mr. Ross to point to me as I bit my nails and listened to the answers of the other students.

"I'm Greek", I said, predictably enough, given that I had been brought up believing that I was Greek, full stop.

Mr. Ross ended the questioning with me and made a profound announcement to all of us in the class. We were not Italian, French, Polish, Greek or anything else. We were all Americans.

This was my first identity crisis and I was only thirteen years old.

At first, we all replaced our statements of "I'm Greek (etc.)", with "I'm Greek-American (etc.)". We then progressed to "I'm of Greek descent (etc.)".

I haven't lived in the US for a very long time so I cannot say if that question is still asked or even if it is politically correct to ask it. I do know, personally, that the identity crisis syndrome has been hounding me ever since the ninth grade in Mr. Ross' class.

Since then, I have learned that the identity crisis syndrome has been around for a very long time and is common in people who leave their homeland to plant roots in another country. The intensity of the nostalgia that people feel depends on many factors, of course, but mostly on why they left and if they will ever go back home again. But generally, we all miss everything that we have grown up with such as the food and the customs, but most of all our families and friends.

The nostalgia syndrome manifests itself with a deep

emotional longing for the homeland and for everyone and everything we knew there. We also call this homesickness. No matter how amazing the new country is, or how wealthy, or how welcoming, the new country simply is not home yet. It takes time to assimilate into a new culture but, with the instant gratification tendencies that characterize the late 20th and early 21st centuries, we want the assimilation to happen quickly, preferably overnight.

And then, something else happens. Just a year or two later, people who have immigrated or moved to a new country have begun to adjust to the new environment so when they visit the homeland, even for just a short time, they experience nostalgia for their new home. And no one understands this, especially if they have not experienced the sensation themselves. It's absurd. It's surreal. But that's the way it is.

My father was one of eight siblings and my mother was one of four. They were both first-generation Greek-Americans born in the US. Actually, my father was born in Greece and came with his family to the US when he was six years old. But he was born as both a Greek citizen and an American citizen in Greece as was his younger brother, my Uncle Nick My grandparents, who had gone to the States years earlier, in the 1890s, married in Lynn and had their first three children there. Then they became nostalgic for Greece. Fortunately for all of us, my grandparents were foresighted enough to become naturalized American citizens before they went back to Greece.

My father was born a few months after the family arrived in Greece and then, two years later, my Uncle Nick was born. It was with Uncle Nick's birth that my grandfather grew nostalgic for the US (does this sound familiar?) and the whole family went back to the States, first my grandfather and then my grandmother with the five children. There, the family planted roots in Lynn where my grandparents had three more children, all girls. They did not go back to Greece again. I suspect that they never really had any desire to go to Greece again but I also suspect that, deep down inside, they missed their homeland. The siblings who had lived in Greece, on the other hand, always romanticized Greece and the formative years that they had spent there.

The only person who did not succumb to the homesickness very much was my grandmother, a down-to-earth and practical woman. She had gone to the States as a single young woman with her sisters and her brother to work and to earn money to buy her dowry. She had never wanted to go back to Greece in the first place and she was not very happy while she was there as a wife and mother. It was bitterly cold in the mountain village in the Peloponnese where my grandfather's family lived. She thought that the landscape had "too many rocks", and she was right. Every day, she would make the descent into the valley to tend the fields and then come up again to the village, a steep climb, at the end of the day. The only benefit that she had was that the village spring was right outside their house. She could get water easily and she didn't have to carry it far.

She and my grandfather, and everyone else who migrated from the Peloponnese to the US in the late 19th and early 20th centuries, left a country that was extremely impoverished. Their motives for seeking opportunity in another country were purely economic. Still, as my mother pointed out to me once, it must have been heart-wrenching to know that the probabilities of seeing their families again were minimal at best.

My grandmother, however, understood and recognized the opportunities that her children would have in the US. When she and my grandfather were preparing to go to Greece with their three young children (and my grandmother was heavily pregnant with my father, their fourth child), she called the Singer Sewing Machine Company to send a technician to help her pack her foot-treadle sewing machine. When the technician saw all the baggage and preparations and heard that the family was moving back to Greece, he said to her,

"Where are you going, Mrs. Demakes? What opportunities will your children have in Greece? They will be tending sheep and goats. Here, at least, they will have the chance to get a good education."

My grandmother never forgot that conversation.

I was born in 1945, just as World War II was ending. My parents decided to speak to me in Greek. All my older cousins had spoken Greek as toddlers and then had learned English when they went to school and became bilingual. Speaking to me in Greek just seemed so natural to my parents. Consequently, until I went to school, I spoke only Greek.

Before I went to school, we were living in a very small two-family home. The family living upstairs from us had a little boy, Joey. Joey was my age and was Jewish so, of course, he spoke no Greek. When we played together, my mother later told me, Joey would speak in English and I would speak in Greek, and yet we understood each other perfectly.

The language situation would change drastically when I started first grade. The College Board, the organization that designs and develops the college entrance examinations in the US, had done a study about children who grew up in bilingual families. The results said that children who grew up speaking both English and a second language did not learn English as well as children who grew up speaking only English.

This study was done just five years after the end of World War II, when immigration to the US had increased exponentially, and may or may not have been propaganda. Whatever it was, however, it impacted the United States in a way that no one could have imagined at the time. One of the dreams that all immigrants had then, and continue to have today, was to provide an outstanding college education for their children. The day that the College Board study was published, parents and grandparents everywhere in the US stopped speaking their native languages to their children and grandchildren. Since the goal was for the children to attend the best colleges and universities in the US and since, according to the College Board at least, being bilingual was an obstacle to admission into the best colleges, English only was spoken from that day on in families across the country. Overnight, one of the links that immigrant families had to their homelands was cut. It was only when immigration from Mexico and Central America increased significantly in the 60s that foreign families would again speak their native languages with their children.

At the time that the College Board published its conclusions, academics and educators were convinced that learning and speaking a second language interfered with a child's cognitive development. Today, however, the attitude about bilingual children has changed significantly. Newer studies show that bilingual children actually excel in many school subjects probably because they use and manage large vocabularies and they switch easily and quickly from one language to the other.

But the damage had already been done. And it was in this dichotomy that I and millions of other children and young adults grew up in America. We were foreigners and yet we were also American. Our parents wanted us to be American, but they also wanted us to be Greek (and here you can substitute any nationality for *Greek*). How could any one of us possibly not have an identity crisis?

My most vivid memories growing up were of belonging to two close-knit Greek families – loud, noisy, and fun; proud to be Greek and, at the same time, proud to be American (and this was before Mr. Ross' civics class exercise). My brothers and I had a total of twenty-two first cousins, seventeen in my father's family and five in my mother's family. Most of us were born in clusters and are all pretty close in age.

My father's family was especially loud, noisy, and fun and looked for any and every opportunity to celebrate an occasion. Whenever we gathered at my grandmother's house (my grandfather had passed away five years before I was born), the din could be heard a block away. But everyone had fun. The men, brothers and brothers-in-law, sat in the living room and talked politics and business. The women, sisters and sisters-in-law, gathered in the kitchen and cooked, served the men in the living room, washed the dishes and looked after the children. The children were everywhere.

We knew we were Greek. Even though some of us were no longer bilingual, our parents still were and they spoke Greek to our grandparents and to each other, especially when they didn't want us to understand what they were saying or when they thought that we didn't understand what they were saying. Maybe we didn't speak Greek but we heard it spoken often enough and understood most of it.

We went to Greek school in the afternoons, after we had left regular school. We went to the Greek church and later to Greek dances at the church. We ate Greek food. We listened to Greek music. Our friends were Greek, especially the friends of those cousins who lived in the part of the city that was close to the church; that neighborhood had many Greek immigrant families. The weddings and baptisms that we attended were Greek. We were brought up to accept that we would marry Greek. That was it. We were Greek. And it wasn't until we went away to college that we were able to put a little distance between ourselves and our Greekness, although the Greekness never really left us. And later in our lives, it enveloped us fully.

When I moved to Greece with my born-in-Greece husband, Elias, I was beset with strong bouts of nostalgia and I became melancholic. The first year was the worst. I missed my family and my friends. I missed hearing English spoken all the time. I missed the *New York Times* and rye bread. I missed picking up the phone and talking to anyone that I wanted to talk to, in English, and whenever I wanted to talk to them. The list was endless.

In addition to that, everything was so foreign in Greece! I wanted to superimpose the grid of my Greek-American upbringing onto the grid of what I was experiencing in Greece, but it was impossible. The grids didn't fit. Nothing in Greece that I was experiencing even closely resembled my experience of growing up Greek-American.

It was cold in Athens and we had no central heating, just a small space heater that we moved from room to room. My husband and I were living in my father-in-law's house with him and with my brother-in-law and his wife. Privacy was non-existent. Privacy, as I learned that first year, is not translated into Greek. Greeks cannot relate to the concept of privacy because there is no Greek word for it.

My Greek was completely inadequate for my new environment. I couldn't keep up with the staccato-pace Greek that was spoken all around me. Even some of the words were different because the language had evolved from the time that my grandparents and their children had left Greece and had returned to the States in 1914.

And to make matters worse, Elias and I had arrived in the middle of the Greek military dictatorship. This was new to me and I was nervous whenever I was out on my own. I was frightened of my own shadow. I was not used to keeping my opinions to myself but I had to learn not to express any opinions because they could get me into trouble.

I tried to compensate for the nostalgia by borrowing books from the library at the Hellenic-American Union. I found a part-time job with a study-abroad program for American students in Greece. These things distracted me but nothing really helped.

Then I became pregnant with our first son, Stefan. Because pregnancy was a new experience for me, all my attention was focused on the pregnancy which helped me to ignore the nostalgia, although I never really forgot it. It was always there, in the background. And when Stefan was born, the nostalgia came back, full-blast. I missed my mother who, in an ideal world, would have been by my side to help me with the baby. But there was no way that she would have left my father on his own in the States and come to Greece for a month or two to help me.

Elias, Stefan, and I went to the States the Christmas that Stefan was a year and a half old. Elias stayed for three weeks and I stayed for a week longer and returned to Greece with Stefan. The nostalgia overwhelmed me again when we landed in Greece and, this time, I could see that it had affected Stefan, too, because he missed seeing my parents and being the center of attention. He was visibly sad and confused. And he was only nineteen months old.

The nostalgia, the homesickness and the identity crises dogged me for years. They were exacerbated by the questions that both Greeks and Americans asked: "Are you sorry that you moved to Greece? Or that you left the US?" "Do you feel more Greek or more American?" There were other questions also, but these questions and their multiple variations were dominant.

It would be years before I could fully embrace both identities without being apologetic for either one. It would be years before I could erase the line that I had drawn mentally between my American identity and my Greek identity and simply be. And it would be years before I would understand that I could accommodate a third identity, my Greek-American identity, and eventually, even a fourth identity, my European identity.

- 2 -

1968 – 1969: The Fates at Work

"When I said that you had to marry a Greek, I didn't mean a Greek from Greece. I meant a Greek-American".

My father

As I look back on the events as they unfolded in 1968 and 1969, I see now that this was when Fate's long-term plan for my life began to appear and solidify. This, of course, is in hindsight. I thought that these events were simply serial incidents, one unrelated incident happening after another, and that I could control or even cancel them. Apparently, I could do neither. And this was when the culture clashes began. Greek-American vs Greek. Greek vs Greek-American.

In March of 1968, I was still a kid, a twenty-two-year-old young woman, living at home with my parents and my brothers and teaching French at Lynn English High School, the same high school that I had graduated from six years earlier. I taught, went out with my friends, shopped a lot, had fun, and went to Greek dances at the church. In short, I was a good Greek-American girl of the 60s, the kind of girl that mothers wanted their sons to marry.

I was also a member of the Helicon Society, an association for Greeks and Greek-Americans who were college graduates. The Helicon Society was a place where young, and not-so-young, single people could meet each other, although it was not only for single people. The Society had monthly meetings during which there would be a lecture or a presentation, a reason for having the meeting. And once a year, there was a formal ball. I was the recording secretary of the association; the president, Michael, was a professor at Boston University.

My first cousin, Janet, and I had planned to go the March meeting. There was going to be a lecture about something academic but I do not remember now what the topic was. What I do remember is that on the Friday afternoon of the meeting, I called Janet to beg off going because "it's Friday, I'm tired, it's been a long week. Did we have a full moon this week? The kids at school were *so* out of control!"

Janet didn't hesitate. "Take a shower and put something nice on. We're going."

I did as Janet said and, a little later, I picked her up and we drove into Boston. I didn't know it, but the fates were already hard at work.

When Janet and I arrived at the meeting venue, several people were already there. My eyes quickly scanned the venue and, in the middle of the room, there was a tall man, about thirty or so and drop-dead good-looking. He was surrounded by at least fifteen women. I waited until all the women had moved away and then walked up and introduced myself.

"Hi", I said as I offered one hand to shake his, holding a tray of cookies in my other hand. "I'm Joan Demakis and I'm the secretary of the Helicon Society. Can I get you a cup of coffee or something else to drink, or a cookie, perhaps?" as I held out the tray.

"Hi, I'm Elias. No, thank you. I'm fine."

And at that moment, Michael walked up and said, "I see that you two have met."

Elias had come to Boston to do post-doctoral research in inorganic chemistry at Boston University (BU). He had just finished his doctorate at Georgetown University in Washington DC. On his first day at BU, he was walking down the corridor on his way to meet the chemistry professor with whom he would be working and stopped short as he recognized someone. It was Michael. Both men had grown up in the same neighborhood in Athens.

Michael and Elias struck up a conversation, talking and reminiscing about home. During that conversation, Michael told Elias about the Helicon Society and what it was, that he was president of the Society, that a meeting was scheduled for that coming Friday, and why didn't Elias come. He told Elias where the venue was and then said,

"There's a girl I want you to meet."

Elias later told me that he had applied for two post-doctoral research fellowships, one at Boston University and another in Florida, in Miami, I think. He had been accepted at both. The Florida fellowship was for one year, and the BU fellowship was for two years. He had decided to go to Florida but, in April 1967, a military junta overthrew the elected government in Greece and installed a dictatorship. Elias changed his plans and went to Boston instead because the one extra year in the BU fellowship program would give him time to see how the situation with the junta developed. Fate?

Elias had graduated from the University of Athens, had served the requisite three years in the army, as an officer, and had worked at *Demokritos*, a prestigious scientific research center in a suburb of Athens. He decided to do a doctorate in the US. He had considered several doctoral programs but settled on Georgetown because he thought that the Georgetown program suited him best, both academically and financially.

He loved being in the US and had acquired the coveted Green Card so that he could travel out of the country and come back again to the States without any hassle although, when I met him, he had not yet traveled outside of the US. His plan had always been to return to Greece when he finished his doctorate and his post-doctoral research and to work at Demokritos. At Demokritos, he could do what he loved best, pure research. The military junta delayed his plans.

In the meantime, however, he made the most of his time in Boston. Chemistry was Elias' element and pure research was what he loved most. Outside of the lab, however, he enjoyed and experienced as much as he could of American culture and life. When I first met him, he had only a trace of a Greek accent when he spoke. His appreciation of the US showed in everything he did and it was almost impossible to detect that he was not born-and-bred American.

It took the two of us a while to synchronize how we felt about dating each other but, once we started, it was a foregone conclusion that we were together. On our first date, he took me to the Acropolis, a Greek restaurant in Cambridge, near Porter Square, close to both Harvard University and MIT. The Acropolis was a family restaurant, but "Harvard professors, romantic couples, and poor college students (usually the romantic couples)"[ii] also dined there. Some professors were Greek as were some of the college students. When I told my mother where Elias had taken me on our first date, she smiled which indicated her opinion. It was good enough for her daughter.

As we were dating, I began to notice some things that were a little different from what I was used to. If we had plans to go out with other people, most of the time it was with Elias' Greek friends so the conversation was mostly in Greek. I was not fluent in Greek and, therefore, could not and did not participate in all the conversations. Sometimes we would be out with my friends, but mostly we went out with his super-smart Greek friends who were getting their doctorates at Harvard and at MIT. That we were socializing mostly with Greeks and that they were all super-smart didn't take me too long to realize. What did take some time to register was that

---

[ii] http://www.visitingnewengland.com/remember.html. Visiting New England

the single Greek women, who were also studying and working in Boston, regarded me with distrust. It was hard for me to spot because some of the things they did or said were subtle. They looked at me with *miso mati* (half an eye). They couldn't understand why this Greek guy, who was smart and good-looking, would be dating a Greek-American woman and not a Greek woman.

As 1968 drew to a close, Gregory and Tassia, a couple with whom Elias had become friendly, invited him to a New Year's Eve party at their home to usher in 1969. Elias decided that this would be the perfect occasion to introduce me to all his friends and invited me to go to the party with him. And this is where I met the whole group, husbands and wives. Somebody took a picture of Elias and me which I still have somewhere in the mass of photographs that are in my closet. Without my knowing it, Elias sent the picture to his family in Greece with the caption "this is the one".

The months passed and we settled into a routine. Then one Saturday evening in May, Elias asked me to marry him. There was one condition. He wanted to go to Greece that summer and he wanted me to go to Greece with him. Since there was absolutely no chance that my father would have allowed me to travel to Greece, as a single woman, with Elias, the wedding would have to happen quickly and it did. Elias and I were married two months later.

Even to this day, I don't know how my mother managed to get an entire wedding planned and executed in that excruciatingly short period of time, but she did. However, before we had any discussions about wedding planning, Elias wanted to come to the house and formally ask my father for my hand in marriage. So, on the Sunday morning after Elias proposed, this is what happened at my house.

First, I told my mother that Elias had asked me to marry him and that we wanted to get married in two months so we could go to Greece. My mother clapped both hands to her face in horror and said she simply could not plan a wedding in two months.

Next, I told my father that Elias had proposed and that he wanted to come to our house to ask my father's permission to marry me. My father's response was,

"When I said that you had to marry a Greek, I didn't mean a Greek from Greece. I meant a Greek-American".

To which I replied, "Too late now, Dad. You should have said something sooner."

And finally, my mother said that I had to go to my grandparents' homes and tell them that I was engaged and that, no, I couldn't tell them by telephone. The reactions at both houses were the same. Everyone was thrilled, and hugged and kissed me and congratulated me. Both my aunts, Nellie and Diana, said that they were surprised that I was marrying a Greek man and not a Greek-American.

Both grandmothers, however, had only one question, "Is he good-looking?"

A week later, it was Mother's Day and my parents used this occasion to introduce Elias to my mother's family and to Grandmother Demakes. We all went out to dinner to celebrate and Elias met my grandparents, aunts, uncles, and cousins. Elias also met with the approval of both my grandmothers. Not only was he good-looking, he became the comparison for good looks in the family. Thereafter, whenever anyone made a comment that some other young man was handsome, my grandmothers would say,

"Yes, but he's not as handsome as Elias".

The next two months flew by quickly. My mother took over the reins of planning the wedding, down to the last detail, together with my aunts. I could see that she was enjoying doing this so I placed myself in her very capable hands and let her have fun. We shopped together for my wedding gown, for clothes, for shoes, and for everything else. *THE WEDDING* became the main topic of discussion at the dinner table, the discussion taking place almost exclusively between my mother and me until either my father or one of my three brothers would interrupt, in complete and utter frustration, with the comment "not of general interest". And this from four males who had dominated, for as long as I could remember, dinner-table conversation with sports talk.

My parents held an engagement party for me. Elias invited some of his friends to the party, including Gregory and Tassia, the couple who would stand up for us. At the end of June, a continuous round of bridal parties and bridal showers began.

The wedding ceremony took place on Sunday, July 13 at the Saint George Greek Orthodox Church in Lynn. The reception was held in our back yard or in the garden as the local newspapers wrote. On the Friday before the wedding, a team of people came to the house to set up the tents, one big tent for the guests and the orchestra, with a dance floor, and a smaller tent for the caterers. It was a gloriously beautiful day with a vivid blue sky and not a cloud in sight. This was very unusual for July in Boston. July is usually hot, humid, and showery.

The next day, the July weather lived up to its reputation and we all woke up to a gray and overcast sky. The tent men came again and put flaps on the big tent to keep the rain out and keep the guests dry, in case it should rain. The caterers' tent already had flaps. Saturday night was a quiet night. There were no parties. Everyone was home where they were supposed to be. Around midnight, the skies opened and, in typical July weather fashion, the water just poured down.

The next morning, the phone rang and my father answered. It was Elias.

"The bride is crying", my father said.

Panic-stricken, Elias asked "The bride is crying? Why?"

My father's response was, "Isn't that what the Greeks say when it rains on a wedding day, that the bride is crying?"

Elias calmed down. He had called to tell me that he had put on his tuxedo and the pants were too short. Elias' aunt (my father-in-law's sister), her four children and their families lived in Detroit. Three of Elias' first cousins came for the wedding. Fortunately, two of the cousins were women and they fixed the tuxedo pants.

The wedding went as scheduled and as planned. People arrived with umbrellas and got a little wet from the unrelenting rain. I arrived at church, wrapped in two white king-size sheets, in a limo with my father. But as the sheets came off and I walked down the aisle with my father, everyone forgot about the rain and beamed at the bride.

My cousin Janet was the maid of honor, a position she felt that she deserved because she was sure that she was the reason that I had met Elias in the first place. My cousin Stephanie was one of my bridesmaids. My other bridesmaid was my friend Margot. Margot and I had been friends from the first day of junior high school when we were just eleven years old.

Margot's Swedish-Irish heritage was obvious. No one would ever have mistaken her for Greek-American. She was very fair and very blond. As Margot walked down the aisle, her parents heard the other guests whispering to each other, "Who's the blond?"

My first transatlantic trip was from Boston to Athens via London on Wednesday, July 16, 1969. I was twenty-four years old, a new bride traveling to Greece on my honeymoon with my Greek husband to meet his family. The scene at Boston Logan Airport was one of jubilation, almost a spillover from our wedding three days earlier. There must have twenty people at the airport to see us off. My parents and my brothers were there as were aunts, uncles, and cousins. Everyone was smiling and happy because first of all, I was traveling as a proper married woman and, secondly, because we all knew that I was coming back to Boston. It was one of the few times, maybe the only time, that I can remember leaving Boston without tears.

Elias and I traveled on Pan American, first class. Tassia's cousin was in the travel business and he had upgraded our tickets to first class. Transatlantic travel had not yet become as common or as frequent as it is today but, even then, I knew that we were traveling in the lap of luxury. I'm sure that champagne was not served in economy class.

It was Thursday when we arrived in Athens the next afternoon. The arrival scene there was a replica of the departure scene in Boston. There were seventeen relatives waiting to greet us, many of them holding flowers for the new bride. The first two relatives to greet us were my father-in-law who was beaming from ear to ear and my brother-in-law, Chris, who I was meeting for the very first time. My father-in-law had come to the wedding but had gone back to Greece the next day to be in Athens so he could meet us when we arrived. He immediately started the introductions, in Greek. I was a little dazed and tired from the trip but I smiled and kissed everyone, and took the flowers that they all gave me. This is how I met sixteen people (not counting my father-in-law who I had already met at the wedding) in just five short minutes.

I later learned that almost all of them had made the trip to the airport from the center of Athens by bus and then had made the return trip home by bus, as well. It was a very hot and dusty July afternoon, but they had put on their Sunday best and taken the hour-long bus ride to the airport just to welcome their nephew and cousin and his bride.

Elias' family was delightful. We arrived at his house which quickly filled up with family and friends who had been at the airport and several who had not been there. Everyone wanted to get a closer look at the *Americana*. I felt like an exotic curiosity. Everyone talked in Greek, loudly and all at the same time. It was impossible to follow the conversation.

My Greek-American Greek bore no resemblance to the more sophisticated and sometimes slangy Greek that I was hearing. But I smiled and nodded politely. It was obvious that they loved their nephew-cousin-friend and that their love for him would extend to his bride.

Even now I still remember each person who was there to meet us that afternoon. Whenever I think of them, my eyes fill up with tears. When my sons, Stefan and Costis, were in their early teens, they asked me what my honeymoon trip to Greece was like.

Without any hesitation, I said, "It was just like a Greek movie but without the music."

The trip was amazing, honeymoon and holiday all wrapped up in one fabulous package. It was summertime, sunny and hot but not unbearably hot, and we had nothing to do but party and have fun.

This was Greece in the 60s, only twenty-four years after the end of World War II and just twenty years after Greece's devastating and divisive civil war. But it was also the time when Greece began to appear on the world's radar screen. The movie *Never on Sunday,* in 1960, had raised everyone's awareness about Greece and the song's catchy tune and naughty lyrics had captured everyone's imagination. The *New York Times* travel section had published three articles about Greece in 1968 and 1969. Two of the articles were about Mykonos and Santorini. Mykonos quickly became the hottest vacation spot on the planet followed closely by Santorini. The third article was about Aghios Nikolaos, a sleepy seaside village on the northeastern coast of Crete, which became a posh resort.

Celebrities had begun making appearances in Greece, despite the military dictatorship, and two of the most well-known were Aristotle Onassis and Jackie O. One night, Elias' aunt and uncle had taken a big group, including Elias and me, to the *bouzoukia* at a very popular seaside nightclub in Glyfada, an upscale suburb south of Athens. Just as we were leaving at 4 am, Onassis and Jackie were arriving.

Elias' wedding gift to me was a seven-day cruise, a fairy-tale in and of itself. We sailed from Piraeus and the next day docked at Istanbul. The stops on the rest of the trip were Ephesus, Rhodes, Mykonos, Santorini, and Crete, and finally back to Piraeus. It was a beautiful trip, romantic and full of memories. In case anyone is interested, my wedding gift to Elias was an Omega watch, a very nice and expensive gift, but prosaic and predictable compared to the cruise.

We did other shorter trips, as well. We went to the island of Paros on our own. This was nice because, as honeymooners go, we were more of exhibit than a couple that was spending time alone before getting into the routine and rat race at home, wherever home was. In Paros, we stayed in a small village called Piso Livadi. I went to Paros again, in 2019, this time with family from the States who had rented a yacht and invited me to join them. It was *déjà vu*. As I sat on the beach with my cousin Nick and looked around at the row of white-washed houses and shops, it dawned on me that this was where Elias and I had spent our time alone on our honeymoon, fifty years earlier.

One of my favorite short trips was to Delphi where I met several of Elias' relatives. This is the area where Elias' family was from, not from Delphi itself but from neighboring villages. I met Elias' eighty-eight-year-old grandmother who looked at me with curiosity at first and then with approval. She had decided that I was good enough for her grandson. She scolded Elias for dragging me up and down the mountains in Delphi to show me all the sights and for tiring me out.

As I look back, I see that our time in Greece was happy, busy, and delightful. It was completely filled with fun activities - going to the beautiful beaches in Athens, dining out with all the relatives, climbing up to the Acropolis and to Lycabettus Hill, going on the cruise, and taking trips to places like Paros and Delphi. And, yes, it was all delightful but it was not real. It was not the real world. Our honeymoon had been like a blockbuster Hollywood movie, like *Roman Holiday*, perhaps, with Audrey Hepburn and Gregory Peck, or other movies that featured a drive on the stunning Amalfi Coast in Italy.

Greece is a very beautiful country but its beauty can sometimes draw attention away from the mundane and routine and from some of the unpleasant realities of everyday life. At least it did then, for me. I was blissfully ignorant, for example, of what life was like living under a military dictatorship and was unaware of the political affiliations of the population. While Elias and I were in Greece, I did notice that the dictatorship was not intrusive (except for the sign that they had put on the top of Lycabettus for the upcoming referendum so that the population would keep them in power), but then again, I was just a tourist and the dictatorship always put its best foot forward for the tourists. Therefore, I didn't know, and couldn't know, who was suffering under the military government. And no one thought it was necessary to tell me.

I didn't see the grinding poverty in which some Greeks lived. I didn't see the small apartments, the two-room apartments where families of four or five and more lived. I didn't see the small kitchen appliances that were small because larger ones couldn't fit in the tiny kitchens. I didn't know that, in the winter, central heating was turned on only for two, three, or, at the most, four hours a day. I didn't understand that not everyone had a car because they couldn't afford one. And most of all, I didn't see the strident anti-Americanism.

While Elias and I were dating, I knew that Elias wanted at some point to return to Greece and that, if we married, we might eventually move there. We had discussed this often but it was still only just a topic, just something that we talked about. On this trip, however, I had the opportunity to observe Greece first-hand. I observed everything, but I did not have a valid reference point to assess what I was observing. I enjoyed our outings with relatives and friends but would these friends and relatives always be available for outings? I enjoyed our evenings at glittering nightclubs but this was a special trip. Would glittering nightclubs be in our regular routine?

After this trip, I thought that I could live in Greece. But could I? Little did I know then that when, three and a half years later, I would move to Greece to live there, the reality of everyday life would bear absolutely no resemblance to the Greece that I had experienced on my honeymoon.

After five weeks in Greece, we flew back to Boston. This time, the mood at the airport was very different. My father-in-law and Chris took us to the airport but there was none of the joy or happiness that had been there when we first arrived. Chris was matter-of-fact and my father-in-law was morose. We were going to the States and my father-in-law and Chris didn't know if or when we were coming back to Greece. Neither did we.

- 3 -

1972: The Move

"There's nowhere you can be that isn't where you're meant to be."

John Lennon

In the years following our honeymoon, life went on as usual, the routine and the rat race. In March 1970, we moved to Fort Lee, New Jersey, where Elias had been offered, and had accepted, a position as chemist in a large chemical corporation. I resigned from my teaching position at Lynn English High School and substitute taught for a while in the towns near Fort Lee, and then found a job in the sales department at Renault USA in nearby Englewood. A move to Greece, any move, had been put on the back burner. Elias and I talked about the move occasionally, but only occasionally.

My brother-in-law had married in May 1970 and he

and his wife, Mary, had come to the US for about a year where Chris enrolled first in an English-language course and then in a computer training program. When they returned to Greece in mid-1972, (where Chris would get a job at the Public Power Corporation using his newly acquired computer skills), Chris wrote to Elias and told him not to even think about going back to Greece. The military junta was still in power. Jobs were still scarce. Pay was still low.

Meanwhile, Elias and I thoroughly enjoyed our time in New Jersey. The George Washington Bridge was just a five-minute drive from our apartment building. From the bridge, it was just a fifteen- to-twenty-minute drive, depending on the traffic, into Manhattan. We spent most of our weekends in Manhattan, exploring its magic. There was so much to see and so much to do. On most of those weekends, we were with friends, and sometimes with my mother's sister, Dee, and her family, or sometimes with my brother, Tom. We were, as the expression goes, footloose and fancy-free. And *the move* was still on the back burner.

In the summer, shortly after Chris and Mary went back to Greece, Elias got another job offer from Demokritos. It was the third job offer that he had received from the center in the ten years that he had been in the States. *The move* changed position and, this time, it moved from the back burner and became a *fait accompli*. Elias wrote to his father and to Chris, who begged Elias not to go back to Greece. It was Chris who begged Elias, not my father-in-law.

Elias and I began having several discussions about whether we should we go or not. Elias' arguments were based on what his brother and his friends were telling him. My argument was different. I had known from the beginning that Elias' master plan had always been to go to back to Greece and work at Demokritos to do research. I asked him how many times he thought that the directors there would continue making offers, which Elias would then refuse, before they just threw up their hands in resignation and stopped making those offers. Apparently, this was what convinced him. Elias made the decision that he would accept the offer from Demokritos and that we would move to Greece. But for the rest of his life, whenever someone asked him what had possessed him to come back to Greece, his answer always was, "Joan wanted to move here."

Chris thought his brother was crazy and, by extension, he thought that I was crazy, too.

The preparations for the move, which was no longer an abstract idea but a reality, were non-stop. We would cross one action off our list and two more would take its place. We resigned from our respective companies. We decided what to take with us and what not to take. We bought American kitchen appliances to take to Greece, the ones that could not and would not fit into the tiny Greek kitchens, and left most of the furniture behind. It should have been the other way around.

The biggest hurdle was telling my parents. They had always known that our moving to Greece was a possibility but it had never seemed to them, or even to us, that it would happen.

My father's reaction was, "Where will your children go to university?" Other than that, both my parents were stoic and, instead of falling apart, they planned a going-away party for us.

We used the few months that we had to prepare for the move to plan our trip, too. Part of our plan was to buy a Renault since I was an employee and would therefore get a discount on the purchase, and that is what we did. We would be able to use the French license plates in Greece for up to two years. The plates would identify us as non-residents and would allow us to defer paying taxes on the car for that time period.

The weeks flew by and our emotions became tense and conflicted. For most of the time that we had lived in New Jersey, I had worked for Renault. It was a job but I had fun, mostly, and met a lot of good people and made a lot of friends. When the time came for us to move to Greece, my colleagues threw me a party. That's when Elias started getting cold feet and I became mortified that he might change his mind at the last minute and then what would I say to my colleagues who had given me a party? Oh, the blessed naiveté of the young! No wonder he would always say that I was the one who wanted to come to Greece!

My second transatlantic trip from Boston took place on the Friday after Thanksgiving, November 24, 1972. This time, instead of flying to Athens, we flew to Paris. We had decided to leave the US immediately after the Thanksgiving holiday thinking that if we left closer to Christmas, we and everyone else would get caught up in an emotional tangle.

The departure scene at Boston Logan was dramatically different from the one in 1969 when we were leaving to go on our honeymoon. It was funereal. My parents and brothers and maybe two or three aunts and uncles came to the airport to see us off. Everyone spoke in low tones; there was no exuberance anywhere. When the time came for Elias and me to begin the boarding process and to head to passport control, we realized that my father had vanished. My brothers dashed off in three different directions and one of them found him in an airport lounge nursing a beer in which he was drowning his sorrow that his only daughter was moving overseas.

My mother had put on a brave face, but it was just a brave face. As we hugged and kissed everyone good-bye, she cupped my face in her hands and said,

"Now that you are moving to Greece, make sure that you learn how to cook real Greek food."

It was her way of telling me that she loved me without actually saying it because it would have brought us both to tears.

None of us knew when Elias and I would be back.

We landed in Paris on Saturday and thus began the month-long trip that was to be an adventure, our last hurrah before we settled down and behaved like grown-ups and started a family.

Paris was lovely. It was exciting! It was a dream come true! We walked a lot and saw all the sights. Notre Dame. The Louvre and the Jeu de Paume. L' Arc de Triomphe. We walked along the banks of the Seine. One of Elias' cousins was studying in Paris and we met up with him. He took us to a restaurant that was either Moroccan or Algerian, and I had my first taste of couscous. It was delicious!

On the third or fourth day that we were in Paris, we went to the Renault factory to meet my French colleagues and to pick up the car. Elias did not want me to drive because the car was brand new and he was sure that I would have an accident and ruin it so the car became Elias' car, *de facto*, even though it was in my name. The traffic in Paris was intimidating, worse than Boston traffic, so I acquiesced and let Elias do the driving.

We left Paris after a week and went to Switzerland, to both Zurich and Geneva. My parents had given me my Christmas present before we left Boston. It was money to buy a real Swiss watch in Geneva. The watch that I bought was in all the fashion magazines that winter because it had no numbers or numerals on the watch face. That watch, which I still have and wear, is the only real memory that I have from Switzerland on that trip.

From Switzerland we went to Munich. It was December and Christmas was in the air. Marienplatz, the main plaza in Munich, was delightful with the clock and its moving figures that moved every hour on the hour and its Christmas bazaar. We wanted, however, to also look at the darker side of Munich and made a somber and sobering pilgrimage to Dachau to pay our respects.

From Munich, we went to Vienna where we met up with Elias' friends, Dimitris and Artemis, who would later become our first son's godparents. We spent only a day or two in Vienna but we spent all our time with Dimitris and Artemis and their children.

We left Vienna and continued on to Salzburg, a beautiful Austrian town. When we arrived in Salzburg, Elias told me that he wasn't feeling well. I had a thermometer with me and we took his temperature and saw that he had a slight fever. In English, I asked the woman who was managing the hostel where we were staying where I could find a pharmacy to buy some aspirin. In German, she directed me to one. The communication was difficult because, in 1972, English was not as widely spoken in Europe as it is now and I didn't speak any German.

The next morning, Elias was still not feeling well so I crooked my finger at him, held out my hand and said, "The keys". And thus, the ownership of the car came back to me. For the rest of the trip, I got a running commentary on my driving. I was going either too fast or too slow, the change at the toll booths was wrong, and so on, but I ignored it. I was having too much fun driving in Europe and I wasn't about to let Elias spoil it.

Our next stop was Italy – Venice, actually. We loved Venice. It was decadent although no one would actually dare say that. It was obvious that a lot of money had passed through Venice. It was glamorous, mysterious, and run-down and, because it was December, the canals didn't smell. We had parked the car in a garage outside of Venice since no cars are allowed in Venice itself. That was fine by us. We walked. We rode in the gondolas. The food was wonderful even though I don't remember what we ate, just that the food was delicious. The sights were magical and the shopping was heavenly. I still have the porcelain flower candlesticks that I bought there and that were so popular in the States that year. They are a lovely memento.

After three or four days in Venice, we set off for Greece. It was now perhaps two or three days before Christmas. Elias and I had decided not to celebrate Christmas in Athens, again so we could avoid the emotional tangle. We purposefully wanted to be somewhere neutral on Christmas Day where the thoughts of what celebrations could have been would not overwhelm us. No place could have been more neutral than Yugoslavia and that's where we were headed after Venice.

We drove to Trieste, and from Trieste we entered Yugoslavia. If we were doing this trip today, we would enter Slovenia from Trieste. I was now in charge of the driving and I loved it. To say that driving in Yugoslavia in 1972 was an experience is a massive understatement. The highway had three lanes – one southbound, one northbound, and one in the middle for passing, for both northbound and southbound cars. Most of the cars were small Yugos (Fiats made in Yugoslavia), the 400, the 500, the 600. They were really no match for our car. And all the drivers were men. The only woman driver on the highway, from Trieste until Greece, was me. That made for a very interesting dynamic.

At one point, I was trying to pass a little Yugo that was in front of us but every time I put my flash on to go left into the middle lane in order to pass the slower Yugo, the driver would move to the left, too. Then I would put my flash on to move back into the southbound lane and so would the tiny Yugo. This little dance went on, with the same little Yugo, for twenty minutes or so. It was then that I saw my opportunity. Much further down, a bus had moved from the northbound lane into the middle lane, coming north, so that it could pass all the tiny Yugos in front of it. I put my flash on and I moved into the middle lane, going south, to pass the Yugo in front of us. Elias folded his hands in his lap and looked down, preparing himself for a head-on collision. Quietly, he said, "We're going to get killed."

To which I replied, "No, we're not. Not today anyway."

I floored the gas pedal and passed the little Yugo whose driver could not believe what he was seeing. In retrospect, I think he most likely didn't trust his car to do anything risky but I must admit that he did make generous room for us to move back into the southbound lane, in front of him, just before the bus whizzed by.

We spent one night in Belgrade and then, on Christmas Day, we arrived in Skopje where we spent another night. Both cities were so depressing (this was 1972) that we didn't even want to think about Christmas.

On the day after Christmas, we left Skopje and headed toward the Greek border. The scenery as we drove south was breathtakingly beautiful – mountainous, green, lush, thick and tangled. There were very few other cars on the highway. In fact, it's possible that it was just us on the road. I was driving quite fast when, suddenly and urgently, Elias told me to stop the car. I did and the car stalled.

We had run into a thin wire that was stretched taut across the road. The wire was at the same height as that of a driver on a motorcycle. If the vehicle hitting the wire had been a motorcycle and not a car, the driver would have been killed, instantly. The wire was secured by two Yugoslav soldiers, one on either side of the road. They were peering down into the gullies, off the road. Apparently, the wire was their communication system and we had almost broken it. Elias got out of the car, visibly agitated. His concern was that the wire had scratched the car. The soldiers were concerned that we had damaged their communication system. Eventually tempers calmed down and we continued on our way.

We reached Evzoni, the Yugoslavia – Greece border which was a much more elaborate affair than any other border we had seen in the rest of Europe as we were driving from one country to another. Here, there was a long stretch on the Yugoslav side with soldiers guarding the border with their machine guns. We crossed to the Greek side after the Yugoslavs had checked all our papers. Greek soldiers were manning the site but they were much more relaxed and nonchalant than their counterparts on the other side.

In Greece, we had to declare the car since we had taken ownership of it in France and it had French license plates. When the car had been declared and our passports had been stamped, Elias went to the currency exchange booth to exchange our Yugoslavian dinars for Greek drachmas. The Greek employee at the currency booth explained that Elias had to go back to the other side to change the dinars as he could not change them on the Greek side. Elias set out for the other side. As soon as he approached the border and began to cross it, several Yugoslav soldiers raised their rifles and pointed them at him, shouting "Alt"!

Elias put his hands up and showed the dinars that he wanted to exchange for drachmas to the soldiers. The soldiers lowered their weapons and Elias exchanged the money.

With that drama over, we began the long drive to Athens. As we drove along, I began noticing how clean

Greece was. The difference between Greece and Yugoslavia was striking. Yugoslavia had looked dingy and dirty but I had not realized just how dingy and dirty it was until we started driving through Greece.

That Greece was poor was obvious, but it was clean and it was pretty. In all the villages that we drove through, the houses were small but well taken care of. In front of every house, there were beautiful flowers in used oil cans that had been repurposed as flower pots. In all fairness to Yugoslavia, the people must have surely tried to add some beauty to their lives but the government was evidently doing all that it could to ensure that the population remained poor and miserable. Beauty was not high on the Yugoslavian government agenda.

At some point, Elias called his father to tell him that we were in Greece and that we would be in Athens in the early evening. My father-in-law told Elias not to let me drive because the driving in Greece was dangerous. I continued driving until we got to Athens and then we switched places because Elias knew exactly where we were going and how to get there. We were going to Elias' family home. Our arrival date in our new place of residence was December 26, 1972.

Our adventure was over. We were now in Athens and the next day would be the beginning of our lives together in Greece. Elias would go to Demokritos in the morning to report for work and I would start assimilating into the Greek culture. The interlude had been lovely and it had served its purpose. We had had a wonderful trip and had seen so much that we would not have seen if we had flown directly to Athens. But the interlude was just that – an interlude. It was a cushion between the departure from Boston and the arrival in Greece, a cushion that protected me from an abrupt and disorienting entry into the Greek culture. The interlude had also served as a cushion that shielded both of us from an acute loneliness on Christmas Day. Christmas, that year, was neutral. It was neither an American Christmas nor a Greek Christmas. It was just another day.

- 4 -

The First Five Years, Generally.......

"Συν Αθηνά και χείρα κίνει." Translation: "Heaven helps those who help themselves."

Aesop's Fables

The actual translation of the quote above is "Pray to Athena but move your arms, too." In one of Aesop's fables, a wealthy Athenian was shipwrecked when his ship capsized during a fierce storm. While the other passengers were swimming to save themselves, the wealthy Athenian began praying to Athena and making promises to her if she would save him. One of his fellow passengers told him to move his arms, too, and start swimming while he was praying to Athena.

I remembered this from my childhood readings of Aesop. It was a moral that my father stressed to my brothers and me and one that I implemented, unwittingly, during my first five years as a resident in Greece.

As I began my assimilation in early 1973, I realized once again that my Greek was inadequate especially now that I was in Greece and few people spoke English. My vocabulary was limited and my grammar was basic. I couldn't really follow a conversation so I was left out of most conversations with Elias' family and friends, not because any of us were being rude but because Greek was the only language that they spoke and I simply could not keep up.

Then I realized that I was cold. It was a different cold from the cold in Boston. It was a cold that pierced my bones. I also noticed that I was very sad whereas Elias was thrilled to be back home in Greece. He had been away for a little over ten years. But I was sad and the homesickness had begun to settle in. It ate at my gut. I cried a lot but by myself so that no one could see.

And, of course there was the privacy issue. There wasn't any privacy. And to make matters worse, Elias' and my clothes as well as our household possessions were still *en route* from the States. We had shipped them in a container and they would not be in Greece for a few more weeks so we could not even move to our own flat because we would have no place to sit or sleep or clothes to wear, just what we had brought with us.

It took only two or three weeks for me to recognize the feeling. I was sinking. I was underwater, way over my head. I was gloomy and sad and I understood that. I also understood that I had to do something to help myself. Otherwise, I would sink to the bottom and drown.

I began leaving the house on some mornings. I would ask my sister-in-law Mary if there was anything that I could do and she would say no. Mary did all the cooking and cleaning. She did everything. I had absolutely no idea of how to navigate the kitchen with its tiny Greek appliances, all of them old, or of how to shop and navigate the Athenian markets. I was literally helpless although I did clean up and wash the dishes after we ate. But I was not independent. And, I had nothing to do.

So, I would just leave. At least I could walk around the neighborhood or take public transportation into the center of Athens and explore the city. My first refuge in the city center was the library at the Hellenic-American Union (HAU). Most of the countries in the world, if not all, have embassies in Athens. Some of the bigger countries also have cultural organizations that work closely with their embassies. The US cultural organization was, and still is, the HAU.

The HAU library was small but had more than enough books to get me through the darkest and loneliest days. I settled into a routine, going to the HAU once a week, borrowing enough books to get me through the week and then, in the evenings while Elias and his family were having lively discussions, snuggling into an armchair in a corner and reading. Of course, this did not help me learn better Greek.

Going downtown regularly taught me how to use public transportation. Public transportation provided me with a visual layout of the city, especially in the neighborhoods that circled the center of Athens. I would get off at Syntagma (Constitution) Square and then walk. I discovered that Athens was the perfect walking city. I became familiar with the streets and their shops and the neighborhoods immediately adjacent to Syntagma Square.

One of the goals that I set to help myself feel a little better was to notice something every day that would make me smile and that I could talk about in the family discussions in the evenings. That something could be anything. It could be a child's smile, a blue sky, a pretty balcony, a colorful flower. I was on the lookout, every time I meandered through the city or even through my own neighborhood, to find something that would put a smile on my face.

This is how I discovered the beauty of Athens' neoclassical architecture with its intricate wrought-iron balcony railings, carved designs on the underside of marble balconies, stunning *art déco* doors and, of course, the beautiful neoclassical buildings themselves. I paid more attention to balconies everywhere and noticed how many of them, small as they were, were filled to overcrowding with flowering plants and greenery. And once I had achieved one smile a day, I upped the ante to two smiles a day.

I also started driving in Athens. Sometimes, I would take the car and just drive. I learned to drive like the Greeks, fast and aggressively. The layout of the city became a mental map, imprinted on my brain, as did the public transportation routes. This was the key to losing my fear of getting lost, although this was almost impossible to do in the Athens of 1973, and to gaining familiarity with my environment.

Demokritos had buses that would pick up employees at specific spots in every neighborhood, take them to work and then drop them off again in the late afternoon. On the days that Elias went by bus to work, I had the car but I have absolutely no recollection of where I went and why. I really wish I could remember where I was driving to.

What I remember from my driving days that year was that the streets were empty or fairly empty, especially in the neighborhoods. I could even find a parking space in front of Elias' family home, most of the time. In downtown Athens, the traffic was also sparse, but the driving was by far more aggressive.

When I went to the States at the end of 1973, one of my cousins was getting married and the wedding was about an hour's drive from Lynn where my parents still lived. My father gave me the keys and said, "You drive".

When we got to the church, an hour later, I gave the keys back to my father, who gave me a disgusted look and said,

"You drive like a cowboy."

And that was after only one year of driving in Greece.

I also started looking for a flat that Elias and I could move into once our belongings arrived from the States. It went without saying that we would stay in the Kypseli neighborhood, close to Elias' family home. I had looked at some flats in other neighborhoods but all my attempts were met with negative responses. We were staying in Kypseli and that was that.

Eventually, I did find a flat on a side street perpendicular to the street that the family house was on. And just in time, because we were notified that our belongings had arrived from the States. We signed a contract with the owner of the flat and, after we got everything through customs, we moved in. It was lovely. There were two bedrooms and a large living and dining room. It was opulent given the tiny flats that many families were living in. And we had privacy. There was no price tag on that.

We unpacked everything and put our beautiful but very large American appliances, stove and refrigerator, in the kitchen. The appliances took up all the space in the kitchen and there was nowhere to put a small table and two chairs so we ate in the dining area in the living room. However, the appliances, silly as this may sound, were a piece of home and, as such, they were comforting because I knew how to operate them. The refrigerator was frost-free, something unheard of in Greece at the time. It burned a lot of electricity, or at least that's what Elias told me.

Now that I had to cook, and had all the equipment that I needed to cook, I began familiarizing myself with the shops and the markets but, again, shopping was not what it was in the States. To begin with, the butcher shops had sides of meat hanging on iron hooks in full view of the customers. In the summer, there were flies flying around and on those sides of meat.

Then there was the green grocer. Mary's mother introduced me to her grocer, his wife, and an employee. I began shopping there because I still didn't know where else to go. After a while, I began to suspect that the employee was not giving me the proper change. He was probably thinking that *"this silly American woman won't notice that I haven't given her the right change"*.

And he was right. I didn't notice, at least not right away, but it slowly dawned on me that this is what was happening. One day, when the employee gave me the change, I had him place the change on the counter next to the cash register and then asked in my most polite tone of voice how much the groceries cost. He told me and I carefully counted out the change.

I said, "You gave me twenty drachmas in change. You should have given me twenty-two drachmas."

The man pretended to be shocked and apologized profusely. Two drachmas equaled about six US cents. It was not a lot of money but that was not the point. And let me correct that. Maybe it did not seem like a lot of money to me but it was to many Greeks because two drachmas could buy a kilo of fresh fish or three loaves of bread. When I counted my change two more times, he stopped skimming. But I asked Mary's mother to point me to another green grocer and she did. And I have been shopping there ever since.

Two events happened in those first three months of 1973 to alleviate some of the emptiness that I was feeling. I visited a Greek friend, Maria, who I had met in the States when she came to visit one of her friends, Tassia. Maria had taken a course in the States, had returned to Greece and was teaching English at Athens College, an elite private school.

Maria was living in another one of the neighborhoods that ring the center of Athens. We visited for a while and then she said that she wanted to introduce me to one of her neighbors, an American woman, Kate, who was running a study abroad program in Athens.

As it happened, I didn't know Kate but I knew about

her. I had already started looking for work in Athens while Elias and I were still in the planning mode in New Jersey. The Greek consul in New York had sent me a list of American businesses in Greece. Kate's study abroad program was on the list with her contact details. I had sent Kate my resume and a letter telling her that I would be in Greece at the beginning of 1973 and that I would be interested in discussing with her the possibility of working for her.

We hit it off and we set up another time to meet and discuss. It would be a part-time job only, but the two mornings a week were enough for me to get out and meet more people, many of them Americans.

And so began my first job in Greece! Those two mornings, or ten hours a week, were a blessing for me. I met so many people and learned a lot from Kate and from everyone else who was associated with the program. Kate had already lived in Greece for a few years and this was an opportunity for me to learn from her the interesting spots in Athens including restaurants, tavernas, shops, and bookstores.

A few weeks later, Maria and I went to a meeting of American women living in Greece although there were Greek women there as well. It was at that meeting that I met the Greek woman who would be my divorce lawyer a few years later. I think that the topic of this particular meeting was the rights of women in Greece, both as married women and as divorced women. This is probably why my future lawyer was there.

Maria was quite adamant that I should join this group. But I myself felt some hesitation and so did not join. I really did not want to be part of an ex-pat group, speaking English all the time. I am confident that it was at this meeting that I made a sub-conscious decision that would directly affect the rest of my life in Greece. I wanted to integrate into Greek society and make Greek friends and learn to speak the Greek language properly.

Integrating into Greek society was not something that I would do overnight and it was not something that could happen quickly. However, I did understand that not joining an ex-pat group would make the whole process of integration easier. Consequently, it was just in the first few months that I began consciously, or maybe even unconsciously, making decisions that would help me acquire a Greek identity.

These were a few of the positive steps and influences that got me through the first few months. There were also negative influences. The biggest one was the military dictatorship. I gradually went from being dismissive of the junta to being terrified of it. Elias, his family and his friends were always admonishing me to *keep quiet,* something that I was not conditioned to do. But the constant finger wagging and scolding worked and I kept out of the way of soldiers and policemen. But how was I to know if someone was undercover?

One day, on the trolley as I was coming home from work, a man kept staring at me. I looked down at my clothes to see if they were dirty. They were not. Then a thought crossed my mind that perhaps he was an undercover policeman and maybe he was going to check my papers, and did I have my papers and if I did, were they the right ones, and if they weren't the right ones, then what would happen to me, and would they put me in jail and if they did put me in jail, how would

I tell Elias. And this went on for the entire trolley ride until I reached my stop.

I got off the trolley, and so did that man. As I hurried up the three or four blocks to get home, I kept turning around to see if that man was still there and he was. I reached my street but I was frightened of going to my apartment building because I didn't want him to know where I lived. Instead, I went to my father-in-law's house and rang the bell. But my father-in-law and Chris and Mary had moved a month earlier to a flat because Elias and Chris had agreed to give the house to a contractor who would tear down the house and build an apartment building there.

The house was empty, and I knew that, but I stood in the doorway entrance anyway, trying to make myself small and pretending that I was waiting for someone to open the door. Just then, the man came by, threw a scrap of paper at me and walked away. I picked up the scrap of paper and saw a telephone number. I was stunned, confused, and still not exactly sure of what had just happened.

Later that evening, when I told Elias and our neighbors what had happened and how scared I had been and why did this man give me this telephone number, they all burst out laughing. He was not an undercover policeman, they told me. He had been hitting on me. I was mortified. Even today whenever I think about this incident, I cannot believe that I had been so naïve.

But the junta was no laughing matter. It wasn't a joke. It was serious and many people had been caught up in the junta's deadly dragnets and were unable to escape. I listened to the Greeks who worked at the study abroad program with me and who talked about the junta. Military dictatorships were not something to fool around with. Some of these people had begun participating in demonstrations against the junta. Whenever I told Elias, he would tell me to stay away from them and not get involved.

"Keep your head down," he would say.

The demonstrations against the junta would continue throughout the year and would come to a head that November of 1973.

Another negative influence came from me. I was constantly comparing Greece to the United States and I began to notice that Elias' friends, especially, were becoming increasingly frustrated, annoyed, and angry with my comments. I converted, in my head, drachmas to dollars to get an understanding of what the cost of everything was because drachmas meant nothing to me but dollars and cents did. One of Elias' friends told me to stop doing this conversion because although I would get the equivalent in dollars, I would not be able to compare the value of one item in Greece with the same item in the States because of the disparity in incomes and other differences in the economics of the two countries.

Also, I would simply compare Greece with the United States or the States with Greece. The most common comment that I would make was,

"But I don't understand. In the States, we do it this way."

And then I would see the looks. When people started walking away, I realized that I had to change gears and be more positive. The first step was to stop criticizing Greece and comparing everything Greek (horrible) to everything

American (fabulous). Eventually, things calmed down, but mostly because I kept quiet.

But the one negative influence that knocked me off my feet was the anti-Americanism that I would come across, all the time. The Greeks blamed the Americans for everything that was wrong in their country, starting with the military dictatorship.

I had only a superficial knowledge of modern Greek history. I had learned a little from my father and was learning some from Elias but the little that I knew was not sufficient to understand the underlying politics in Greece. Greece had suffered greatly in World War II and had been occupied by Nazi Germany. The end of that war was closely followed by a civil war that divided the country as only a civil war can do.

A large percentage of the population was leftist and the Communist Party was very visible in Greece's politics. The leftists accused those on the right of being pro-American and therefore responsible for all of Greece's ills. The political right was friendly to the US, making the political left even angrier.

I had heard comments and innuendos several times but had paid little attention because I didn't fully understand what they meant. The first time that I encountered truly strident and vitriolic anti-Americanism that was, as I had discovered, very prevalent in Greece at that time, was one summer evening when Elias and I had gone to Delphi and Itea where some of his family lived. We had gone out to eat with Elias' cousin and her husband and another couple who were friends of theirs. It was in the summer of 1973, one year before events in Cyprus would change everyone's perceptions, mine included, of the US / Greece political relationship.

The man, who I had never met and would never see again, began a tirade against the United States. He was rude and loud and spoke directly to me, in Greek, in an accusatory tone of voice, blaming me personally for everything that the United States had done to Greece. It was the States' fault that Greece had a military junta, it was the States' fault that Greece had not become Communist after World War II, (that was actually Churchill's influence), and it was the States' fault that the Communists had not won the Civil War. And by extension, everything was my fault, too.

Was any of this true? I don't know. But as I would find out over the years, it didn't matter if what the anti-Americans said was true or not. What mattered was that they believed it was true.

That evening, I felt alone and completely on my own. Elias didn't speak up. I was so furious with him afterwards; he said that he hadn't wanted to add fuel to the fire. Whatever. The cousins didn't speak up. The man's wife didn't speak up to tell him to stop. If I had been able to, I would have got up and walked away. But we were at a taverna on the outskirts of a small village and where would I have gone? Still, sometimes when I think about it, I think that that was just an excuse. Just sitting there and listening to his diatribe was cowardly and weak. I wish that I had stood up and walked away, even if it was just to sit at another table by myself, or that I had stood up and yelled back, in English, and broken a dish or glass or both on the table. I did have a choice, I tell myself. Then again, this person's diatribe was in Greek and I could not have possibly responded, in Greek, to his manic outburst. Again, this was just another excuse. Any move by me would have indicated to everyone that I was brave enough to stand up for myself and that I did not accept or condone this man's boorish and bullying behavior. But I didn't get up. I just sat there.

Over the years, I have learned to speak up and have reached the point where I now can argue effectively, in Greek, with someone who is, as I like to say, speaking out of both corners of his mouth at the same time. But I am not an arguer. I do not like arguing for the sake of arguing, especially when the conversation is about politics. But more than that, I am now bored with anti-Americanism. It's pointless. It's silly. It's out of context. It doesn't matter. And I am just not interested in wasting my time and energy on these arguments. And, besides, anti-Americanism today is not what it was fifty years ago.

After Greece joined the European Union, the Greeks were looking forward to the day that they could travel to the United States without going through the long and grinding process of applying for a visa. Greece wanted to be like the rest of Europe and, for the rest of Europe, getting a visa to travel to the United States took just a few days, not six months. But the rest of Europe did not rant against the States as Greece did.

A few years ago, a rocket was fired at the American Embassy, which is on a major thoroughfare in Athens, from a building across the street from the Embassy. The rocket had been fired early in the morning and fortunately for everyone, and I mean everyone, there were no casualties.

A few days later, I was in a taxi driven by a woman. She asked where I was from and when I told her that I had been born in the States, she tried to start the usual anti-American conversation. Her biggest gripe was that the Greeks still had to go through a long visa process to take a trip to the States, something that she herself wanted to do so she could visit her sister in Brooklyn. My response was that maybe if the Greeks stopped firing rockets at the American Embassy, then the US government *might* consider changing the visa process.

I have spent far too much time for far too long being angry and upset with incidents like these. I resent being the receiving end of everyone's whining about the US only because I am American. I've stopped reacting to anti-American comments. I stop conversations before they even start. Or if they do start, they fizzle out when I don't respond. A non-committal "hmmmm" usually does the trick. The Greeks' relationship to the States has always been a love-hate one. They all love traveling to the States and shopping there and they love studying and working there, but they hate powerful countries and, to the Greeks, the US is too powerful. But that's something that the Greeks need to figure out by themselves.

The first five years in Greece were constructive, although I didn't realize it at the time. I was learning the culture, and I had begun to make a few friends and they were Greek. The hardest times for me were coming back to Greece after a holiday in the US. Even though I was adjusting to Greece, I still missed the States very much. Coming back required a re-adjustment to get back into the rhythm of Greece – the language, the sense of familiarity, the shopping, and basically everything.

But there were also happy times in those five years, very happy times. Both my children were born in that time frame, Stefan in 1974 and Costis (Constantine) in 1977. My parents came twice, in those same years. My brother Tom came twice. Some of my cousins came to visit.

One of the most memorable visits from my cousins was in August 1973. My first cousin Connie came with her husband John and my first cousin Johnny came with his wife Callie. And I was in seventh heaven. It was the first visit from the cousins and it was the harbinger for all family visits that followed. The icing on the cake was that Connie, Callie, and I were all pregnant although I would officially find out in September that Elias and I were expecting. And, as an added bonus, Connie's sister-in-law, Timi, who was also living in Greece with her family, gave birth to her second son while Connie and John were here.

I drove a lot during the cousins' visit but if Elias was driving, I would give him directions where to go, which streets were one-way and what the alternative streets were to get to our destination. I guess it had helped that I had done a lot of driving on my own at the beginning of the year.

For two weeks, I spent all my time with the cousins. We went out to eat, we went to the beach, we went shopping, and we laughed a lot. I had missed my cousins' company and the laughter so much. It was a beautiful piece of the US in Athens and it was so much fun. It was also fun to discover that I had learned, in just eight months, enough about Athens to show it off. I really enjoyed that, too.

Giving birth to my two children was the biggest highlight of the first five years. The funny thing is that I never expected that having a baby in Greece would be a highlight. It was a huge surprise. Of course, becoming a mother was a unique and emotional experience, unlike any other. But there were other factors, too.

First of all, I had a wonderful doctor – low key, unflappable, and kind. What else could I ask for? The American wife of one of Elias' colleagues had recommended him, and he was perfect because he spoke English and he had studied in the US. Secondly, when I had Stefan, I had a private room and I stayed in the maternity clinic for seven nights. It was a heavenly vacation. When I had Costis in 1977, the maternity stay was six nights. I remember being disappointed and asking the doctor why I could only stay for six nights. He just smiled.

Two or three years after Costis was born, a friend called me. She was the wife of one of Elias' childhood friends. Hara and her husband were trying for a second child but were having a difficult time. Hara had had two miscarriages in one year and her doctor was not particularly sympathetic to her. She called me to ask for my doctor's name and number because I had spoken so highly of him. I gave her the information that she wanted and then I called my doctor to tell him that a very good friend of mine was going to call him for an appointment.

A few months later, after she gave birth to a healthy baby girl, a group of us had gone out to dinner and Hara was singing the praises of our doctor and told us a story about him. She had gone to his office after I had given her his phone number. He told her and her husband not to try for another pregnancy for a few months and to let her body rest. So, Hara waited and in a year's time, she was pregnant again. She went back to the doctor who examined her and he told her that she should stay in bed and that he would come to her home once a month, and more frequently as the due date drew near. The doctor's office was in downtown Athens. Hara lived in a suburb north of Athens. But every month, he went to her house to examine her and, every time he went to examine her, his wife was always with him. I liked that story and still tell it to my friends. It's a lovely testament to the doctor's character and is probably one of the reasons that having both babies in Greece was such a positive experience for me.

There were funny incidents, too. My favorite is the story of putting our Renault through customs. In 1974, when I was pregnant with Stefan, Elias decided that we should declare the car, pay whatever taxes were due, and put Greek license plates on the car. His concern was that we might be drawing unnecessary attention to ourselves with the French license plates. We had gotten through almost a year and a half without any major problems although we had been stopped a couple of times. Elias didn't want to risk a second year without Greek plates.

He found out where the customs office was. I had to go with him because the car was in my name. It was about one month, maybe less, before my due date.

One of Elias' colleagues (the one with the American wife) had given Elias an excellent piece of advice. "When you want to get something done in the public sector, keep asking different employees for information. Eventually someone will say exactly what you want to hear or what you need to know. That is the person you should deal with." This is what we did at the customs office.

In the nearly year and a half that I had been in Greece, I had become aware of how Greek pregnant women behaved. They stuck their stomachs out as much as possible, arching their backs to protrude their stomachs more, with one hand on their stomachs and the other hand supporting their backs at the waist, all topped off with a suffering expression on their faces. This posture was designed to get everyone's sympathy and attention and to get immediate assistance. This is the posture that I adopted when I went to the customs office. The reactions were instantaneous. People (all men) gave me their places in line and, in less than five minutes, I was at the head of a one-hour line. Others asked me if I was okay, if I needed to sit down, if I wanted a glass of water. I realized that Greek women were experts at getting exactly what they wanted, when they wanted it. Why did I have to be a strong independent American woman when I could just as easily play the part of a damsel in distress?

Elias had done his research, following his colleague's advice, so we knew what I was supposed to do. I filled out reams of papers and signed them while Elias stood a few inches behind me nervously coaching me and, at the same time, explaining to the other men why I was the one doing the work and not him. He patiently told them that I was the owner of the car and, therefore, I had to sign all the paperwork. About twenty minutes later, the employee with whom I had been talking told me that the office needed to process the papers and for us to go back the next day when everything would be ready and we could pay the taxes due.

The next day, I waddled slowly back into the customs office, stomach out, suffering expression on my face – ready to go. The first thing that the employee did was to hand me a form to fill out. I looked at the form and then said that I had already filled it out the day before. He looked at me with disbelief as if to say, *"You didn't really think that we would be that organized and have all the papers in order, did you?"*. Instead, in a matter-of-fact tone of voice, he said "Please fill it out again."

I filled out the form and, in a few minutes, we were done. Elias paid the taxes due. I don't remember if we got the Greek license plates from there or if Elias had to go somewhere else but, basically, we were done. Lesson learned? Stick out my stomach, waddle slowly, look exhausted. And everything will get done promptly.

Forget the one or two smiles a day. That night, I had a huge grin on my face. Maybe I had started to become Greek. Or maybe I had begun to appreciate the winning combination that I myself had. I was American, pregnant, and a car owner, and all these factors had opened the doors for me.

This is a good time, however, to say how thankful I was, and still am, to all those men at the customs office that day. They were polite and kind, caring, respectful, and protective. It was Greek masculinity at its absolute best. Even though most, if not all, of these men have probably passed away, this would also be a good time to say,

"I'm sorry for conning you that day. But you did put a big smile on my face."

- 5 -

…….. and Specifically, 1973 – 1974

"Sometimes you put walls up not to keep people out, but to see who cares enough to break them down."

Socrates

Friday, November 16, 1973. Elias and I were driving to the airport. I was taking a late morning flight to the States to see my family. I hadn't seen them for an entire year! Elias and I were expecting our first child and as soon as I had entered the second trimester of my pregnancy, the doctor had given me the green light to travel to Boston. I would be there for a week on my own. Elias would come a week later and then we would return to Athens together. Neither one of us had any inkling that all hell was about to break loose in Athens in the next few hours.

I was a little nervous. The military junta was still firmly

in power although some students had been demonstrating for the past week, since the past Tuesday, in and around the Athens Polytechnic. Those demonstrations were a niggling concern at the back of my mind but I was much more nervous about getting through customs and passport control at the airport. I think that I had a little more money on me than I was supposed to have. Elias had coached me before we left home and told me that if anyone asked me how much money I was carrying, to state the amount that I was allowed to have.

I am, however, the world's worst liar so when, at the airport, the police officer asked me how much money I was taking with me, I told him the truth. It was just about $100 or so more than the permitted amount. The officer frowned and I turned around to look at Elias, beseechingly. Elias in turn looked worried, concerned and anxious, and maybe he did take a step towards me and the police officer to clarify things, if necessary. The police officer saw this, and noticed as well that I looked completely helpless (I suppose this meant that I was not smuggling money out of the country??) and waved me through. I turned around again. Elias had calmed down.

The military junta had been governing Greece since April 21, 1967, when two colonels, the now infamous Georgios Papadopoulos and Stylianos Pattakos, activated a top-secret NATO plan that had been drawn up to defend Greece in the event of an enemy attack. Instead, the colonels used the plan to stage a *coup d'état* and to install themselves as heads of the government.

My first experience of being in a country with a military dictatorship was in July 1969 when Elias and I came to Greece on our honeymoon. I was a new bride and a new visitor to Greece and, therefore, I was blissfully unaware of the political undercurrents and completely ignorant of what a military dictatorship was or meant. Nothing bothered either Elias or me because we were honeymooners and, anyway, we were going back to the States in just a few weeks.

We were still in Greece when a planned referendum took place in late July. The referendum was to be a vote of confidence for the colonels. The sign on Lycabettus urging the population to vote *NAI* (*yes*, in English) worked because the colonels got 99.x% of the vote.

When Elias and I moved to Greece the day after Christmas in 1972, my real experience of living with the junta began. For the first time in my life, I was not comfortable in situations where I did not know anyone because I didn't know what was appropriate to say and what was not. I was suspicious of everyone and was constantly concerned that my papers might not be in order and that I could be questioned. A constant underlying tension defined each and every day.

I had grown up in a completely different environment in the States and had never been afraid of speaking up or of speaking my mind or of stating my opinion. What I was experiencing now in Greece was the complete opposite of what I was used to and I did not know how to handle it or to process it because I had no point of reference. One evening, we had gone out with Elias' friend, Dimitris, who was visiting from Austria. The conversation turned to the dictatorship and I said something very sarcastic. There was dead silence in the car. When we reached our destination and got out of the car, Dimitris turned to me and said,

"Don't *ever* say anything like that again in front of *anyone*, ever again. *Ever.*"

I arrived in Boston that afternoon of November 16 and was greeted with hugs and kisses. My father had told my mother how happy he was that I had decided to come to Boston because he could not have gone through another day without seeing me. We were all smiling and simply thrilled that I was back home.

In Athens, however, all hell was breaking loose, steadily and fiercely. Students, who had been demonstrating at the Polytechnic since Tuesday, November 13, had always been at the forefront of all the anti-dictatorship demonstrations despite the arrests, the trials, jail, and worse. This time, they seemed intent on pushing as far and as hard as they could and on Wednesday, November 14, the students at the Polytechnic moved into and occupied a building at the university. They were quickly joined by high-school students and blue-collar workers. In a flash, what had been a student protest changed into a popular uprising against the dictatorship. The junta pushed back by mobilizing the police and the military.

The next day, the first broadcasts from the Athens Polytechnic began and students urged the people to join them in a general strike and a general uprising. Students from other universities all over Greece set out to join the students at the Polytechnic.[iii]

[iii] http://news247.gr/eidiseis/afieromata/17-noemvrh-1973-to-xroniko -ths-eksegershs.1496921.html

This is a newspaper article, published on November 17, 2016, that chronicles

On Friday, November 16, the day that I flew to Boston, crowds of people began gathering in the streets, church bells began ringing, and the general atmosphere was one of a popular revolt. At 2 pm, the gates to the university closed.

In the early afternoon, twenty-five Greek and foreign reporters went to the university to hear an announcement read by the students. Photographs were not allowed. A little later, clashes between the students and the police began.

At around 8 pm the authorities began using tear gas. The First Aid Center was filled with injured people and the Polytechnic radio station broadcast appeals for medicines, doctors, and ambulances.

At 9 pm the demonstrators set up roadblocks around the Athens Polytechnic, using automobiles, buses, and trolleys, making it almost impossible for the police to advance.

At 9:30 pm, a curfew was announced. It would be effective until further notice. An hour later, police tanks rolled into the crowds around the Polytechnic, with the police throwing tear gas at the demonstrators at first and then tossing tear gas canisters inside the gates of the university.

Around midnight, a huge demonstration, with

---

the events that led to the uprising and the events of the uprising itself. Since I was not in Athens when the uprising happened and the military took action against the demonstrators, I have used the information in the article (from the newspaper NEWS) to relate what happened on November 16 and 17 in 1973. It still takes my breath away to read about the uprising and the bravery of the demonstrators who dared to lift their heads high. The article is in Greek and I have translated the parts that describe the timeline of events. The article also includes the photograph of the students on top of the gates of the Polytechnic, celebrating the fall of the junta, in July 1974.

thousands of people, began moving forward on Alexandras Avenue toward the Athens Polytechnic.

Not everyone was tuned into the students' broadcasts and not everyone was fully aware of the history unfolding. Friday evenings were "boys' night out" for Elias and his colleagues at Demokritos. That particular Friday evening on November 16 was no exception. Surely they had all heard something about what was going on at the university but, if they had, they didn't pay too much attention, if any at all. To be fair, they were all working in a suburb of Athens which was quiet. They had all been working that day, and it's certain that what was going on in the center of Athens was not covered either on the radio or on television. The men all went out for dinner and, around midnight, they all set out in different directions for home.

It was a dark night and Elias saw the army tank in front of him just in time to avoid crashing into it. He slammed on the brakes and the car stalled. He got out, yelling and flapping his arms, and started cursing and swearing at the soldiers to be more careful, and why had they stopped the damn tank in the middle of the street in the first place without any lights on *for God's sake*. And this from the man who had been telling me for an entire year not to speak up and to keep my head down. Fortunately, for the future generations of our family, the soldiers were calm and polite and said,

"Sir, go home. You have not heard the news. There is a curfew in place and you need to go home."

A little after midnight on what was now Saturday, November 17, the army tanks began moving out of their barracks and making their way to the vicinity of the Athens Polytechnic where police were clashing with civilians and students. Fifteen minutes later, the tanks made their first appearance at a junction a few blocks from the university. Athens had become a battlefield with the Polytechnic at the center.

A little before 1 am, the tanks turned onto Patission Street (where the main entrance to the Polytechnic is) and tanks, soldiers, and police all circled the university.

The demonstrators started retreating a little after 1 am to avoid the tanks. Many were able to hide in apartment buildings nearby where the main entrance doors had been left ajar by residents to allow demonstrators to find safety.

At about 1:30 am, there were still demonstrators outside the Polytechnic and sharpshooters took position on the rooftops of buildings around the university. In the meantime, the Polytechnic's radio station was broadcasting appeals to the soldiers, telling them that they, the students, were unarmed and that they would welcome the soldiers with applause.

Three tanks were outside the tall gates of the Polytechnic on Patission Street. Negotiations were taking place between the police and the students when at about 3 am, one of the tanks outside the gates backed up and then moved forward, attacking the gates with ferocious momentum, breaking through them and flattening them.

When the tanks entered the courtyard of the university, the demonstrators were grouped together by soldiers and, with their hands up, they were escorted out of the Polytechnic by Army Special Forces. A little after 3:35 am, according to witnesses, the Polytechnic had emptied out and ambulances began moving the wounded and the dead from the area.

At 5 am the tanks left the Polytechnic and moved to a park nearby. Athens looked like a war zone and everywhere there were fires, damaged and destroyed roadblocks, and blood. All public buildings were surrounded by the police.

At 7 am, people still in the street were chased away from the sidewalks across from the Polytechnic but at 7:30 am, demonstrations began again.

At 11 am, martial law was imposed.

One week later, on Saturday morning, November 24, Elias' Olympic Airways flight left for Boston. His flight was the last one out of Athens Airport and, when the plane left, the airport closed down for one week. It was a mini-replay of the April 21, 1967 *coup d'état* when the colonels had closed Greece down. Now another officer, Brigadier General Dimitrios Ioannides, had pushed aside Papadopoulos and Pattakos and had installed himself as the new military dictator of Greece.

Elias and I were in Boston for two weeks. I was immensely relieved that Elias had left Greece and was in Boston but neither of us was calm. The two weeks in Boston together were stressful. I was so happy to be back in Lynn surrounded by family and friends, but Elias and I were anxious about the situation in Greece. The only thing that alleviated our anxiety was that we felt the baby move for the first time.

Every night, with the lights out, we would talk, softly and quietly so as not to disturb my parents, about what to do. Perhaps we were also speaking softly so as not to frighten each other or ourselves. Should we go back to Greece? Should we stay in Lynn? All our belongings were in Athens. How would we get them out if we decided to stay in the US? And, if we stayed in the US, where would Elias work? The news from Greece was not good. The new dictator was more brutal and more ruthless than the two who he had thrown out.

We decided to take our chances and go back to Greece.

The atmosphere in Greece had changed dramatically. I could see it in the looks on people's faces, in the way they walked. They were nervous and jittery. They looked up whenever they heard a helicopter fly over. We heard rumors about the number of dead from the night that the tanks had crashed into the university. We heard rumors about the dissenters who had been jailed and were being tortured. I heard stories from friends about *their* friends who had had miscarriages during the revolt. We kept our heads down.

The weeks rolled by, and on April 24, 1974, our first child, Stefan, was born. We thought that he was the most beautiful creature that we had ever seen, God's perfection. His birth blocked out the anxiety and the stress of living with the junta, even if only briefly. The day after our baby was born, Elias came to the clinic to see us and he brought me a newspaper. I read that the military dictatorship in Portugal had collapsed, after fifty years of rule. I felt sad that our Stefan had not been born in freedom.

The days went by and we began planning for Stefan's christening. His godparents, Dimitris and Artemis, who we had visited in Vienna, were coming to Greece for the summer so the christening would take place at the end of July. My parents made their plans to come to Greece to attend the christening. But, once again, political events intervened.

On Monday, July 15, 1974, I went to a concert at the Herod Atticus theater under the Acropolis. Gina Bachauer, an internationally renowned classical pianist, would be performing. At the Herod Atticus theater, I met up with my cousin Connie's sister-in-law, Timi. Both of us had been looking forward to this concert for weeks and so had many others, judging from the number of people who had gathered in front of the ancient theater.

The concert was scheduled to begin at 8 pm but at 8 pm the gates had not yet opened. People became a little edgy, in a nervous way but not at all in an impolite way. Timi and I both had small children at home and were anxious about the delay. Timi's mother-in-law was watching her children and Elias was with Stefan. The whispering got a little louder and a little agitated and we heard rumors that there had been an assassination attempt on Archbishop Makarios, the first President of Cyprus, but that Makarios had managed to escape and was in London. A theater employee came out at some point and announced that, due to illness, Mrs. Bachauer had had to cancel the concert. But the real reason for the cancellation was indeed because of the events in Cyprus. The Greek government didn't want people milling around and perhaps causing trouble.

Trouble came anyway. A few days later, on Saturday July 20, a good friend of ours called to tell Elias to turn on the radio. Turkey had invaded Cyprus. The Turks used the attempted *coup* against Makarios as an excuse to invoke a clause in the Treaty of Lausanne and to invade Cyprus. They disembarked on the northern shores of Cyprus and marched to the middle of the island, cutting it in half. Hundreds of Greek Cypriots were forced to leave their homes with their elderly parents, their young children, and whatever they could carry with them. Boys as young as twelve years old had to drive the family cars as all men, except the very old and the very young, had been called into the Cypriot army.

The panic in Greece spread like wildfire. Men didn't know if they would be called up to serve in the Greek army and be shipped to Cyprus to fight there. Those men who had been called to report for duty had no uniforms and, worse, they had no weapons. Rumors were flying that the boxes that supposedly held the weapons contained only stones. Those same rumors alleged that the colonels had sold the weapons to African countries.

As for me, it was the first time that I had seen war, if not first-hand, then almost first-hand. I didn't know if Elias or my brother-in-law would be called up. There was so much confusion. And worst of all, the US and the UK seemed to be supporting Turkey's invasion of the island. The news on the television said that every time Greek fighter planes took off to stop the Turkish planes from flying over Cyprus, British planes intercepted them.

The US Ambassador of Cyprus was killed by a stray bullet that had ricocheted off a wall in the American Embassy. The bullet had not been intended for the Embassy or for the Ambassador. My mother was horrified that an American had been killed. I was horrified that the Greeks were prevented from providing much needed support to Cyprus. It seemed that my worst nightmare, which had always been that I would be in the middle of a conflict between Greece and the United States, was on the verge of becoming a reality.

Then something extraordinary happened. Because the colonels were unable to deal with the repercussions from the invasion in Cyprus, they resigned from their governmental positions or simply went underground. General Phaidon Gizikis was installed as the puppet head of the military government until someone with political experience could take over and restore democracy in Greece. Gizikis was a colorless officer but perhaps the perfect person to hand the country back to a constitutional government because he himself had not been sullied by the junta.

All this happened in just two or three days. Everything was happening with breakneck speed. By Tuesday, July 23, Athens was rife with rumors. One rumor was that King Constantine would come back and the password to convey that message, in case our telephones were tapped, was *"simera ta makaronia einai Corona"* (today we are having Crown macaroni). Another rumor said that Constantine Karamanlis was coming back from his self-imposed eleven-year exile in Paris. And, indeed, this is the scenario that played out.

On Tuesday afternoon, July 23, people flooded the streets and cars honked their horns. When Elias came home from work in the late afternoon, we left Stefan, who was all of three months old, with my father-in-law and then walked to the Polytechnic where throngs of people had gathered to rejoice and to celebrate the fall of the military junta. Students had climbed to the top of the gates which just eight months earlier had been crushed by the tanks. This was a photo-opportunity and I fully expected to see this picture in all the international newspapers the next day or the day after but I didn't. I could never understand why.

From there, Elias and I walked to Syntagma Square and again there were crowds of joyous and happy people, shouting slogans, celebrating the return of Karamanlis. Elias and I briefly considered going to the airport, together with thousands of others, to greet the plane but changed our minds because we did not want to leave my father-in-law alone with Stefan for too long. In the end, we made the right decision.

Constantine Karamanlis arrived in Athens on Wednesday, July 24, 1974, at 2 am. Giscard d'Estaing, the President of France, had put France's presidential airplane at Karamanlis' disposal so that he could fly back to Greece. The airport in Athens was mobbed with police and with civilians. Karamanlis was immediately taken to Parliament where he met with legitimate political leaders who had been sidelined, exiled, or imprisoned during the junta. At 4:15 am, he was sworn in as Prime Minister of Greece by Serafim, the Archbishop of Greece.

The sad and fearful period of the military junta had ended and the hard work of restoring Greece to a constitutional democracy had begun.

We baptized Stefan on Thursday, July 25, 1974, the day after Karamanlis arrived in Greece and was sworn in as Prime Minister. Stefan's christening was at 6 pm in the church where Elias had been an altar boy. After the christening, everyone went home to listen to Karamanlis' first address to the nation. It was a historic moment and it was one that nobody wanted to miss. We would celebrate Stefan's christening another night.

My parents came to Greece in September 1974 to visit Elias and me and to see their first grandchild. They had missed Stefan's christening but maybe that was for the best. If they had come in the middle of the Cyprus crisis, there would have been no way to predict what could or would happen. Instead, two months after the restoration of democracy in Greece, Elias and I were much more relaxed than we had been living under the junta, and we could truly enjoy my parents' visit without fearing for anyone's safety.

Those first two years in Greece, 1973 and 1974, were filled with breathtaking changes that happened at breathtaking speed and so much had happened in such a short period of time. The first five years generally were a period of constant adjustment and upheaval but those first two years included events that most people never see in an entire lifetime.

Towards the end of the first five years, in September of 1977, my parents made a second trip to Greece, this time for the baptism of our second son, Costis (Constantine), my parents' second grandchild who was named after my father. It was a happy event and we went out to dinner after the christening to celebrate.

The first chapter of my life in Greece had closed.

- 6 -

Growing up Greek-American

"A cousin is a little bit of childhood that can never be lost."

Marion C. Garrety

Fig 1: Some of the cousins on Christmas
Day, 1950, at Grandmother Demakes' house.

There are seven girl cousins in the Demakis / Demakes family.[iv] My two oldest girl cousins passed away very early on – (Nina, at the age of seven, before I was born, and Jean, at the age of twenty, when I was just three or four). The girl cousins then became evenly outnumbered by the boy cousins at a ratio of 2:1. The bond holding the girls together was always remarkably strong and has remained that way even now that we are no longer young.

In November 2015 I went to Boston for a wedding. My cousins, Nina and Louis, were marrying off their daughter Christina. I hadn't been to Boston for almost two years, and it was not just a wedding that I was going to. It was an opportunity to see my mother's family again, all together, although some family members were not there.

As soon as I arrived in Boston, the Demakes / Demakis girl cousins rallied and it took just a few calls for us to settle on a date for lunch. It turned out to be the day before I was returning to Greece. A few more calls later, we decided on the logistics and transportation details. We all met at a bistro in Marblehead, a small but very beautiful seaside suburb north of Boston. My brother Greg and sister-in-law Joan were living there at the time and, since I was staying with them, the bistro

---

[iv] My Grandfather Demakes spelled the family name with -es at the end, but many non-Greeks pronounced our name with two syllables – Dee Makes – rather than with three syllables. As a consequence, my father and his oldest brother spelled our name as Demakis but my other two uncles continued to spell it Demakes. The rest of us, for the most part, manage to keep things straight.

was a convenient place to meet.

Cousin Janet picked me up at Joan and Greg's house. Cousin Helen picked up Cousin Jean and together they picked up Cousin Joanne. Cousin Elaine was not feeling well[v] and so did not meet us for lunch and Cousin Connie was wrapping up her vacation in the Caribbean, arriving that evening. She would pick me up the next day to drive me to the airport and we would have lunch together before she dropped me off at Logan.

When Janet and I arrived at the bistro, Helen and Jean were already there, as was Joanne who was outside making a frantic phone call because she thought she had lost her house keys which, luckily, she found in the car. As we all settled down in the restaurant, a small cozy place with about six or seven tables, we studied the menu trying to decide what we wanted to order. I said something about a salad and Joanne said that that was what I always ordered whenever we went out for lunch. We made our choices and placed our orders with the young woman who was waitressing that day.

I looked around. The restaurant really was small and all the tables, about seven, were filled. Despite that, there was not too much noise. There was a low hum from the conversations taking place all around us. The bistro itself was warm and smelled invitingly good.

When Joanne told us that she had found her house keys on the floor of Helen's car, we all relaxed and started asking each other how everyone was and how their families were. In

---

[v] Elaine and Jean both passed away in 2019, just a month apart from each other.

about five minutes, we were in normal mode. We had hit our stride and were now talking loudly and laughing raucously. The food arrived and, in between bites, we continued our chatter. At some point, the conversation turned to me and to Greece and how were we, the Greeks, all doing and how were we managing with the financial crisis. Once we finished with the formalities, we started telling family stories.

This happens every time I meet my cousins, men and women. We finish with the formalities and then we discuss our families and our experiences of growing up in this particular family. Helen made a comment about not wanting to complain about her childhood because she had nothing to complain about, and I agreed because I didn't have anything to complain about either. But we all had stories that we wanted to tell and share.

Joanne started first. Joanne has visited Greece several times. I don't remember exactly how many times she has been here but it's a lot. Every time she came, she spent a significant amount of time and money in the jewelry stores, adding to an already large collection that she had of Greek jewelry. She vowed that day that she was done shopping for jewelry because she said that she had more than enough rings, bracelets and chains. Joanne loves Greece, and not only because of the shopping. She simply loves Greece and she always preferred coming here rather than traveling to other countries.

The last time she was here, she came with her friend Laura. They stayed in one of the big hotels in downtown Athens. That trip was the one when she blasted out all the electricity at the hotel. Here's what happened. She had brought an American hairdryer with her. She plugged it into the socket without a transformer and the entire hotel went black.

We were all laughing about this. Only Joanne and I knew the story so it was new to the others. When we finished with Joanne's story, we started in on the other family stories and our laughter was getting louder. At one point, I became aware that the three people, one man and two women, sitting at the table next to ours, were looking at us.

"Oops," I said. "I'm sorry. We're making a lot of noise."

"That's ok," one of the women responded. "We're enjoying listening to your stories about Greece."

"Are you all friends?" the man asked.

I looked at Helen first and then back at the man and said, "Yes, we're friends but our primary relationship is that of first cousins."

The man couldn't believe this. His jaw dropped. I saw an opportunity here and said "Let me introduce ourselves. I am Ioanna (my name in Greek), this is Ioanna (Joanne), this is Ioanna (Janet), this is Ioanna (Jean) and this is Eleni (Helen). The four of us (as I pointed at the four Ioannas) were named after our grandmother Yannoula."

This opened up a conversation between the two tables. It turned out that the man was Greek and had a jewelry store in Mykonos where he went with his wife, one of the women at the table, every summer. As soon as she heard this, Joanne was ready to hop on the next plane to Athens and take a connecting flight to Mykonos.

"But you just said that you had enough jewelry and you weren't going to buy any more." I told her.

"I changed my mind."

In September 2018, I went to another wedding, this time

to Cousin Janet's wedding. Her husband Nick had died a premature death several years before and she was remarrying, much to the delight of her family. Her new husband, Brian, is not Greek. He is Irish and the Irish are just as clannish as the Greeks. Most of the Demakes / Demakis cousins were at the wedding. We had come from everywhere. We were celebrating Janet's happiness, circling the wagons.

Janet had requested that the DJ play the traditional wedding song from Greek weddings, loosely translated as *How Beautiful Our Bride Is.* When we heard the first notes of the song, we all got up to dance with Janet and her husband Brian, and Janet led the dance just as we had learned from our aunts so many years ago. When she sent out her thank you notes, she wrote that what she liked best of all at the wedding was that we all got up to dance the Greek wedding dance with her and Brian. And here, I would like to say that Brian was such a good sport about this.

After the dancing, the photographer took a photograph of the Demakes / Demakis clan. There are at least fifty of us in the photo.

In all immigrant families, there are two centers of gravity or two points of reference. One is family. The other is a community gathering place. We'll start with family.

My family is big, very big. It's also loud and noisy. And it's also loving and supportive. Most immigrant families in the US, even into the third and fourth generations, are the same as ours. Change the names, the language, the religion, the country of origin, and they all circle the wagons the way we did, and still do.

Growing up, we were family and we were *Greek* family. And even though we may have resisted sometimes, we were proud to be Greek family. We were a tribe. The whole family congregated at my Grandmother *(Yiayia)* Demakes' house at least once a month because there was always something to celebrate. Anything so everyone could get together.

This is where we learned to dance Greek dances. Yiayia's house had a very long corridor and my aunts used to lead the dancing, taking us all in a line up and down the corridor, teaching us the steps while the Greek music played on.

Yiayia's house is where the cousins went for vacation every summer. We were each allotted a few days to spend there in July or August and maybe another cousin would be there as well. My cousins Helen and Janet lived on the ground floor of the two-family house with their parents and their older brother Tommy, so we had plenty of company.

Yiayia's house is also where many newlyweds spent the first few months of their married life together until they had a place of their own. The attic was filled with furniture that they would borrow and then return so someone else could use it.

Later, I would wonder how the in-laws, Yiayia's sons-in-law and daughters-in-law, and later the husbands and wives of the first cousins, managed getting used to this family which could be overwhelming. But the in-laws loved the family, most of them, anyway. They loved the noise, the revelry, and the closeness. They loved being part of this family, and the family loved them back.

Elias loved being part of my family and, even after

we divorced, whenever he went back to the States, he would make a point of visiting with my parents and with my cousins, too. He loved them and they loved him back.

Even now, so many years later, I see the friendships among the next generations of the family including my sons' friendships with my cousins' children and their children with the rest of the family. There is a bond that they all recognize and that cannot be broken because we are family. We are a tribe.

My mother's family is smaller than my father's family, and not as noisy and certainly not as loud. They were also a tribe but a smaller tribe than my father's family. Consequently, the memories that I have from that family are different. The Demakes / Demakis family spilled over with first cousins. In the Jenis family, the first cousins were a total of nine, including my three brothers and myself. The memories, however, of my grandparents and my aunts and uncle remain indelible in my mind.

I would go to my Jenis grandparents' house for weekends when I was a little girl and would be pampered and spoiled. My grandmother was an outstanding cook and my favorite meal at her house was chicken and potatoes roasted with oil and lemon and a bowl of avgolemono soup as a starter.[vi] My Aunt Nellie would spoil me, too. She would send me to the corner store to buy a package of powdered Kool-Aid which we would dissolve in a pitcher of ice-cold water.

[vi] Avgolemono soup is rice cooked in chicken broth and topped off with a frothy egg and lemon mixture that has been whipped and folded into the soup.

Heaven on earth.

I remember that on Saturday afternoons, my aunts, Nellie and Dee, would listen to the Metropolitan Opera and Maria Callas on the radio. At the age of five, I cannot say that I truly appreciated opera and neither had I begun to listen to other kinds of music. But those Saturday afternoon radio transmissions from the Met were the beginning of my appreciation of culture.

I was the first grandchild in the Jenis family and although my grandparents and aunts loved all the grandchildren, I was still the first and, therefore, not only the most spoiled but also the one with the most memories.

Probably the best part of belonging to these tribes was that the appreciation of family started at the top. My Jenis grandparents and my Demakes grandmother were devoted to each other. Every week, my grandfather would take my grandmother for a leisurely drive, usually to the cemetery or to pick wild greens, and he would invite my Grandmother Demakes to go with them.

My uncle George, my mother's only brother, was a close friend of my Uncle Nick, my father's youngest brother. My Jenis aunts, Nellie and Dee, and my father's youngest sister, Diana, were best friends. And my Aunt Dee's daughter Nina married Louis, my father's nephew's son, cementing even further the ties between the two families.

The Jenis family and the Demakes / Demakis family had very different personalities. The Demakises argued about everything. They could not even agree on how to spell their last name. But they were always the best of friends.

The Jenis family was more low-key probably because the Jenis family was less than half the size of the Demakes / Demakis family. The Jenises were also quieter. Yet, despite the differences in their personalities, the two families got along beautifully.

In 1953, Diana and Dee traveled to Europe together. It was almost unheard of at that time for young women to travel to Europe alone. I always refer to my two aunts as the original backpackers because they wanted to go to Europe and they just went. Dee quit her job at the General Electric and Diana quit her job working for her brothers at the sausage factory.

The two women were in Europe for at least three months, maybe longer. One of the countries that they traveled to, of course, was Greece. They had promised themselves that they would make a pilgrimage and meet their relatives.

Once they arrived in Greece, the two young women hired a taxi to take them to my Demakes grandparents' village of Logganikos, high in the mountains of Lakonia in the Peloponnese. The trip to the village from Athens, in a taxi, took twelve hours. This was 1953, eight years after the end of World War II and just four years after the end of Greece's civil war. Basically, there were no roads to speak of but the roads that did exist were narrow, bumpy, unpaved and dangerous. All along the side of the roads were little memorials with icons and crosses, to indicate that someone had died in a car accident there. After one particularly harrowing hairpin curve, Diana and Dee crossed themselves in the back of the taxi and said, "Please God, we didn't come to Greece to die."

They had flown to Greece from Italy. Tim, one of the Demakes family's Greek cousins, met them at the airport. His father had been advised that the girls were traveling to Greece and when they were arriving and told his son to go the airport to meet them. Tim was reluctant, but went anyway.

This is how Tim met Dee, my mother's sister and Diana's close friend. Once he greeted the two young women, he was always with them. A romance between Tim and Dee began but the two friends went back to the States as planned despite Tim's pleas to Dee to stay. But Tim and Dee wrote to each other and in one of his letters, Tim proposed. Dee flew back to Greece and the couple was married in November 1954. My cousin Nina was born in 1955 and Diana flew to Greece again, this time to be godmother to Nina. Another connection between the two families.

The other center of gravity or reference point was the church. Church was not only about religion, a common bond in every immigrant group. It was also about congregation, gathering together as a community. It made no difference what everyone's origins were, whether they were from Northern Greece or from the Peloponnese or from one of the islands. Everyone was from Greece. And that was what brought us all together.

The church played a definitive role in our lives. First of all, the children all went to Greek school which was a two-hour class twice a week at the community center. Greek-American parents sent their children to Greek school after public school was out for the day in the hope, mostly futile, that they would learn to speak and read some Greek. Most of the teachers were Greek grandmothers whose ability to discipline was minimal, at best.

We did learn some Greek but, most of all, we made friendships that have lasted forever. We were bored silly in the classes which took place in the afternoons after our regular school but we managed to write notes to each other and hold long conversations, whispering back and forth. Our church was, and still is, in an area of Lynn known as West Lynn. Until the late 40s and early 50s, most Greek immigrant families, including both my parents' families, lived in West Lynn, resulting in strong relationships and friendships. In the 50s, families began fanning out into other areas of Lynn and to other suburbs which were less crowded and better off. The friendships remained, however, and the tribes stuck together.

We were not the only kids going to a religious institution after regular school. The Jewish kids were going to synagogue to learn Hebrew and the Catholic kids were going to church for catechism lessons. It was something of a badge of honor to have some kind of religious activity after school, or any other activity for that matter.

As we got older, our attention turned to socializing and the accepted way to socialize was to go to church on Sundays and to the church dances. Sunday services were a given. My father would drive my brothers and me to the Sunday service and then visit his friends at their factory for a Sunday morning coffee. When the service and Sunday school classes were over, he would come back to the community center and pick us up.

The best socializing, however, was at the church

dances. Some of the young men were in Greek bands, playing the bouzouki or the guitar and singing Greek songs, in Greek of course. Our parents would drop us off and, for two or three hours, we would dance non-stop until they came to pick us up. But we were also looking around and taking note of who was there, sizing them up. More than one couple met on that dance floor.

And of course, that church is where we all got married. When Elias and I were planning our wedding, we had to meet with the priest before the wedding. I had two requests for him. One was to do the entire service in Greek only and the other was to have our elderly priest co-officiate, even though he was retired. Elias was shocked that I had specified these two requests; he thought it was unbecoming. But our priest was not bothered in the least. When some of my non-Greek friends complained that they couldn't understand the service, I asked them if they had understood that I was getting married. They said yes, and I answered that that was the only thing that mattered. And having Father Argyrides there to co-officiate was a sign of respect for him from me because he had been the priest of our church for as long as I could remember.

At some point, and as we grew up, we, the cousins, started to resist a little. The Greekness and the closeness were sometimes a little too much, a little too cloying. We had very little room in which to move around. Everywhere we went, people knew who we were. We could not stray from the straight and narrow. We couldn't smoke. We couldn't even swear. We were the

Demakeses / Demakises. And even though we didn't realize at the time that we were a tribe, we certainly felt as though we were in Greek club[vii], all the time!

We all went to college around the same time and discovered a world that was very different from the one in which we had grown up. It was a sophisticated world where there were people from other countries and other cultures and who spoke other languages. They had different political views. They read different books. Our college experiences were eye openers and, although our parents wanted so much for us to have a good, solid college education, they knew that there could and might be some unwanted and unexpected influences.

Growing up in any immigrant family in the United States is filled with constant pushing and pulling. The family, whether they are immigrants or first generation born in the States, push their children out to integrate into the American world and then pull them back into the fold at critical junctions so that the children won't lose their connection to the family and traditions. The children are also pushing and pulling, pushing to get out of their restricted environments so that they can explore the world around them, and pulling their parents with them to approve of their plans to have a little more freedom.

I am second generation born in the United States as are my brothers and my first cousins. We were all pushed to

---

[vii] As Paris Miller, Toula's daughter in the movie *My Big Fat Greek Wedding 2,* famously said, "Every day of my life is Greek Club."

integrate into the American culture and the 40s, 50s, and 60s were an ideal time for that. Our primary language was English although some of the cousins were fortunate to learn really good Greek from their grandparents. Unfortunately, I was not one of them. My parents wanted us to learn perfect English so that we could get into the best American universities.

Additionally, all the cousins were brought up with limited job choices – the boys could take over the family business, if there was one, or become a lawyer, a doctor, or an engineer. My Greek friends tell me that the "lawyer, doctor, engineer" options were the same in Greece at that time. The girls' options were even more limited. We could become teachers only because eventually, in our primary jobs, we would be wives and mothers. The biggest push of all was for the boys - a top-notch college and either law or medical school.

As we were pushed, however, to integrate into American culture, other issues intervened. We wanted to go to school dances during the school year or to the beach in the summer with all the other kids from school or to the movies with our friends. And obviously, some of our friends were Greek-American, but not all of them. It was then that our families wanted to pull us back.

The biggest pull from our parents came while we were in high school, with school dances and dating. Our parents wanted us to go to the dances and to date but they didn't want us to date non-Greeks. The mantra that we heard all the time was that we would marry Greek, and we heard that mantra from the time that we were teenagers. Also, at the time that most of us were in high school in the 50s and 60s, the two biggest worries for all parents were a pregnant teenage daughter and a drunk driver teenage son. These two worries were a huge pull for our parents.

To counteract the possibility of meeting and falling for a non-Greek, our parents sent us not only to Greek school, to church, and to the church dances six or seven times a year, but also to the church festival and to the Greek AHEPA[viii] conventions once a year – hoping that we, the girls, would meet a good Greek boy and the boys would meet a good Greek girl. And by good Greek boy or girl, I mean a good Greek-American boy or girl.

When I was eighteen, my parents went to the New Year's Eve party at our church. They took me with them. This was the Greek-American version of a debutante presentation without the long white gown or any of the other debutante paraphernalia. But the message was clear. My parents were presenting me to Greek-American society in Lynn. I was now officially of marriageable age.

This put enormous pressure on us, the cousins. Yes, we wanted to get married eventually, but all in good time, and if the prospective bride or bridegroom was not a good Greek-American girl or boy, then so what? But that's not how our parents saw things. It was the classic push and pull although the boys had a little more freedom than the girls had.

[viii] AHEPA is the American Hellenic Educational Progressive Association, a fraternal organization founded in 1922.

My mother's first cousin Dee, who is just eight years older than I am, got engaged at the age of twenty to a young Italian-American man. Dee had met Vinnie through Vinnie's sister who was Dee's classmate at college. People would say "Did you hear? Dee is engaged." And inevitably, someone would whisper "He's not Greek". This is what our parents wanted to avoid but the pull sometimes was not as strong as the push. Dee and Vinnie had a long and brilliant marriage, by the way. And their two children, sixty years later, revel in and enjoy both their heritages.

This was the model with which I came to Greece and the one that I expected to find. Elias' family was certainly close but not in the way that we were. They did not circle the wagons the way that we did. Everyone in Greece was Greek and their Greekness did not make them different, as it made us in the States, and as it made every ethnic group different in the States. In Greece, they were family. In the States, we were tribes.

The other dynamic that I encountered in Greece was the dynamic between the Greeks and the Greek-Americans, those who stayed and those who left. It's taken me a long time to understand that dynamic and the way each group looked down on the other. Even Elias was dismissive of the Greek-Americans.

"What were you?" he would ask me once in a while, rhetorically. "You were all dishwashers."

On the other hand, the Greek-Americans didn't truly understand the psychology of the Greek people who had lived through the two World Wars, the Catastrophe of Smyrna, and a civil war, all in the space of fewer than fifty years. The Greek-

Americans were incredibly proud of the Greeks for fighting so bravely in World War II but, in all fairness to the Greek-Americans, it is impossible to understand the consequences of such wars on any society if one has not lived through those wars.

Janet's wedding was at the end of August and I stayed in Boston for two weeks. I saw my whole family ranging from the oldest member to the youngest. Another major highlight of that trip was the festival that my church, the Saint George Greek Orthodox Church in Lynn, was holding on Labor Day weekend, the first weekend in September, as it does every year.

The festival is a big event in Lynn and the surrounding suburbs. People come from miles around for the food and the music, the dancing and the fun. The festival lasts for three days, and every member of the church volunteers to make each year memorable. I went with Connie and Joanne on the second day of the festival and there were hundreds of people there. A Greek band was playing and people were dancing or just milling around to talk to people who they hadn't seen for a while. Joanne got up to mingle and came back and said that two of her good Greek-American friends were there if I wanted to see them. It had been at least forty-five years and maybe longer since I had seen Stella and Julia. But it was wonderful to see them again and to visit with them, the feeling of familiarity still there.

A few minutes later, another woman came up to me and said, "Hi, Joan. I'm Stacia, Amalia's daughter. We lived on the first floor of your Jenis grandparents' triple-decker. Do you remember me?" And, of course, I did remember her.

Another memory that I have from that visit to Boston that summer is having dinner at the country club with my brother Greg and sister-in-law Joan and my cousins Tom and Peachie. Greg and Tom are members of the club and everyone knows them. As we walked into the crowded dining room on that summer Saturday evening, a woman who I did not know or if I had met her before, I didn't remember her, came up to me and asked "Are you the Demakis that lives in Greece?" That surprised even me. That was the power of the tribe.

Fig 2: Easter 1951 at Grandmother Demakes' house.
Front row: Me, Johnny and Philip C., Tommy L.,
Helen, my brother Tom, and Janet. Back row: Aunt
Mary, Grandmother, Aunt Diana, Aunt Julia.

- 7 -

Growing up in Boston and Lynn

"Here's to dear old Boston, the home of the bean and the cod, where Lowells speak only to Cabots, and Cabots speak only to God."

John Collins Bossidy [ix]

It has been said that it can take a lifetime to make a friend in Boston but that once you have established the friendship, you will have that friend forever. On the other hand, if it has taken a lifetime to make that friend, how much time is left to enjoy the friendship? This is probably why Boston's snobbery is legendary.

Perhaps it is the frigid winter weather and the snow

[ix] From a toast given by John Collins Bossidy at the 1910 alumni dinner at Holy Cross College.

that never ends that put a holding pattern on making new friendships. Perhaps it is the city's history including the Tea Party, the USS Constitution, Bunker Hill and the Freedom Trail, that sets Boston apart from other cities. Perhaps it is the fact that most of the passengers on the first sailing of the Mayflower settled in what is now Boston and its environs.

There are many beautiful cities in the US, each one with a distinct personality of its own. But Boston is Boston and it is unique. It is a pretty city, situated on the Atlantic Ocean and punctuated by the Charles River which separates it from Cambridge. One of the oldest residential neighborhoods in Boston is Beacon Hill, with winding cobblestoned streets and beautiful three- and four-hundred-year-old brick residences that remind one of old England. They require a lot of maintenance and money but give the city a certain cachet.

Boston is home to the Boston Common and to the Boston Public Garden, both large parks and both British imports. The Boston Public Garden is famous for the swan boats which have made that elegant bird the city's iconic signature. The real swans are in the Lagoon in the park. They are taken from the Lagoon in the fall to protect them from the freezing winter weather and are brought out again in May where they are welcomed back with a parade.

The Public Garden is also home to the sculpture of the family of ducklings made famous in Robert McCloskey's children's book, *Make Way for Ducklings*. It is full of blooming flowers and flowering trees in the summer and is the perfect place for children to play and for taking wedding pictures.

Boston is probably the only city in the US where you can start out driving from Point A, take four right-hand turns and not end up back at Point A. Boston's streets are former cow paths and no effort was made to straighten them out, probably because the streets were defined by the houses and stores that had already been erected. When I was growing up, Boston was, in my opinion, the city of the worst drivers in the States. Someone asked me why that was but I don't know the answer. It just was.

I didn't travel much outside of New England until I got married. Shortly after we were married, Elias and I drove to Detroit to visit his aunt and his first cousins. We pulled into a gas station in Detroit – it was rush hour and I was driving – and after we had filled the car up with gas, I gradually started to pull out of the station, waiting for an opening in the rush-hour traffic to get onto the road. Much to my wondrous surprise, cars stopped to let me pull out. I was so shocked that I didn't react right away. I can still remember Elias saying, "Go. Go. GO!!!!" In Boston, I might have waited at least an hour for a break in the traffic or for some non-Bostonian to stop.

Another memory is from several years later, in 1989, when I was driving home from my graduate school program. The boys were in the car with me. The infamous Friday afternoon 3 pm bumper-to-bumper traffic was worse than horrendous and there, in front of me and to the right, was a little Volkswagen Beetle with Vermont license plates. The Beetle was in the right lane, trying to change lanes and move to my lane, the middle lane. One desperate young man, who thankfully was a passenger and not the driver, was leaning out the window and waving his arms, pleading for someone to make room for the Beetle in my lane. I slowed down and, much to the annoyed honking of the drivers behind me, let the flustered Vermonters change lanes.

However, as Einstein used to say, everything is relative. I went back to the States in November of 1973 to see my family after a year of living and driving in Athens. I had had the car mostly to myself that year. I had learned the streets of Athens and I had learned to drive aggressively, like an Athenian.

The driving culture in 1973 was completely different in Greece than it was in the States. Young people in the States got their licenses at the age of sixteen and drove the family cars. In Greece, cars were still a luxury and only a few people were able to afford them. Most of the Greeks who became car owners were in their thirties, forties, and fifties. They were proud to be behind the wheel of their own cars but they didn't have the same driving skills as a person who learns to drive at a much younger age. They were nervous, uncertain, and impatient, and sometimes had a heavy foot on the gas pedal.

But driving in the Greek environment influenced me and, after just one year of driving in Athens, when my father told me that I drove like a cowboy it meant that he could see the difference.

Boston reinvents itself every twenty-five to thirty years. One of the biggest changes that I remember growing up was the construction of the Mystic River Bridge, the one that looks like a child's erector set. Up until that bridge was built, the only real access to Boston from the North Shore was through the Sumner Tunnel. The bridge changed all that and became popular with the North Shore crowd, although they still used the tunnel, especially if they were going to Logan Airport but mostly out of habit. The Mystic River Bridge speeded things up and traffic usually moved relatively quickly.

In the early 60s, the Charles River Park apartment complex was built, next to the Massachusetts General Hospital (MGH). At that time, MGH was only one building and was just beginning its expansion, an expansion that seems to never end. The Charles River Park apartment buildings in the West End were the *in* place to live. As all the North Shore suburbanites drove by the complex to get onto the Mystic River Bridge in the evening to get out of Boston and go home, there was a huge sign in front of the complex that said, "If you lived here, you would be home now." However, in order for some people to live in those glamorous new apartments, poorer neighborhoods, mostly Italian and Jewish, were torn down as part of a late 50s urban renewal project and the residents began moving out of Boston. Many of them moved to Lynn.

It was after the new apartment building complex was built that everyone, Bostonians and suburbanites, noticed the magnificent landscape in front of and around the complex. Storrow Drive is a very busy thoroughfare that goes by the hospital and the Charles River Park apartments, taking drivers *to* the bridge as they are leaving Boston or *from* the bridge as they come into Boston from the North Shore. Across from the apartment complex, on the other side of the thoroughfare, is the Charles River Esplanade, a state park where the famous and fabulous Boston Pops Orchestra gives a July fourth concert every year, accompanied by spectacular fireworks. The setting is stunning.

Boston reinvented itself again in the late 70s and early 80s. In 1970, Elias and I moved to Fort Lee, New Jersey, a small town then, on the banks of the Hudson River. The first time I went back to Boston after we moved to Fort Lee, I thought to myself, "How provincial". Just a few months of living in New York, even if it was on the New Jersey side of the Hudson, had changed the way I looked at Boston.

The next time we went back, however, I noticed some significant changes. And in just a few years, by the time we started traveling from Greece, in the late 70s and early 80s, Boston had transformed itself from a stodgy city, stuck in its English architectural past, into a very sophisticated metropolis. The whole US began taking notice of Boston and people started flocking to Boston to live there. They were attracted by jobs at the hospitals and the universities. After a while, it also became one of the most expensive cities to live in. Although other cities may have been trendier at different times, Boston was still Boston.

After the transformation of the 70s and 80s, the next big project was the Big Dig. Bostonians will never forget the Big Dig. And neither will anyone else. The Big Dig was Massachusetts' grand plan to make Boston more accessible and easier to drive into and to drive through. The key words here are *grand plan*. There were overruns in time estimates, budgets and costs.

The Big Dig was completed in 2007, officially. Many drivers are still intimidated by the new roads and the new signage and several drivers still get lost. I wouldn't even think about driving into Boston now. It is so much easier to take public transportation. I think that many people coming from the suburbs also prefer not to drive into Boston and, who knows, maybe this was the goal of the grand planners and engineers all along.

My brother Paul told me that Boston is currently in the middle of another transformation. This time they are building skyscrapers. Whatever they do, I hope that the planners and the engineers remember that Boston's main attraction is its uniqueness and that they will leave space for the parks to show and that the new buildings will not eclipse the traditional Boston architecture.

My mother and her sister, my Aunt Nellie, started taking me to Boston, once or twice a year, when I was five years old. We would take the narrow-gauge train from Lynn Central Station to North Station in Boston. From there, we would end up downtown, although I don't remember how. I was entranced. Boston was a wonderland to me, even in its stodgy version.

We would go to Schrafft's for lunch. I loved that restaurant and would order a grilled cheese sandwich and a coca cola whenever we ate there. We always bought a loaf of cheese bread from their bakery to take home with us. Schrafft's on Boylston Street is gone now but I still remember its enticing aromas.

From there, we would go shopping, starting with C. Crawford Hollidge, an elegant store for linens, ladies' undergarments, beautiful dresses for women and gorgeous children's clothes. I remember that there were no cash registers or cashiers. Instead, there was a dumbwaiter which was a small freight elevator. The customer would give money to the salesperson to pay for her purchase, the salesperson would put the money in the dumbwaiter and, in a few minutes, the dumbwaiter would come back with change and the receipt.

The two big department stores in Boston were Filene's and Jordan Marsh. Filene's offspring was Filene's Basement which was famous for its sales of bridal gowns at incredibly discounted prices and the crush of women who would wait for hours before the store opened to be one of the first to try on a gown. Jordan Marsh was famous for its fabulous blueberry muffins. Both stores are closed now. There were Bonwit Teller and Charles Sumner, two stores with beautiful women's fashions and, finally, Shreve Crump and Low with beautiful jewelry, and gorgeous silver and bone china dinnerware. This is where I set up my wedding registry. The shopping is still fabulous in Boston but that era was one of a kind.

Most of all, I remember my mother and my aunt tutoring me on how to dress by looking at the wealthy Bostonian women to observe what they wore and how they behaved. My mother and my aunt would point out a woman and tell me how I could identify her as wealthy.

"This woman is a wealthy Bostonian. Look at how she dresses. Low-heeled sensible black shoes but expensive, a tweed skirt - expensive, a cashmere sweater - expensive, and a string of pearls – very expensive. Nothing flashy. Simple and understated, but expensive."

The tweed skirt had most likely been hand-loomed in Australia from wool sheared from Merino sheep and then purchased from the venerable Brooks Brothers emporium. The pearls had most likely been pried from oysters by pearl divers and sold at Shreve Crump and Low. The shoes were not

Louboutin, but they were undoubtedly a high-class American brand. The cashmere sweater needs no explanation.

That is how I learned to dress (most of the time). Understated. Simple. Almost plain. It was an example to emulate because the women that my mother and my aunt pointed out to me were the ones who held the keys to their family vaults. And this was Boston snobbery at its finest.

Boston is, and always has been, a city of the best – the best universities and colleges, the best hospitals, the Boston Symphony Orchestra, the big four sports teams (although the Red Sox took a while to get back to the top), the Boston Museum of Fine Arts, and the Children's Museum. The Freedom Trail guides both native Bostonians and tourists along the sites of the American Revolution which started here (in nearby Lexington and Concord, actually).

Boston is home to some of the finest educational institutions in the world. I grew up with Harvard and MIT in my back yard. Both colleges were just a forty-five-minute drive from home (this was before the Big Dig). I cannot impress enough the impact of living in the shadow of these institutions. They were the invisible gold standard that all parents set for their children and to which we, as high-school students in Massachusetts, all hoped that we would be admitted. It was our parents' dream and it was our dream, too. When I was in high school, several students in my senior class, including me, applied for admission to Harvard and / or to MIT. Only one of my classmates actually did gain admission to Harvard and the rest of us were in awe. But because we had aimed for the sun and the moon, those of us who had not been admitted to Harvard or MIT landed on a star and got into another great college instead.

Boston is a college town, not in a small-town sense, but in a big city sense. In addition to Harvard and MIT, there are Tufts University (with its outstanding Dental School), Boston University, Boston College, Brandeis University, the University of Massachusetts, Suffolk University, Northeastern University, Berklee College of Music, and Simmons University, as well as smaller colleges such as Emmanuel and Wheaton. There are students all over the city, from all over the world, and perhaps this is one of Boston's major attractions.

I studied at Boston University (BU) and I loved several things about it. One was its diversity – even more than fifty years ago, the diversity was plain to see. There were students from every country in the world, of every religion, of every race. There were students who lived in the dorms, and there were students who commuted from Boston's suburbs. BU was diverse and egalitarian. BU's admissions process, when I was a student there, gave everyone a chance to study, and then it was up to the students to get through the rigorous curriculum or not. At that time, Boston University was the great leveler.

Another thing I loved about BU is that it was, and still is, a city college. I am partial to city colleges and universities because the whole city is the campus. BU does have a campus but the campus is not a defined separate entity, fenced in or walled off from the rest of the city. The city is BU's campus and, as students, we had access to everything a cosmopolitan city has to offer – theaters, cinemas, music, restaurants, bookstores, and more.

I commuted to BU for the first two years and then lived in one of the smaller dormitories, the French House, for the next two years. One night, four of us, all young women from the dorm, decided to go see two Ingmar Bergman films, back-to-back. We walked about a half hour to the movie theater, the four of us talking non-stop. Then we saw the two Bergman movies. The walk back was markedly different. This time, we were so shattered by the movies that we had just seen that none of us spoke a word.

On Friday afternoons, when it was performing in Boston, the Boston Symphony Orchestra would do a dress rehearsal of their Sunday afternoon concerts. Students were admitted free of charge to the dress rehearsals so, again, my friends and I would go occasionally, depending on our study and exam schedules. And both Kenmore Square and Fenway Park were just a short walk away from our dorms in case someone wanted to take in a Red Sox game rather than a BSO concert.

It wasn't only the city activities that attracted us. Living in the dorms on campus gave us the opportunity to do a lot of things that we couldn't do as commuters. Several professors would give evening lectures that anyone could go to even if we were not taking that professor's class. My friends and I were always on the lookout for interesting philosophy and history lectures. It was a good way to broaden our interests and to think about taking a course from some of these professors.

Commuting was a different story. Students who lived within an hour's driving distance to the university often drove in, mostly for economic reasons. Perhaps their parents were not able to pay the dormitory fees. There was a distinct difference between the students who lived on campus and those who did not. For those who commuted, participation in many of the social and educational activities was limited because there simply was not enough time to do the extra-curricular activities and still be home at a reasonable hour (before midnight). But there were other perks.

I lived on campus in my junior and senior years but commuted during my freshman and sophomore years. I drove in every day with another classmate who lived in Lynn. George had a car and wanted three other students to drive in with him. We paid him a small sum every week to cover costs, gas and tolls. I was George's first passenger. Someone in my extended family circle had told George to call me. I think that he was the nephew of one of my mother's friends. I then recommended two other friends who lived close by, Margot and Stanley. George would pick us up every morning and drop us off every evening. The four of us bonded and driving into Boston beat taking the bus or train and then the MTA, Boston's subway.

The four of us talked non-stop both ways. Margot was my friend from the seventh grade in junior high school and was later a bridesmaid in my wedding. I met Stanley when he and his family moved to the neighborhood and we were in junior and senior classes in high school together. We all talked about everything and laughed a lot, too.

The most enduring memory of our commutes is from the Friday afternoon of November 22, 1963. We were driving home. It was the weekend and there was so much traffic. Usually, we had the radio on but on this particular afternoon, we were talking about something that must have been extremely interesting because we had turned the radio off. As we were driving up Storrow Drive to get onto the ramp leading to the bridge, I happened to look around at the other commuters. We were passing by the Charles River Park apartment complex. I commented to everyone how serious the drivers in the other cars looked.

"No one is smiling," I remember saying.

It wasn't until George dropped me off at home and I turned on the radio to listen to some music that I learned the reason why the drivers in the other cars had looked so somber. President Kennedy had been assassinated.

The Charles River separates Boston and Cambridge, with BU on the Boston side. Sometimes, on a warm spring or early summer day, one of our professors would take our class, if the class was small enough, across the highway on the overpass to sit on the banks of the Charles and we would have our class there. It didn't happen very often but it was a nice break when it did happen.

The "school across the river", as some of our BU professors referred to Harvard, is on the Cambridge side of the Charles. So is MIT. Across the river, Harvard generates its own special magic. One says "Harvard" and all the bells and whistles go off. Harvard does have a traditional gated campus, covered in ivy and walled in from the bustle of Harvard Square. Its reputation is decidedly different now from what Henry Adams[x] described in his autobiography, *The Education of Henry Adams.*

---

[x] Henry Adams was the grandson of John Quincy Adams, the sixth President of the US, and the great-grandson of John Adams, the second President of the US. He printed one hundred copies of his book, *The Education of Henry Adams,* privately in 1905. In 2009, Digreads.com Publishing converted it to an e-book.

"The next regular step was Harvard College. He (Henry Adams) was more than glad to go. For generation after generation, Adamses and Brookses and Boylstons and Gorhams had gone to Harvard College, and although none of them, as far as known, had ever done any good there, or thought himself the better for it, custom, social ties, convenience, and, above all, economy, kept each generation in the track. Any other education would have required a serious effort, but no one took Harvard College seriously. All went there because their friends went there, and the College was their ideal of social self-respect."

The Education of Henry Adams was written in 1905. A lot has changed since then. But it is still worth reading Chapter IV about Harvard College.

Harvard is extremely selective in its admissions process but once a student is accepted, it is very rare for Harvard to ask any student to leave because of low grades. Its rarified atmosphere is cultivated by students, faculty and administration. But Harvard does reach out to students who do not have the social, economic, or educational background that most people associate with Harvard. In its effort to be diverse, the college looks for students who are outstanding in their own milieu. Maybe they have had interesting summer jobs or maybe they have done some outstanding volunteer work. Maybe they are budding artists and writers or maybe they have achieved perfect scores on their college entrance exams. Or maybe they come from poor immigrant families. Whatever that something is, Harvard is always on the lookout for that exceptional student who Harvard thinks will thrive in its environment. One of those students was my father.

Dad went to the US in 1914 on a boat that took three weeks to sail across the Atlantic from Patras. He and his mother and four siblings were berthed in fourth class on the ship, with dried bread and cheese that my grandmother had packed from the village as their meals. My grandfather had already returned to the States a year before and was waiting for them at Ellis Island in New York in a horse and carriage. When my father walked off the ship with his family, his shoes hung around his neck so he wouldn't wear them out. My grandmother had tied them together by the shoelaces. Dad was six years old.

My father grew up in the classic immigrant family where the grandparents spoke no English and the parents spoke a few words, haltingly, to get by. Still, the children were pushed to excel and achieve and work towards a better life. If the family had many children, usually the first boy and / or first girl were taken out of school early, after the first two or three grades in primary school, to help their parents with the chores and with raising the younger children.

Dad and his brothers and sisters, the ones who stayed in school, went to the local schools. They did chores before they went to school in the morning, and then again when they came home in the afternoon. My grandparents had begun a small family business where they made and sold Greek sausages. The boys would go to the customers in the mornings and take their orders and, after school, they would deliver the orders to the customers.

But they were still expected to excel, and excel they

did. My father's older brother, my Uncle Louie, was accepted at MIT to study chemistry. Two years later, my father was accepted at Harvard, to the graduating class of 1931. Both my father and his older brother had graduated from Lynn Classical High School as did their younger brother, Nick, who also went to MIT. Dad had finished at the top of his class at Classical High.

When Dad had finished his first semester at Harvard (he commuted every day to Cambridge, taking public transportation), my grandfather told him that he didn't have the remaining Seventy-Five dollars to pay the second semester tuition at Harvard and that my father would have to drop out. Total tuition in 1927, when my father began his freshman year at Harvard, was Three Hundred dollars. My grandfather had paid Two Hundred and Twenty-Five dollars for the first semester.

The United States, at that time, was just two years away from the beginning of the Great Depression. Even before the Depression, many families were heartbreakingly poor.

"Louie is in his third year at MIT and it would be a shame to have him drop out now that he is more than halfway through," said my grandfather.

"If I can manage to get a scholarship and you don't have to pay the tuition, can I stay at Harvard?" asked my father.

"Yes," was my grandfather's response.

So that morning, when Dad arrived at Harvard, he went to see the assistant dean for the freshman class. The young dean was not much older than my father himself. He asked my father why he wanted to leave Harvard. Was it for financial reasons?

"Yes," my father replied.

"What grades did you get in the first semester?" the dean asked.

"Two As and two Bs".

"Wait here," the dean said. "I'll be right back."

When the dean returned a few minutes later, he told Dad that Harvard did not want him to drop out, that they would provide a scholarship to him for the rest of the first year, and for the next three years. They would also refund the tuition for the first semester. Given these new conditions, would my father be willing to stay at Harvard?

My grandfather was surprised. He had not expected this result, but he had already given his word to Dad. He was thrilled when a check for Two Hundred and Twenty-Five dollars arrived in the mail from Harvard. And so it was that my father continued his studies at Harvard and graduated *cum laude* in 1931, in the middle of the Great Depression.

Dad then went to Suffolk University Law School at night, and drove the truck for the family business during the day. He opened his law office in Lynn, practiced law, and participated fully in both the Saint George Church and in the Lynn community. On his seventy-fifth birthday, he reminisced about the people who had helped him throughout his life. One of the first people who came to mind was the assistant dean at Harvard. Dad contacted Harvard and, after several telephone calls, got the telephone number for the now former dean who was living in upstate New York. On the day that Dad called him, the dean was celebrating his own birthday.

Dad introduced himself and told the surprised man

the purpose of the call and thanked him for supporting a poor student more than fifty years earlier at a critical junction in that student's life. The scholarship had enabled my father to continue his education at Harvard and to pursue his dream of becoming a lawyer. At some point during the call, the dean's daughter came on the line and told Dad that her father could not continue the conversation because he was crying.

Dad was at Harvard in the middle of the Depression. My grandfather's reaction to my father's scholarship was mixed. He was happy that my father's work had been recognized at Harvard but he would miss the income that my father might have contributed to the family if he had been working rather than studying. This was the case with my mother who, more than ten years later, also graduated at the top of her class at Lynn Classical High School.

Her teachers and the principal at Classical tried to encourage her to apply to Radcliffe College which was the women's college attached to Harvard. My grandfather Jenis was opposed to the idea. He knew how capable my mother was but paying tuition for four years so that my mother could attend college was simply out of the question. The teachers and the principal at Lynn Classical even paid a visit to my grandparents and begged my grandfather to let Mother apply to Radcliffe. The teachers and the principal had all agreed amongst themselves that they would pay my mother's tuition over the four-year period. And again, my grandfather said no.

"You don't understand. It's not that I cannot pay the tuition, which I cannot. It's that I cannot afford to miss out on the one dollar each week that she will bring home to the family if she is working."

Here I want to thank those wonderful, caring teachers who thought so much of my mother and her potential that they would have paid her tuition.

"Lynn, Lynn the city of sin
You never come out the way you came in

You ask for water, but they give you gin
The girls say no, but they always give in

If your (sic) not bad, they won't let you in
It's the damndest city I've ever been in

Lynn, Lynn the city of sin
You never come out the way you came in."

Author Unknown

I learned my manners in Boston. I learned how to dress by observing the wealthy Bostonian matriarchs. I went to university and to graduate school in Boston. But in Lynn I learned to get along with everyone. It was in Lynn that I had my first real jobs and where I got my first library card. It was there that I learned what diversity was. My two best and oldest friends were from there. I am, and always will be, a Lynn girl, through and through.

While my parents were growing up, Lynn was in its heyday. It had a thriving shoe industry, probably the best in the world at the turn of the century. When I tell friends from outside Massachusetts about this, they look at me skeptically but, when they visit the museum and see the history of the city's shoe industry, they are amazed.

The other industrial mainstay of Lynn was the General Electric plant. Lynners called it, and still call it, the GE. The company became the General Electric in 1892 when the Edison General Electric company in New York State and the Thomson-Houston company in Lynn merged. Both my grandmothers worked at the GE when they arrived from Greece. They didn't speak any English but they were able to do the work if someone showed them how. They left the company after they started their families and they didn't work there again, but they were still able to collect small pensions.

Just four years after the merger that created General Electric, the company became one of the twelve stocks that made up the original Dow Jones average. By the time that the US entered WWII almost fifty years later, the GE Lynn plant had transformed aviation. It dominated the aviation industry and continued to be dominant even after WWII, absorbing much of Lynn's workforce.

Lynn has a beautiful shore line. It is known as Lynn Beach but that name doesn't even begin to convey its natural beauty and splendor. Lynn Beach is on the Lynn Shore Drive, a beautiful street with large mansions on one side of the street and the beach on the other side. It is a perfect alternative to driving through the industrial part of the city. The mansions were built by the shoe barons in the late 1800s and in the early 1900s. They are stately homes and are a lovely complement to the promenade that people walk along or jog along by the beach.

Downtown Lynn, in the 30s and 40s and even in the 50s, had a wonderful shopping area. It didn't have the glamour of Boston but it was possible to find just about anything there. There was, and still is, an English-style park extending from the commercial center of the city to the western more industrial part of the city. At the beginning of the Common is the Lynn Public Library, a large lending library with a reading room filled with the requisite large wooden reading tables.

I cannot remember the timeframe for this particular bit of information but at some time in the 60s or 70s, a list of the largest libraries in the United States was published. The Library of Congress in Washington DC was, and still is, the largest. Second was the New York Public Library and third and fourth were the Boston Public Library and Harvard's Widener Library although I don't remember now which was third and which was fourth. In Massachusetts, the third largest library after the Boston Public and the Harvard Widener was the Lynn Public Library.

When I was growing up in the 50s and 60s, Lynn began a downward spiral. Two factors contributed to this downward trend. One was that the shoe center of the world relocated to Europe at the end of WWII and the United States was now importing shoes from Spain and Italy. Both those countries were known for their leather goods. Production of leather shoes and handbags increased in those countries and the production of shoes in Lynn slowly decreased.

The second factor was the construction of the North Shore Shopping Center (now the Northshore Mall) in Peabody, a small suburb just a few miles north of Lynn. It opened in September 1958 as an open-air shopping center which meant that stores were accessible only from the street or sidewalks. In 1958, it was the biggest shopping center in the country.

Immediately, the mall became the place to be, the place to shop. The local downtown shopping centers began to wither, Lynn's downtown shopping center included. For Lynn, one answer to the slow death it was going through would have been to build an exit somewhere in the city to connect with the highway on which the shopping center was located. That exit would have meant going through the street on which we lived and everyone on the street would have lost their homes, hopefully with some reasonable compensation to allow the residents to relocate.

Lynners were concerned with the probability of increased traffic, even though it would have increased business for the city as well, as new restaurants, gas stations, and services would have been required. In the end, the negatives dominated because no one wanted to lose their home. Thus, the Lynners voted against the exit in a referendum that gave everyone a chance to express their opinion but, at the same time, signed and sealed Lynn's death certificate.

The result of those factors, however, was that downtown Lynn, which had been a vibrant shopping area albeit small, deteriorated and died. Stores closed, one after another. The boarded-up storefronts gave Union Street, the main shopping street, a desolated and abandoned look. As the years passed, the residential streets downtown began to breed crime. Later, those streets would be havens for drug addicts.

The smaller suburbs to the north of Lynn suddenly

looked prettier and trendier, tidier and safer. Those suburbs built small strip malls which became extremely popular with the suburbanites when they didn't want the hassle of going to the new shopping center and looking for a precious parking space close to the stores, especially during the holiday seasons.

The houses on the Lynn Shore Drive began to look seedy and unkempt as the wealthy shoe merchants left the city for greener, calmer, and wealthier suburbs. Some of the houses were in need of a renovation, although a simple paint job would have made a difference. Even the promenade along the beach looked forlorn.

In addition to the downturn in the shoe industry and the focus on the new shopping center, Boston's urban renewal project in the West End dislocated residents there and many of them moved to Lynn. On its own, this event may not have been a problem. But as part of the overall downturn, the relocation of the West End residents added to the city's financial burden.

Lynn had always been a diverse city and, because it was a relatively small city, with a population of about 100,000 when it was at its peak, it was easy to see the diversity. There were fewer enclaves with specific ethnic groups than in the larger cities and even those enclaves that did exist were close to each other in proximity, erasing, or at least lessening, the illusion of an enclave or a ghetto.

My mother grew up on a tiny street called Shepherd Place in West Lynn. Shepherd Place doesn't exist anymore. It was demolished and razed in one of Lynn's urban renewal projects. When my mother was growing up there, that tiny little street had perhaps eight or ten rickety wooden triple-deckers, as the classic New England three-story houses were known, with outside staircases and wooden balconies that tilted dangerously downward.

But to me, Shepherd Place was the most romantic place in the world. I loved going there because it meant visiting my grandparents and my aunts. I am the only one of my siblings and cousins with memories from that neighborhood. My brother Tom, who is two years younger than me, is the only other one who remembers something from my grandparents' house. His memory is of my grandmother's brother, Louis. Tom remembers that whenever we would go to visit, he and Uncle Louis would go out to that dangerously tilted balcony in the back, wet a piece of bread, and throw pieces onto the garage roof for the pigeons. Otherwise, no one else has any memories. Even Tom cannot remember if my grandparents lived on the second or the third floor. I was desolated when he told me that the street had been razed. This is what I remember most from when I was little.

The neighbors on Shepherd Place were families of Greeks, Italians, Jews, and Blacks, and they all got along. As children have done throughout the ages, my mother, her siblings and her cousins tortured the older residents mercilessly whenever they could. There was one elderly man in particular who lived next door to them and who was the main target of their silliness. They had made up a little ditty about him:

"Mr. Brown
Went to town
With his pants
Upside down"

The children would then collapse into spasms of laughter and giggles and run away, leaving poor Mr. Brown shaking his head.

My grandparents' triple decker housed three Greek families. My grandparents and my aunts and uncle and my grandmother's brother lived on the middle floor. My mother lived there, too, until she and my father got married. On the top floor were my grandmother's sister and her husband, their two daughters and their son. The cousins were inseparable, especially the girls. One of my favorite black and white pictures from the late 30s or early 40s is of my two aunts, Nellie and Dee, and their two upstairs cousins, Irene and Anne. The four of them, standing in front of the triple decker, look so carefree. Aunt Nellie once told Stefan that when they were young, they didn't realize that they were dirt poor because they didn't know any better and they simply had a good time amongst themselves.

On the ground floor was another Greek family, Amalia and her two children, perhaps ten or fifteen years older than me. The distinguishing features that I remember about Amalia are her gravelly voice and her loud raucous laugh that you could hear up to the top floor. Stacia, the woman I met by chance at the Greek festival in Lynn a few years ago, is Amalia's daughter. And even though Shepherd Place has literally been wiped off the face of the map, my mind still floods with memories whenever I think about it.

Lynn produced two phenomenal Greek-American athletes.

The two that I mention below were phenomenal not only because of their athletic ability and prowess but also because they were Lynn boys and first-generation Greek-Americans born in the US.

Lou Tsiropoulos, the basketball player who played college basketball in Kentucky, went on to play for the Boston Celtics for three years. Tsiropoulos had graduated from Lynn English High School before attending college in Kentucky.

Actually, one of the best memories that I have relating to Lou Tsiropoulos is not about the basketball star himself but about his mother. One Sunday, I had gone to church and had driven there with the family car. On the way home, I saw two tall, stately and dignified grandmothers, dressed in their Sunday best, walking home. One of them was my grandmother. I did not know the other lady. I stopped to pick up my grandmother and, of course, the other lady, too, but my grandmother politely declined because she wanted to walk with her friend, Mrs. Tsiropoulos. I will always carry that picture in my mind of the two proud Greek grandmothers with their flowered hats on heads held high.

Tom's memory is more about the basketball star himself. My parents enrolled Tom one summer in a summer basketball camp in Lynnfield, a small town near where we lived. The camp was run by Lou Tsiropoulos.

The other phenomenal Greek-American athlete was the Golden Greek, Harry Agganis. Harry (Aristotle) Agganis graduated from Lynn Classical High School and then went to Boston University where he played varsity football. He was the first athlete in BU history to be named All-American.

When Agganis graduated from BU, he had an opportunity to play football for the Cleveland Browns but his first love was baseball. He signed with the Boston Red Sox and began playing with the team in April 1954, as the first baseman.

The next year, in May 1955, just a month after the baseball season had begun, he got pneumonia and was hospitalized. He was released from the hospital and went back to Fenway Park to play for the Red Sox, but two weeks later he was hospitalized again, this time with a viral infection. He was beginning to recover and was asking to be released from the hospital so he could go home. But on June 29, 1955, while he was still in the hospital, a blood clot in his leg dislodged and went to his lungs. He died instantly, of a pulmonary embolism.

The entire country was in shock. No one could believe that the twenty-six- year-old Golden Greek had died. The Greek-American community, the sports world, no one could believe that in just a few seconds, one of the greatest all-around athletes ever was gone.

Thirty thousand people came to Lynn for the wake and for the funeral. The grief, the sadness, and the disbelief were palpable. People were crying in the streets. This was Lynn's boy and all of Lynn went into mourning, but the whole country was crying for him.

Tom remembers that he was at summer camp that day. The camp counselors would each take five kids in their cars at the end of the day, and drive them home. That day, one of the counselors was driving the kids from Lynn back home, an hour's drive from the camp. As the kids, including my brother, piled into the car, they noticed that their counselor was crying.

"What's the matter, Mr. Palumbo?" the kids asked. "Are you crying? Why are you crying?"

"Do you kids know who Harry Agganis is?" Counselor Mel asked in turn.

"Yes, of course we do."

"He died today. He was a great athlete and a wonderful person."

Tom said that Counselor Mel cried all the way back to Lynn.

Harry Agganis belonged to everyone. Later, a book was written about him, *"The Golden Greek, An All-American Story"*.[xi] Harry was exactly what the title said, the Golden Greek. His was the quintessential all-American story.

[xi] Nick Tsiotos and Andy Dabilis, *The Golden Greek, an All-American Story*, Brookline, Massachusetts, Hellenic College Press. 1995.

- 8 -

1981: A Watershed Year

"If you can't explain your theory to a bartender, it's probably no good."

Ernest Rutherford

1981 was the year that my life changed. Dramatically. It was the year that I separated from my husband. It was the year that I found a full-time job in a high-profile Greek multinational company which was on a list of the top 500 multinational corporations. It was the year that Greece joined the European Union. But most of all, it was the year that I spread my wings and started to fly.

The previous years had also been full of changes. In 1979, Elias and I went to the States for a year with both boys. Elias was a visiting professor that year at Boston University. I think that we were both champing at the bit to leave Greece and go back to the States for a while. It was a wonderful year for all of us but in different ways. Stefan went to kindergarten there. Costis learned to speak English there. Actually, both boys learned to speak perfect, almost unaccented English. We were staying with my parents so grandparents and grandsons had the ideal opportunity to get to know each other. I relished being with my whole family again, and so did Elias. And Elias, of course, was in academia which he loved. It was a win / win for everyone.

But, despite the double distractions of being with my family again and being in the States and not in Greece, our marriage was slowly unraveling. When we returned to Greece at the end of August in 1980, back to the usual routine, it became obvious that the marriage was no longer viable and had become the biggest collateral damage of our move to Greece almost eight years earlier. One year later, in October 1981, Elias and I separated.

Separation and divorce were not as common then in Greece, or in the US either, as they are now. This was a completely new thing for me to learn how to manage. I had learned how to be the good Greek housewife and how to handle the nostalgia that washed over me every so often. I had even learned how to handle the anti-Americanism, especially when it was directed at me. Now I had to learn to handle the criticism that came with separation and divorce because, as both a foreigner and a woman, I was, of course, the one responsible for the break-up in the eyes of Elias' family and friends and in the eyes of my family, too.

The outbreaks of nostalgia disappeared overnight. I

had so many things to do and to take care of. For the first time, ever, I was in charge and therefore had zero time and energy to waste on nostalgia. Stefan was in the second grade and Costis had just begun kindergarten. I had to make sure that they were adjusting to their schools and to schoolwork and that, at the same time, they were also adjusting to the separation. They were the only ones who had the full focus of my attention. There was no attention left over for anyone else, critics included. I left the critics, all of them, to their own devices.

After the children, the second priority was finding a place to live. We had been living in a flat in a building where Elias' family lived. Obviously, I had to leave that flat because it belonged to Elias, but I wanted to stay close by so that Stefan and Costis could stay in the same school and so that they could walk, when they were just a little older, to their father's flat.

And, of course, everything - where we would live, how we would live, and everything else, too - was determined by the financials. I wasn't working and did not have any income. About a month before Elias and I separated, however, I found a job at a Greek company. I knew where Elias and I were heading and that I would need to work and I had started looking for something before the children started the new school year. I was not particularly optimistic about the whole enterprise of job-hunting, but I got spectacularly lucky when an application for a secretarial position in a law firm led to a position as secretary, one of several, in the office of the owner and managing director at one of Greece's largest and most prestigious companies, Motor Oil Hellas. This job provided me with a salary that helped me, in turn, to provide for the children. It also bestowed a magical aura on me because when people heard where I was working and for whom, they were immediately impressed. Actually, they were so impressed that they would stop dead in their tracks when I told them. That alone was enough to stop the critics from their never-ending moaning and groaning about the separation.

In September 1982, I found a flat that met all my requirements except for one. It didn't have central heating. But I moved there with the boys anyway. Elias and I worked out a schedule for being with the children and things fell into a routine. In September 1983, I left the company to teach in a private American school in one of the posh northern suburbs. My rationale was that I would have the summers to be with the boys. The problem was that the school downsized one year later, giving up the live-in facilities that it had as a boarding school, and became a day school only. The school needed fewer teachers and, since I was last in, I was also first out. I called the company that I had left a year earlier and asked if I could come back. The answer was yes.

The move back to the company was a good move. I had a good, high-profile job that paid well. I gained confidence in myself and realized that I was a competent working mother, focused on my job and attentive to the boys. Stefan and Costis were flourishing in school and were adjusting to having divorced parents. They didn't like it but they accepted it. And their attitude motivated Elias and me to cooperate with each other for the well-being of the children.

Probably one of the biggest changes in our lives, although

it was not visible at first, came with Greece's entry into the European Union. On January 1, 1981, Greece officially became a member of the EU. This was the achievement of Prime Minister Constantine Karamanlis whose government had applied to the EU for membership, and who had pushed and persuaded the European leaders, mostly Valéry Giscard d'Estaing and Helmut Schmidt, that Greece belonged in the EU. To the Greeks, Karamanlis said *"Anikomen eis tin Dysi"*. (We belong in the West.) Membership in the EU guaranteed that Greece would be in western-oriented territory.

Membership in the EU put a layer of confidence and sophistication on Greece and the Greeks. It gave the Greeks, including me, a sense of community and a sense of belonging to something bigger than ourselves. It may have even given us a sense of security and safety. And in a way, there was safety in being part of the EU. First of all, it reduced tremendously the possibility of aggression among the member nations. There was now a European Parliament where differences could be discussed and resolved. Secondly, the European Union provided a larger front than any country could provide for itself individually. This front was a barrier to external aggression although there were still ways for people to slip into the country and do immeasurable damage. There were still ways for countries to harass and badger Greece. But as part of a larger community, Greece had support in addressing these issues.

What I liked best, however, about Greece's joining the European Union was that Europe and, by extension, the entire world, became accessible to all Greeks and not just to the wealthy or to the very educated. Borders were no longer the fearsome obstacles that they had been for so long, with so many questions asked, so many forms to fill out, so much possibility of being turned away. Suddenly, travelers were either Schengen or non-Schengen; they were either European Union or non-European Union.[xii] It helped that we had European passports (issued in Greece). It was empowering to pass through passport control of any member country and simply hold up our European passports. It was almost as if we were traveling from one state to another in the US.

It took a few years for the Greeks to understand that they had a freedom of movement within Europe that they had never had before. They could look for work in Europe. Young people could study in Europe. The whole dynamic of what it meant to be European had changed.

I happened to be on a business trip in Slovenia a few weeks after Slovenia had been admitted to the European Union, in 2004. Slovenia had been part of Yugoslavia since World War II. In the early 2000s, the seven countries that made up Yugoslavia began breaking away and becoming independent. I asked a Slovenian colleague how he felt about his country now being a member of the EU. He was diffident.

"I don't expect anything to change for me." he shrugged.

"True," I replied, "but things will be different for your children. They will grow up knowing that they can study and

---

[xii] Schengen is a treaty that was signed by European Union members in the Netherlands. It refers to the EU passport-free zone that covers most of the EU countries and functions mostly as a single jurisdiction zone for international travel purposes, with a common visa policy

work anywhere they want to in Europe. That's how your life will change."

Stefan and Costis graduated from university in Greece and then, after they had completed their mandatory military service in Greece, both went to graduate school in the UK at outstanding, world-renown academic institutions. Stefan worked in London for three years after he finished graduate school. Costis worked in Italy, first in Pisa and then in Turin. Then his company sent him to London to re-open the office that they had closed in the wake of 9/11. From there he went to graduate school in London and from graduate school, he went to Silicon Valley. Like all other children who grow up in the EU, my sons had opportunities that they may not have had if Greece had not joined the European Union.

For me personally, the 80s were a revelatory decade. Although the divorce period was a very difficult period for all of us, it was also the beginning of an extraordinary independence for me – meeting people, working in an exciting professional environment, understanding that I finally had economic power, and realizing that, yes, I could survive and do anything that I wanted. I enjoyed being on my own and making my own decisions without any interference or any requirement to live up to someone's expectations. I was far away from my own family and far enough away from Elias' family. I flapped my wings, hesitantly, dusted them off and started flying, a little wobbly and unsteadily at first, but with more confidence as time went on.

I learned how to deal with the Greek tax office (hint: I approached the Greek tax office as I would have approached the IRS in the US – respectfully and obediently). I learned to deal with pompous and self-important employees in the public sector. I became an integral part of the Greek work force, contributing to Greece's GDP. I learned to be the "head of a household". It was exciting stuff.

In 1987, I decided, confidently enough, that I was ready to fulfill a dream that I had starting thinking about in the mid-70s – to go to graduate school and get an MBA. I did my research and decided upon a very specific and specialized one-year MBA program at a small women's college in Boston. It was not an easy decision to make but if those wings were to get any practice, it was a decision that I needed to make. It would mean starting all over again in the workplace once I had the degree, but I would think about that later. At that specific time in my life, I had reached a *now or never* moment.

- 9 -

The Magic of the Parthenon

"Beauty depends on magnitude and order."

Aristotle

There are two anecdotes that I like to relate to my friends and family in the US; they are about how Greece was created. The first anecdote tells how God planned to create the world but, before He created His grand design, He decided to create a small prototype first. The prototype contained seas and mountains, trees and rocks, sand and mists, flat and fertile plains and hilly terrains, hot and cold. When He finished the prototype, He sat back to admire it and then created the world, using the prototype as His model. He was very pleased with the result and decided to keep the prototype for Himself. He placed the prototype in the geographical location that He thought suited it best and called it Greece.

The second anecdote is similar but, in this one, God had already created people who were ambling and stumbling around in space with no particular place in which to settle down so He decided to create a world for them where they could settle. Once He finished creating the world, He began taking groups of people and placing them in different areas and regions. "You are the French," He said, "and this is France. You are the Germans and this is Germany." (Remember, this is only an anecdote.) He did that with most of the groups of people and then He took the remaining peoples and placed them all in one geographic area. It turns out that these peoples were Greeks, Bulgarians, Romanians, and other Balkan groups. The Greeks immediately started to complain, saying,

"You never pay any attention to us. You always pay attention to everyone else. Why can't we have our own country?"

They whined and complained and continued whining and complaining until God couldn't take it anymore and said, "Enough! I can't stand listening to you any longer. Here, you can take this place. I was keeping it for myself but I would rather give it to you than listen to your whining."

And that is how the Greeks got Greece.

In March 2017, a web site, *BusinessInsider,* published a poll that it had taken, asking several architects world-wide to vote for "the one building that in their opinion defines building design, inspired them to become architects, or that they simply consider to be a stunning piece of architectural art". The Parthenon was voted "the Most Beautiful Building in the World" by a large margin. One of the architects who participated in the poll said that "the Parthenon is the quintessential beautiful architectural form", and went on to say that the Parthenon gave architects their "initial ABCs of architecture" that architects keep trying to use and improve upon today.

When the *BusinessInsider* poll was published, it immediately made headlines all over Greece. I first saw it on Facebook where two sites – *Greek Gateway* and *Growing Up Greek Style* - had posted it. *Greek Gateway* embellished their announcement with an Instagram photo of the Parthenon, lit up in that beautiful yellow lighting that shows it off to its full advantage, and the caption: "God spent a little more time on Greece." (Although I am not sure if the Parthenon was on God's agenda when He designed His grand plan.)

There is something magical about living in the same city where the Parthenon, the most copied building in the world, stands as a sentinel on the Acropolis, the city's second-highest hill (the highest is Lycabettus Hill). There is something magical about basking in the warm glow of the Parthenon's fame. We may not think about it all the time or talk about it all the time, but I am sure that all Greeks have a deep reverence for the monument that has withstood time and is held in veneration throughout the world. I like to think that living in the golden embrace of the Parthenon makes us better people.

An architect friend said that the phrase "the most beautiful building in the world" does not even begin to connote the true value of the Parthenon. He believes that the

Parthenon is the closest that humans ever got to perfection. It was a demonstration of what humans can really do when their motivation is to do their very best. Dedicating the temple to Athena, the goddess of wisdom, made perfect sense. Using their wisdom, Athenian society made it possible for democracy, philosophy and the arts to flourish and to reach their peaks during the Golden Age of Pericles. This is what the Parthenon represents. The Parthenon is the most beautiful building in the world because it is the one building in the world that came closest to perfection.

The entire Acropolis site is a wonder to behold. The Propylaea – the splendid entrance to the Acropolis – lives up to its definition in English: a monumental gateway.

The Erechtheion, a temple that was dedicated to both Athena and Poseidon, is on the north side of the Parthenon. Inside the temple, there was a shrine to the god Hephaistos. The Erechtheion is famous for the six Caryatids that hold up the porch on the north side of the temple. The Caryatids are beautifully carved maidens that are known throughout the world, not least because one of them is housed in the British Museum.

When I moved to Greece, I must have gone up to the Acropolis at least fifteen times the first year that I was here to show my visiting family and friends the Parthenon. Each time I went, I would go off by myself for a few minutes, sit on one of the marble stones scattered around the site and gaze at the Caryatids. They were, and still are, the most beautiful sight that I have ever seen.

In 2004, in time for the Athens Olympic Games, new

lighting was installed on the Acropolis to show the world the beauty of the Parthenon. It had been lit before, prior to the 2004 Games, but this new lighting bathed the entire site in a soft yellow that highlighted its magnificence.

A few years later, as I was coming home from work one evening, I noticed something very different on the Acropolis. The lighting showed a structure that I had not seen before, a structure that seemed to spill over the steep slope. The effect was one of astonishing beauty. I had not been aware of this temple or of its restoration until I began asking friends what had changed on the Acropolis and they told me about the Athena Nike temple. That temple added a new dimension to the sacred site; it filled it up and rounded it off. It completed the Acropolis site.

The Athena Nike temple is on a steep slope of the Acropolis, on the southwest side, to the right of the Propylaea as one goes up to the Parthenon. Construction of the temple began in 480 BC and was completed in 420 BC. It was built on the remains of an earlier temple dedicated to Athena Nike but which the Persians had destroyed. The new temple remained intact until 1686 AD when the Turks destroyed it and dismantled it, using the stones and other material for their defenses. In the 1830s, two foreign architects excavated the temple and later, after the temple was re-erected from its remaining parts, a series of restorations and reconstructions brought the temple back to its former grace and beauty.

When the restoration of the temple of Athena Nike was completed in 2010, the lighting was extended to include that temple, too. The temple is a jewel as we look at it from afar and close up, as well. I never get tired of looking at the site, craning my neck to get just a glimpse of its glory.

The Parthenon, of course, is also the ultimate view – now. This was not always the case. When Elias and I came to Greece for our honeymoon in 1969, one of his cousins invited us to her flat to visit with her and her husband in the Plaka where they lived. The Plaka is Athens' Old Town. Today it is one of the most expensive real estate areas not only in Athens and in Greece, but in Europe, as well. In 1969, it was seedy but its charm was still evident. It had the charm that old neighborhoods with old buildings have; it was full of history and it was in the immediate vicinity of the Acropolis. In fact, I think we could see the Parthenon from a window in Vicky's flat. But Vicky was less than enthusiastic about living there – it was considered a cheap place to live. The flat itself was a rickety third-floor walk-up, but I still thought it was charming.

We made, of course, the requisite pilgrimage to the Acropolis during that honeymoon period. We went one time only as we were in Athens for just five weeks. But it was that one time that set the pattern for me to sit on a marble stone and gaze for ten or fifteen minutes at the Caryatids in the Erechtheion. I was enchanted with the graceful beauty of the six maidens who held up the porch of the temple effortlessly, with their simple but beautiful Greek gowns and their beautifully plaited hair, all carved in marble.

In 1969, we could actually step inside the Parthenon and walk around and admire the friezes and metopes. When we came back to live here, this was no longer the case. Officials were concerned that the vibrations from the millions of feet that walked inside the temple every year would cause irreparable damage and that it would eventually crumble.

In 1969, the Parthenon was simply the Parthenon, beautiful and graceful, accessible to all, with nothing to mar its beauty. When we came back at the end of 1972, scaffolding had been erected and a crane had been installed on the site. Both the crane and the scaffolding have been permanent fixtures ever since.

There was probably much more danger of permanent damage to the Parthenon from the pollution than from tourists' feet. The street in front of the entrance to the Acropolis is lined with stunning, stately residences on one side of the street, across from the Acropolis, but the street itself, in 1973, was always clogged with traffic.

In 1973, many, but certainly not all, of the residents of Athens seemed to be indifferent to the Acropolis. Perhaps Athenians were unimpressed by the imposing presence of the Parthenon or perhaps they were simply jaded and had become blasé about living in the shadow of this unique monument. In any case, in early 1974, another of Elias' cousins invited us to her house for dinner one Sunday on a cold January day. She had invited the whole family so there were about twenty-five people in all, maybe more. I was six months pregnant at the time and the thick cigarette smoke bothered and annoyed me so I went out onto the balcony to breathe some fresh air.

Haroula and her husband owned a three-family house in the area of Theseion which is next to the Plaka and where many of the old ruins are. The apartment building itself was nothing special; it was not luxurious. It was an ordinary concrete building, with nothing exceptional to distinguish it from any other concrete apartment building in Athens. The neighborhood was border-line rundown and, like the Plaka, it was seedy and looked worn. It was revitalized, probably at the same time as the Plaka was, and today one can sit in any café or restaurant in Theseion and enjoy a perfect view of the Parthenon. Haroula's house had such a view in 1974, before the revitalization.

I went out onto the balcony to get that breath of fresh air that I was craving and came face to face with the Acropolis and the Parthenon. I actually could not believe what I was seeing. The Acropolis and the Parthenon were literally across the street from Haroula's building.

I went back inside and asked my husband, and everyone else as well, "Have you all seen the view from Haroula's balcony?"

Someone said, in a very nonchalant and languid manner, "Yes, it's the Parthenon."

"NO," I said, insistently, "HAVE YOU SEEN THE VIEW FROM HAROULA'S BALCONY?" I was not only insistent. I think that I may have raised my voice a bit and was also a little rude.

But I got their attention. Everyone turned to look at me, with a look of amusement on their faces, smiling indulgently at the American who was so impressed with something that they took for granted, something that was part of their everyday lives. That blasé attitude has since changed.

The Plaka in the 60s and 70s was in a steady state of decline.[xiii] Before then, it had been a genteel neighborhood where many of Athens' well-to-do families lived. At the end of the 70s, the government took an interest in intervening in the historic neighborhoods in the center of Athens and one of those was the Old Town. In fact, the area was declared a historic part of the city center and it was then that serious actions were taken to clean it up. It had been overrun by shabby tourist businesses that included discos, neon signs, loud nightclubs and strip joints, none of which showed any respect for the history or the historic significance of the area. Most of the former residents had fled and the only residents who remained were the ones who were not able to leave because they had nowhere else to go.

The revitalization and preservation of the Plaka began in 1979, first under the aegis of Minister Stefanos Manos, who was the deputy Minister for Housing, and then under Antonis Tritsis who was the mayor of Athens in 1991 and 1992. The Plaka was declared a "historic and traditional area", thus protecting it from further decline. Several of the residences became part of the preservation effort.

Streets were pedestrianized and traffic was reduced significantly. In 1983, forty-two nightclubs were shut down. In the following years the residents who had left out of despair slowly returned and the neighborhood acquired a kinder and gentler profile. People were no longer afraid to walk around

---

[xiii] http://www.nytimes.com/1982/12/26/world/athens-restoring-a-historical-area.html

in the streets in the evenings. And a few savvy people made investments in real estate, while the property prices were still low. They renovated homes that were in a terrible state of disrepair, restoring them to their former elegant simplicity.

A few years later, when Greece was hosting the 2004 Olympic Games, the government implemented another project. This project was the unification of archaeological sites in the center of Athens, with a series of walkways around the Acropolis, the Plaka, and Theseion.[xiv] The original project was a much grander design than what was actually completed. The grander design would have included unification with Syntagma Square and with the Panathenaic Stadium where the first modern Olympic Games took place in 1896.

That design was put on hold because there wasn't enough time or money to complete it for the 2004 Games. Then Greece was hit by the worst financial crisis it had been through since World War II and, of course, this project became impossible for any Greek government to implement.

However, the walkways that were in place for the Games are by themselves magnificent. The project began in 1997. Dionysiou Areopagitou Street, the street on which the entrance to the Acropolis is, was pedestrianized as were the streets on the west and north sides of the Acropolis, creating a walkway almost all around the Acropolis. The effect of eliminating vehicular traffic on these streets and allowing only foot traffic was stunning. The noise from the snarled

---

[xiv] http://www.athens24.com/the-unification-of-athens-archaeological-sites.html

traffic evaporated and it was possible to walk down the middle of the cobblestoned streets without angry drivers honking at pedestrians to get out of the way. Suddenly it was possible to hear the crickets chirp, to smell the flora, and to admire the olive trees which are hundreds and thousands of years old. Suddenly, it was possible to get a faint idea of what it may have felt like to wander around the old footpaths of ancient Athens and the Agora when Athens was a small city-state, in the time of Pericles.

A plot on Dionysiou Areopagitou was designated for the new Acropolis Museum, across the street from the Acropolis. Construction began in 2003 and was completed in 2007. It didn't open in time for the Olympic Games but still, it is now a major attraction for both the Greeks and the tourists.

In the early 2000s when the Plaka had been renovated and restored, and the walkway around the Acropolis had been completed, Haroula invited the cousins, once again, for dinner. It was a warm September evening, on a night with a full moon when the archaeological sites were open to the public (and still are). Dinner would be served on Haroula's rooftop terrace.

On that evening, and subsequent September full-moon evenings at Haroula's home, the men carried folding chairs and folding tables up to the terrace and the women carried the food. We placed the food on the tables, buffet-style, and placed our chairs in a line, facing the Parthenon, watching the full moon slowly rise and take its place over the Acropolis. And that's how we were that evening – sitting next to each other, eating our food quietly, and engaging in minimal conversation because we were all so utterly enchanted and engrossed with the view. The attitude on those evenings was in stark contrast to the blasé attitude that I had encountered at Haroula's house in 1974.

The view from the terrace was breathtaking, even more so than from Haroula's balcony. Every time I was on the terrace, I had the feeling that I could reach out and shake hands with the tourists who were on the Acropolis, admiring the Parthenon

In 2008, when I was seriously looking for a flat to buy, I made a list of specifications to keep myself from getting over-enthusiastic whenever I saw something that I thought was impressive. The flat that I would purchase would have to meet a minimum of 80% of those specifications, one of which was a view. The word "view" is vague and could be anything. It could be a view of the sea, a view of a park, or a view of the Parthenon, in which case the price of the flat entered the upper stratosphere.

I called a real-estate agent to see a flat that was in one of the neighborhoods near the Plaka and a block down from the Acropolis. It was in a nice neighborhood but the view was the concrete wall of the apartment building next door. The agent suggested seeing another flat, brand-new, with all the latest materials and technology. It was a lovely apartment but the view was one of the busiest main streets in Athens, with the accompanying noise. It would be impossible to sit on the balcony and relax.

He suggested that we see yet another flat, this one still under construction. I asked him how big it was and what the price tag was. He told me that it was 145 square meters (approximately 1,450 square feet) and that the price tag was 1,400,000 Euros.

I almost rejected seeing it, out of hand. After all, there was no way that I could afford the price. Then I thought, "Why not?". It was an opportunity to see what this kind of money bought. We trudged up to the sixth floor as there was no elevator yet. I walked around the flat with the realtor. I had only a vague sense of what the completed apartment might look like.

Then we walked out to the veranda and I stopped short in my tracks. The Parthenon was right in front of us even though the apartment building was on a street that was one street behind Dionysiou Areopagitou. The view was magnificent. If I had been able to afford it, I would have bought it on the spot although I had serious visions of playing hooky from work, frequently. How would I have been able to tear myself away from the view to do something as prosaic as work?

The Parthenon is a temple. It was dedicated to the goddess Athena, the virgin goddess. A first temple was built shortly after the Battle of Marathon and was destroyed in 480 BC by the Persians who also destroyed the temple of Athena Nike. In 480 BC, the Persians were at war with the Athenians. The Athenians won the war with the Persians and the Spartans conceded sovereignty on the seas to Athens.

The Parthenon that we all know now was built in 447 BC, in the age of Pericles. It took only nine years to build that magnificent monument. Fifty architects worked on the Parthenon, but the two who were responsible for its design and the execution of the design were Kallikrates and Phidias.

The marble used to build the Parthenon came from Penteli Mountain, one of the three mountains that ring Athens. One hundred fifty artisans, experts in handling marble, came from the islands of Paros and Naxos and from Asia Minor to work on the Parthenon. An interesting piece of trivia is that Socrates, the famed philosopher, also worked on the construction of the Parthenon. He was a sculptor by profession and was engaged in the work on the Acropolis.

A statue of the goddess Athena, made of gold and ivory, was built and then placed in the center of the temple. The temple became a place of worship to the goddess but, in addition to the worship of Athena, the temple also served as the treasury of Athens. The city-state of Athens kept its money there, under the protection of the goddess. Eventually, the treasure was used up by the Athenians to finance their war with the Spartans. And at some point, the gods of ancient Greece were replaced by newer and more formal religions. But the Parthenon and the goddess Athena remained intact for 2,500 years.

If the Parthenon could talk, it would have one hell of a story to tell. Over the years, the sanctity of the Holy Rock, as the Acropolis is referred to, was violated and desecrated several times.

In 267 AD, the Herulians, barbarians from Northern Europe, invaded Athens and set fire to the Parthenon. The ravages of the fire are still visible today; the beams supported by the columns are blackened.

During the Byzantine Empire and in the last decade of the sixth century, the temples in Greece were converted to

Christianity and a church was built inside the Parthenon. It was dedicated to the Virgin Mary, and was called *I Panagia I Athiniotissa* (The Virgin Mary the Athenian).

Then the Franks came. They treated the Acropolis as a fortress and the Parthenon as a castle. They built a tower, known as the Tower of Belloc or the Frankish Tower, in front of the Propylaea, sometime during the seventy years preceding the Ottoman conquest. Fortunately, it was dismantled in 1874 as part of a larger project to clean up the Acropolis which had suffered from the ravages of time as well from the indignities to which various invaders and occupiers had subjected it.

In 1456, the Ottoman conquerors came to Athens and built a mosque inside the Parthenon, complete with a minaret. Houses to accommodate Turkish families, the Turkish guard, the Sultan's harem and the administrator of Athens were built on the Acropolis and surrounded the temple of Athena. Entrance to the site was forbidden to Christians unless they had a special permit.

In 1687, when the Turks and the Venetians were at war, the Turks stored their gunpowder in the temple, believing that the Venetians would respect the sanctity of the site and not attack the temple. However, the Venetians bombarded the Parthenon with their lighted arrows and with mortar, causing the gunpowder to explode. On September 26, 1687, the temple blew up causing severe damage to the Parthenon and to the sculptures. The Parthenon had been intact for 2,500 years; in minutes, its roof was blown off and one of its sides was destroyed as was the statue of Athena.

Fragments of the metopes, friezes and sculptures scattered over the site, leaving them vulnerable to looting.

When the Ottoman Empire fell, many Greeks began to smuggle the fragments out of the country where they were coveted on the black market. But it was the Venetian Morozini who was the first to steal archaeological monuments and artifacts from the Parthenon and take them to Venice for his own use.

The most infamous and ruthless vandal of them all, however, was Thomas Bruce, the seventh Earl of Elgin. From 1801 to 1812, he removed friezes, metopes, and sculptures from the Acropolis, including one of the Caryatids in the Erechtheion temple and, allegedly with the permission of Ottoman Empire officials, took them to England where he wanted to decorate his own residence and the residences of his friends. Eventually, the marbles were sold to the British Museum where they are today.

There is disagreement about whether or not the Sultan actually signed a *firmani*. The word *firmani* is Persian and entered the Greek language during the Ottoman occupation of Greece, where it came to mean an order of the Sultan. Some sources say that a *firmani* was written but was not signed by the Sultan. Indeed, the original *firmani* has never been found, only a copy which was not signed by the Sultan himself but by one of his subordinates.

Various experts on the Parthenon say that Lord Elgin bribed many Turks working for the Sultan in order to remove the archaeological artifacts from the Parthenon. Others, including a guide I listened to during a tour of Byzantine churches in the Plaka, say that the Sultan did not grant permission to Elgin. Therefore, Elgin, in order to avoid being caught smuggling the ruins out of Greece, and so that the Sultan would not see him taking the ruins down from the

Acropolis, had his workers chisel the artifacts to remove them from where they had been for so many years and then threw them over the side of the Acropolis where they broke into pieces. Even today, his colossal disrespect for and indifference to the priceless value of these marbles is astounding.

The Caryatid that he removed from the Erechtheion was the second from the left in the front row. It is said that when the workers removed her, the other five Caryatids cried all night in sorrow. It is also said that when the workers packed her into a crate to be loaded onto a ship for England, the workers could hear cries and moaning from the wooden crate. Being superstitious, they told Lord Elgin that they would no longer work on packing the Caryatid and would not load it onto the ship. This is what most likely saved the other five from being stolen.

I told my son Stefan this story. He had always wondered why only one Caryatid was stolen and not all of them. His theory about the noise from the crate is that a cat most likely got trapped while the Caryatid was being packed and then caterwauled all night in a desperate attempt to be freed.

Lord Elgin loaded some marbles onto one ship, which sailed successfully to England. He loaded the rest onto another ship but against the advice of the captain who said the weight was too heavy for the ship. The ship sailed anyway and, during a storm near the island of Kythira, the ship sank and it was only several years later that the crates began surfacing, allowing some of the marbles to be rescued.

Lord Byron, one of Greece's greatest admirers and supporters, was appalled with the looting that Elgin had done. He called on the goddess Athena to place a curse on Elgin. It must have worked because the tide of Lord Elgin's fortunes changed. British public opinion turned against him. His health deteriorated. His finances were depleted and he tried desperately to sell the marbles to make some money. Finally, he was put in jail where he spent the rest of his life.

There is one other story that I want to tell and that I read about recently, a beautiful story, as I researched the Parthenon. It is a story of yet another indignity to the sanctity of the Parthenon and the Acropolis. The story itself could be apocryphal. It has never been confirmed but neither has it ever been completely denied. Most likely it is a story that was told to bolster the morale of the Greeks whose country had once again been invaded, this time by the Nazis.

As the story goes, a young man, seventeen years old at the time, was serving in the Greek army as an evzone. The evzones are the elite Presidential guard and are known for standing guard over the tomb of the Unknown Soldier in Syntagma Square. The young man apparently was stationed on the Acropolis, guarding the flag. This is one of the reasons that the story has never been confirmed. There were no soldiers guarding the flag on the Acropolis and even if there were, they were not evzones.

However, to continue the story, the young man, who was most probably Konstantinos Koukidis, was at his post on Sunday, April 26, 1941, when the Nazis marched into Athens. April 26 was one week after Easter and was the Sunday of the Doubting Thomas.

The next morning, on Monday April 27 at 8:45 am, a contingent of Nazi officers climbed up to the Acropolis to raise the Nazi flag, thus announcing to the Greeks that their country was now under German control. The Nazi officers ordered the young Greek solider to lower the Greek flag so that they could raise the Nazi flag. In one version of the story, the young man said not a word but instead, after lowering the Greek flag while singing the Greek national anthem, wrapped the flag around himself and jumped six hundred feet off the cliff of the Holy Rock to his death as the Germans watched in disbelief. In a second version of the story, Koukidis refused to lower the Greek flag. A Nazi officer lowered the flag, folded it, and gave it to Koukidis who wrapped it around himself and jumped off the cliff, as the Germans looked on in shock.[xv]

It has been said that the young man's sacrifice of his

[xv] http://www.protothema.gr/stories/article/678057/konstantinos-koukidis-oiroas-pou-epese-apo-tin-akropoli-me-tin-elliniki-simaia-ligo-prin-upsothei-i-svastiska

This article is in Greek. Apparently, there were several eyewitnesses who saw Koukidis jump to his death from the Holy Rock and many of them rushed to the spot where he had fallen. His body was battered beyond recognition and his uniform was in shreds. According to Kostas Kostopoulos, a researcher for the Resistance, Koukidis' body was found on Thrassilou Street in the Plaka. There was no identification on him except for a postcard with the name of the recipient: Konstantinos Koukidis.

A few years ago, Kostas Kostopoulos found an elderly cobbler whose father used to sell ice in the Plaka area in 1941. The father and a friend of his picked up the body of Koukidis, wrapped in the Greek flag, covered him with a blanket, and put him in a wagon that the father used to sell ice. They took him to the First Cemetery where they buried him. This is what the old cobbler told Kostas Kostopoulos.

life for his country prompted the German command to raise the Greek flag next to the Nazi flag. If this is true, and I have not been able to confirm it, then Greece would have been the only country occupied by Nazi Germany in World War II to have its own flag flying next to the Nazi flag.

In any event, and despite the fact that the story may only be apocryphal, there is a plaque in the Plaka, near the Parthenon, that memorializes this story and the young man who was at the center of the story.

On the night of May 30, 1941, just barely more than a month after the Nazis marched into Athens, two young Greek men, Manolis Glezos and Apostolos Santas, climbed up the steep hill on the east end of the Acropolis, behind the Parthenon. In the dead of night, they lowered the Nazi flag and folded it. The next morning, the Germans who had been guarding the Acropolis were stunned when they saw the bare flagpole. The Greeks, however, were inspired by what Glezos and Santas did and some consider that their action may have been the beginning of the Greek resistance to the Nazis.

In 2008, I bought a flat in one of the large neighborhoods that ring that center of Athens. The flat has a lovely view of a park where teenagers play soccer and children ride their bicycles. A view of the Parthenon would have been beautiful – maybe in another lifetime. For the time being, I am content to admire it from a distance from wherever I can see it, knowing that it will always be there for me to revere.

The Acropolis site is clean now. The original metopes, friezes and sculptures, including five of the original Caryatids, are housed in the Acropolis Museum, across the street from the Parthenon, where they are displayed in their magnificent splendor. The British Museum made plaster cast copies of the marble friezes taken by Elgin and sent them to Greece. They are displayed next to the original marble friezes that have been saved and restored. Wherever there is a blank space in the display area, it means that that particular frieze has been permanently lost.

The Greek flag flutters serenely, undisturbed, in the breeze on the east end of the Acropolis. The Parthenon is now accorded the respect and reverence that are commensurate with its symbolism. It will always be, for me, the definition of the glory and the magic of Greece. It truly is the most beautiful building in the world.

- 10 -

The Glory of Greece

"Μολών λαβέ." (Come and get them.)

King Leonidas I of Sparta
at the Pass of Thermopylae to Xerxes I,
King of the Persians.

Democracy had its beginnings in ancient Greece. Greece's antiquities are the world's cultural icons. Thousands of books have been written about the politics, the language, the wars, the mythology, and the philosophy of ancient Greece and almost as many have been written about contemporary Greece as well. The result is that everyone knows something about the ancient history of Greece and about Greece's contemporary history, too. It is impossible not to know something.

I love many things about Greece and the Greeks, but at the

top of any list that I make about what I love best is Greece's history. Greece's history is magnificent and it is glorious. It stretches back more than three thousand years and reaches into the present. It encompasses the Golden Age of Pericles, the Byzantine Empire, and the period of the Ottoman Empire occupation of Greece for 400 years. It includes the 1922 military fiasco in Smyrna, two world wars, a civil war, and a dictatorship. And it includes the present, with membership in the European Union, the refugee crisis, and the current crisis in the East Mediterranean.

Throughout this history, there is an unbroken thread that connects ancient Greece with the Greece of today. The Greeks quarreled with each other in ancient Greece, and they still do. The Greeks argued incessantly in ancient Greece, and they still do. The ancient Greeks never agreed on anything and, even now, the Greeks today agree with each other only rarely. Sometimes I wonder if perhaps all this arguing and quarrelling was the impetus for the birth of democracy which gave all free men in ancient Athens the opportunity to just get on a soapbox and talk.

When, however, the ancient and medieval Greeks had their backs to the wall or a knife at their throats, they were united in overcoming any and every difficulty and obstacle in their way. And the same holds true today. The Greeks quarrel and argue but, if they are collectively threatened by an outside force, they come together to beat back that force.

I have watched life and circumstances change in Greece during the past fifty years. Life has not always been easy for Greece and the Greeks, but the Greeks have always held their heads high. In all the time that I have lived here, I have observed three things.

One, as I mention above, is the way that the Greeks come together when they are threatened by an outside force. Their unity is impressive. They come together with a steely determination that is dogged and visceral. No one understands it. No one expects it. But its real beauty is that no one sees it until it is too late.

The second thing that I have noticed is that the Greeks have a quiet dignity in the way that they endure hardship or face criticism. The Greeks see the hardship and they acknowledge it. They hear the criticism and they record it. But they put their heads down and get on with the job at hand, whatever that job is.

And finally, what I have noticed all these years is that no one expects anything from Greece although neither does anyone expect that the Greeks will dig their heels in, even with a passive resistance. Greece is simply not taken into consideration in many undertakings. Is it because Greece is a small country? Is it because it is neither a financial nor military powerhouse? Is it because others think that Greece is disorganized? Or corrupt? (This seemed to be the common opinion about post-World War II Greece.) Whatever the reason, Greece is often overlooked in discussions or initiatives where Greece could be a positive contributor, as has been proven time and time again.

For about ten years, beginning in 2007, things were very difficult for Greece. It struggled through the worst financial crisis that any European country had gone through since the end of World War II. The International Monetary Fund and the European Working Group policed Greece's finances mercilessly. The world press ridiculed and humiliated the Greeks endlessly. For a long time, a favorite question, accompanied by a smug smirk, was, "Aren't you Greeks ever going to pay your taxes?"

Common world opinion, at that time at least, was that the Greeks were lazy and incompetent. The Greeks bore the sarcasm and the ridicule stoically and, most of the time, tuned it out.

Unemployment was staggeringly high for several years. Anyone who could get out, got out. Young men and women, professional men and women, left the country to try their luck elsewhere. Those who stayed were paid pitifully low wages, pensioners saw their pensions all but disappear, and all of us have been taxed beyond reason although the situation has begun to improve. Still, the conditions are harsh, especially for the younger generations who are defeated before they even have a chance to make their way in the world. They don't get married. They don't have families. They are tired and they are not even thirty years old yet.

Yet, during the crisis and despite the crisis and because of the crisis, the Greeks would always find a café to sit in and nurse a one-Euro coffee with friends for three or four hours. There was an unspoken collaboration between the cafes and the customers. Customers paid one euro for their coffees and the cafes let them drink that one coffee for as long as they wanted.

This was Greek resistance at its best and this is what

annoyed the Europeans during the crisis, especially the Germans and the British.

In recent years, there has been an unprecedented influx of refugees and immigrants. Greece has managed this challenge with grace and dignity for the most part. Greece and Italy have been the main ports of entry in the European Union for people coming from war zones in the Middle East or from extreme poverty and political upheavals in Africa and Asia. The refugees are seeking a better and more peaceful life and they make the journey at great risk to themselves and their families. Although the processes in place for receiving the refugees and immigrants may not be perfect, Greece has shown a humane side to the men, women, and children who are hoping to put war, terror, and poverty behind them.

One November evening in 2015, I was watching the news and waiting for Stefan to come for dinner. I was traveling to the States the next day to attend a wedding. The news was mostly about the refugees and the immigrants and it was dismal and grim. Lightweight inflatable boats and dinghies were capsizing in the Aegean Sea in November's rough weather. Those who had not been rescued had drowned. Two months earlier, the lifeless body of a three-year old boy from Syria had been washed up on a beach in Turkey, very near a Turkish beach resort. The dinghy carrying the boy and his family and other refugees had capsized shortly after leaving the Turkish coast. The television channels were still showing, repeatedly and relentlessly, the images of the little boy lying face down in the shallow water at the edge of the beach. His hands were straight down by his sides, his palms facing up, and his sneakers were still on his tiny feet. It was heartbreaking to watch.

I reached for the remote to shut off the television. But just before I shut it off, another video came on. The video showed two Greek fishermen who had just rescued a little boy. The boy had fallen into the sea with his family when their little dinghy capsized. He was sobbing and kept saying that his father and his brother had drowned. The two fishermen had wrapped him in a heavy blanket and were trying, in broken English, to calm him down. Was it the broken English? Was it the gentleness with which the fishermen treated the little boy? Whatever it was, I smiled. But I reached for the remote again.

And then a third video came on. This was the video that washed away all the sadness, despair, and distress that I was feeling. There were three Greek grandmothers[xvi] in Lesvos (Mytilene), all dressed in black, a crying refugee baby, and the baby's visibly relieved mother standing nearby. The refugees had landed on the beach near where the grandmothers live. The mother's clothes were sopping wet from swimming and walking from the boat to the beach. She had been trying to feed the baby with a bottle but the baby was crying, reacting to the wetness of his mother's clothes and his own clothes, too.

The three grandmothers were sitting on their favorite

[xvi] http://www.pappaspost.com/video-greek-grandmothers-whose-photo-went-viral-were-children-of-refugees-themselves/

bench nearby, watching the latest wave of immigrants being helped onto the beach. They decided to help, too. They took the baby from his mother's arms. One grandmother fetched dry clothes for the baby and changed him, another one fed him, and the three of them sang lullabies to him in Greek. The baby, who was now dry and had snuggled up to someone dry and calm, stopped crying and drank his milk.

The picture was priceless. These three good women had found a solution when no one else could even think of one. There is nothing at all romantic about being a refugee but neither is there anything romantic about being a resident on an island that, because of its proximity to Turkey and the Mideast, bears the brunt of the refugee influx. And yet, the humanity and compassion that most Greeks have shown to the refugees, in the wake of a devastating financial crisis, is an example for the rest of the world.

When I first came to Greece at the end of 1972, there were two holidays that I knew only a little bit about. I had learned about them in Greek school although I hadn't really understood the significance of those holidays then. After we moved to Greece, I watched all the movies and documentaries on Greek television about these two holidays so that I could understand them and understand their significance.

One of those holidays is celebrated on March 25. This is both a national holiday, Greek Independence Day, and a religious holiday. It is the Annunciation, the day that the angels announced to the Virgin Mary that she would give birth to Jesus. The other holiday is celebrated on October 28, the day that Greece said *OXI (no,* in English*)* to Italy and entered World War II. It is also a religious holiday, the feast day of *Aghia Skepi,* or the Feast Day of the Protection of the Holy Mother of God. Many Greeks are not aware of this feast day (nor was I) but it is an important religious celebration.

When I sat down to write this chapter, it was two days before the holiday that celebrates my favorite period in Greece's history – World War II and Greece's role in that war. The holiday is *OXI* Day and it celebrates the Greeks' bravery, determination, and backbone. It may possibly be the only national holiday in the world that celebrates the beginning of a war rather than the end of a war. In any case, October 28 is my favorite Greek holiday.

The story, which has now become a myth, begins on October 28, 1940, when the Greeks supposedly said *OXI* to the Italians. This is the myth that has prevailed throughout the years. The actual story is much more interesting.

On October 28, 1940, at about 3 am, the Greek Prime Minister, Ioannis Metaxas, was awakened by a call from the guards outside his residence. The guards informed the Prime Minister that the Italian ambassador, Emmanuele Grazzi, had arrived at the residence and wanted urgently to meet with the Prime Minister himself. Prime Minister Metaxas dressed quickly and received the Italian ambassador in his living room.

The ambassador then proceeded to read a letter from Mussolini who demanded that Greece allow passage to the Italian army to march through Greece, beginning at 6 am that same morning. It was an ultimatum for Greece to surrender and accept Italian control and, therefore, Axis control, as well.

Metaxas took the message from the Italian Ambassador and considered it briefly. He then looked up at the ambassador and, according to the history that has come down through the years, said *OXI* (No). However, the Prime Minister's ten-year-old daughter, who had woken up with the commotion, had quietly come downstairs and had hidden behind a door next to the living room where her father and the Italian ambassador were meeting. According to Metaxas' daughter, who told her story years later, her father responded in French (the diplomatic language of that time), and said,

"*Alors, c' est la guerre.*" (This means war.)

The Italian Ambassador responded, "*Ce n' est pas necessaire, Mon Excellence.*" (This is not necessary, Your Excellency).

Again, according to the Prime Minister's daughter, her father replied, "*Non, c' est necessaire.*" (No, it is necessary.)

Ioannis Metaxas was a general in Greece's Armed Forces and a dictator. Because he was a dictator, the story of what actually happened in the early morning hours of October 28, 1940, has been hotly debated by politicians and historians for many years. Some say that it was not Metaxas who said the metaphorical *OXI*, but someone else. Others say that Metaxas did not want to say *OXI* to the Italians because he sided with the Germans but if he had done otherwise, King Paul would have removed him from the position of Prime Minister.

Ambassador Grazzi, however, offered a different view of the events. In his book, *The Beginning of the End. The*

Campaign Against Greece,[xvii] Grazzi says that when he gave the ultimatum to Metaxas to read, he (Grazzi) watched the Prime Minister's hands, which were trembling, and his eyes, which were filled with tears. After their brief conversation, Grazzi left the Greek Prime Minister's residence. He recalled that he left feeling the deepest respect for "the proud old man" who preferred sacrifice to enslavement. Only nineteen years earlier, in 1921, Greece had celebrated its first 100 years of independence from the Ottoman Empire. Grazzi said that he was humbled and felt a tightness in his chest because of the hatred that he had for his profession.

Thus, tiny Greece went to war with the Axis powers. In the morning, all the Greek newspapers announced the war in a blaring headline with one word only - *OXI*! Within a few hours, the Greek army was crossing the border into Albania. The troops were poorly equipped, much more poorly than the Italian troops who they were fighting. The fighting was fierce. The terrain was difficult and treacherous. And on top of that, the Greeks were outnumbered, by some estimates of at least ten to one. But the Greek troops held their ground and pushed the Axis troops, Italians and Albanians who had moved into Epirus in Northern Greece, back into Albania.

All of Europe was in awe of Greece's heroic efforts. When the Greeks went to war with the Italians, the only other European country that was at war with the Axis powers was England. All the other European countries that were not

---

[xvii] Ambassador Grazzi's book was translated into Greek in 1980 and published by Hestia Publishers and Booksellers.

fighting with the Nazis had been invaded and were occupied by Germany. The two glaring exceptions were Spain and Portugal, both ruled by dictators who did not want foreign influence from either side, Axis or Allies, in their countries.

It has been said that Hitler was furious with Mussolini at the unexpected turn of events with the Greeks. Who knows what Hitler expected – perhaps that the Greeks would fold in one weekend? In any case, for the first time since their war began, the Axis powers had met resistance and this apparently led the Germans to rethink their strategy and to pour more of their soldiers into the war.

The Greeks' resistance shattered the idea that Germany was invincible and the story of the Greek army fighting the Axis powers became a story of David fighting Goliath. The story made its way into all the major newspapers around the world and inspired world leaders to praise Greece and its heroic people.

It was Winston Churchill's words, however, that elevated the efforts and the bravery of the Greek soldiers to mythical proportions.

"If there had not been the virtue and the courage of the Greeks, we do not know which the outcome of World War II would have been. Hence, we will not say that Greeks fight like heroes, but that heroes fight like the Greeks."

Stalin also praised the Greeks, thanking them because their resistance gave the Russians time to prepare for their defense. Georgy Zhukov, the Soviet Field Marshall under Stalin, said that the Greeks had delayed the Germans from invading Russia. Indeed, estimates are that the Greek resistance to the Italians and the Albanians delayed the German invasion into Russia by at least six weeks.

The Greeks defeated the Italians and the Albanians but the cost was high. So many dead and so many wounded, including my future father-in-law who had been wounded. Historians have written that the Greek army, following its defeat of the Italian army, walked back from Northern Greece to their homes, a heroic feat on its own, and that many soldiers who survived the fighting died of cold, frostbite and starvation. And then, just when the weary and worn-out Greek soldiers had returned to their families, Germany invaded Greece and occupied it.

Why is the Feast Day of the Protection of the Holy Mother of God celebrated on October 28? Traditionally, it is celebrated on October 1 in most of the Orthodox Christian world although some countries celebrate this holiday on October 14. Only Greece celebrates it on October 28.

In 626 AD, when the city of Constantinople was threatened by the invasion of the Avars (Turkish-Mongolian nomads), the miraculous intervention of the Theotokos, the Holy Mother of God, saved the city from the invasion. It was then that *Aghia Skepi,* the feast day of the Holy Protection, was established on October 1 to celebrate the miracle.

Several years later, on October 1, 911, Saint Andrew was praying in an all-night vigil at the Blacharnae Monastery in Constantinople. After several hours, he lifted his eyes and had a vision of the Virgin Mary who had entered the church. The Theotokos had knelt in prayer with tears streaming down her face. She removed her veil and spread it over the entire congregation in a symbolic act of protection and then rose to heaven in a blaze of light, leaving her veil behind.

When the Greek soldiers returned from the Albanian front, they told of the many miracles that they had seen, convinced that the Theotokos had protected them. In 1952, the Church of Greece moved the holiday of *Aghia Skepi* from October 1 to October 28 so that the government could honor the Holy Mother for her protection of the Greek soldiers and the Greek people during World War II.

In her book, *A Hidden Child in Greece: Rescue in the Holocaust,*[xviii] Dr. Yolanda Avram Willis describes her childhood on the run with her parents and her younger brother. Dr. Willis was born Yolanda Avram, of Jewish parents, in Larissa, in central Greece. When the Nazis invaded Greece in 1941, immediately putting the entire Jewish population in Greece in mortal danger, Dr. Willis was six years old.

The Avram family hid in Crete and hid also in Athens. They were helped by hundreds of Greeks (and this is most likely an underestimation), who forged documents for them, who took them to the mountains during the German invasion, and who hid them in their homes. Dr. Willis' story is about the Greeks who saved her family's lives and the lives of other Jews.

[xviii] Yolanda Avram Willis, *A Hidden Child in Greece: Rescue in the Holocaust,* 2017, Author House, USA.

The stories tell of the pasta factory owner who hid the family on a flower farm and of the baker who worked at the pasta factory and hid young Yolanda in his home with his family, pretending to the outside world that she was his goddaughter.

She tells the story of the Athens Police who "kept giving my parents Christian IDs". She tells the story of Archbishop Damaskinos who alerted the Chief Rabbi of Athens that the Germans were coming for him and to disappear with his family. The rabbi gathered all the treasures from the synagogue and hid them in the archbishop's residence and offices where they remained until the Nazis left Greece.

Mrs. Willis tells the story of Metropolitan Bishop Chrysostomos of Zakynthos and Loukas Carrer, the mayor of the island of Zakynthos. The German Kommandant of the island had demanded a list of the Jews living on the island. After being threatened with house arrest if he did not comply with the order to produce a list of the Jews with all their information, the bishop appeared at German headquarters, together with the mayor, right before the expiration date of the order.

The Kommandant looked at the document and saw just two names on it – the bishop's name and the mayor's name.

These incidents are not the only ones related by Dr. Willis in her book. There are several such stories, each one more beautiful and impressive than the one before.

I had heard several stories from my husband and his family and his friends about their experiences in the war. The stories were all deeply personal and, although they fit into the overall history of Greece during World War II, they were mostly about their suffering and the brutality of the Nazis during the war. Except for one story.

Elias discovered, by chance, and I honestly do not remember how, that one of his elderly uncles had played a significant role in saving the Jews in Athens. That uncle has since passed away. He never revealed to his family the role that he played but I assume that he never spoke about what he did because he did not want to put his family in danger. Thus, the secret remains although his family does know now. But with great admiration for this uncle, and to pay him the tribute that he deserves, I will say that what he did was not only enormously important but truly grand and selfless, as well.

There were many such selfless actions on the part of the Greek people all over Greece, both on the mainland and on the islands. People hid Jews in their homes, claiming them as distant relatives from the countryside or, if they were in the countryside, as distant relatives from Athens. And everything these humble people did put themselves and their families in great danger. But they never gave up or stopped doing whatever they were doing.

One of the interesting things that I became aware of while reading Dr. Willis' book was that many of the people helping the Jews were fighters in the Resistance. Greece was, even then, divided into left and right, and most of the resistance fighters were leftists. The Resistance had a strong and large network and was able to locate, almost in a moment's notice, a person or a family willing to help. I do want to be clear that it was not only the leftists that helped. Anyone who wanted to help did offer their assistance, regardless of their political affiliation.

Also, I want to admit here that, after reading Dr. Willis' book, not only did I learn much more about the Greek resistance movement during the Nazi occupation of Greece, I also developed an admiration for the leftists. But I do not want to paint a pretty picture. Not all Greeks were selfless, either in defense of the Jews or in the defense of Greece itself. There were Greeks who spied for and collaborated with the Nazis. They were, however, in a tiny minority which is why Greece survived the horror of occupation, for a second time in its long history.

One of the saddest episodes for me in Greece's modern history is the Civil War which took place right after World War II, from 1946 to 1949. The leftists had fallen in love with the Russian Revolution, and with Stalin, too, and believed that the communist model that had resulted from the Russian revolution would solve Greece's woes.

All of Europe after World War II was in shambles. France, Germany, Belgium, Italy, Great Britain, the Netherlands, Poland – the list of countries that needed to stand on their feet again after the devastation of the war includes almost all the countries in Europe. Spain and Portugal, as I mentioned earlier, did not ally themselves with any power during the war and thus escaped the killing and misery of the war. They had to deal with another misery, the two fascist governments that dominated them, in Spain for twenty-five years, and in Portugal for half a century.

Greece was no different from the other war-torn countries. The devastation was everywhere; people were starving and inflation was rampant. And to cap this off, before even giving themselves a chance to recover from what they had lived through just a few months earlier, the Greeks went to war with themselves.

I have read very little about Greece's Civil War and it really does not matter because I hear about it all the time. And every time I hear someone's story, it is a different version from the other versions that I have heard. No matter what anyone hears or reads, someone else will disagree with it. Most of what I know, or think that I know, comes from stories that I have heard from people who lived through it or who had relatives who lived through it.

Elias told me the story of his own father and of his father's cousin, Elias' uncle or *theios*, Leonidas. Theios Leonidas was a colonel in the army and one time, when he was on leave, he decided to go to see his cousin (my father-in-law) but he was cautious and careful because he did not want to be captured by the leftists or, worse, killed by them. Also, he did not know where my father-in-law stood politically. He risked the visit and the two cousins had an emotional reunion.

The Civil War left an indelible mark on Greece and the Greek psyche. The mark is still there but perhaps not enough time has passed yet. Perhaps that mark will always be there. It is a divisive mark and one which does not allow for quick healing, unfortunately.

Several years ago, I bought an old stone house in a village in the mountains of the Peloponnese. It was close to the village where my father was born and I had the feeling every time I was there that I was home. I started going there once or twice a month to see my investment and to start planning a major restoration of the house.

One February, I was there for a weekend, visiting friends and family. On Sunday, I went to church. The day was cold and damp, with a light drizzle. The cold was a chill that went right through my bones but I went anyway as I had never been to this particular church for a Sunday service.

The Church of the Holy Apostles was built around 1300 AD. Its architecture is classic Byzantine; it is made of stone and the windows are accentuated with a thin red brick trim. It has two domes which is unusual because most Greek Orthodox churches have one dome. Outside, there is an interesting detail. There is a structure, the bottom half of which is the old bell tower, left over from the Byzantine era. The top part of the structure is a minaret that was added by the Turks during the occupation of the Ottoman Empire. When the archaeologists renovated and restored the church several years ago, they made a decision to leave the bell tower with the minaret as it was. I am glad that they did as it adds an extra dimension to the site.

Inside, it was so damp that I could see the moisture on the walls. I had dressed warmly and, fortunately, I had paid particular attention to my feet which were especially warm. The inside of the church, at that time, was mostly unchanged since 1300 – stone walls, a stone floor, no insulation and no heat. About ten or twelve people had braved the weather to attend the service. I tried to ignore the cold and to focus on the service. As the priest intoned the prayers and we all rose in rhythm to cross ourselves and then sit down again, several times, I became aware of a strong emotion overwhelming me. Maybe it was the language and the service. Maybe it was the ten or twelve worshippers. If they had not been there, the priest would still have done the service. But who would have heard it? Without them, no one would have heard the Greek language or the Greek Orthodox service. But with those worshippers, both the language and the religion were kept alive.

Many Greeks are angry that their ancestors did not fight sooner to overcome *the yoke of slavery*. Again, many books have been written about both the Byzantine Empire and about the Ottoman Empire and its occupation of Greece. I cannot, and will not, give a full historical description of those periods. I do, however, have my own perspective on that period of time, a perspective that may be different from that of the Greeks who were born in Greece.

The Byzantine Empire left the world with priceless treasures, different from those inherited from the ancient Greeks. It left the incomparable Byzantine churches which are recognizable from their unique architecture and construction (for example, the thin red brick trim around the windows). It left a new religion founded by the Emperor Constantine in Constantinople (the city of Constantine) and an incomparable art form with the magnificent Byzantine icons. It left a beautiful language. It left a cuisine that is in a class of its own. But most of all and, again, for better or for worse, it left the world with the concept of Byzantine politics, a phrase which has come to mean sneaky, backhanded, treacherous, conspiratorial, labyrinthine.

If you talk to the Greeks about the Ottoman Empire and its occupation of Greece, they will tell you that because of the Ottoman occupation, both the Renaissance and the Industrial Revolution passed over Greece, with the result that Greece remained a backward country and did not develop either an industrial base or a different idea of art and philosophy as most western European countries did, especially England, France, Germany and Spain.

Then again, four hundred years is a very long time. It would have been possible for the Greeks to lose both their national and religious identities in that period of time. But they did not. It is said, although this has not been confirmed by historians, that they had secret schools where priests and scholars taught the Greek language to children. The priests also held secret religious services. And the Greeks persisted.

When the Greeks came to the realization that *the yoke of slavery* needed to be thrown off, they did exactly that. They formed, carefully and secretly, underground resistance groups to fight the Turks for their freedom, one of the most important, active and influential being the *Filiki Etaireia*. The Greeks fought bravely and fiercely to gain their independence. And when they did finally begin their revolution for independence, on March 25, 1821, they opened their eyes and did whatever they could to bring Greece into the modern world.

When I was growing up, my mother told us that Tuesday the 13th was a day on which we should not begin or end anything. It was a day of bad luck, something like Friday the 13th. Tuesday, May 13 was the day that Constantinople fell to the Ottoman Empire and the Emperor Constantine IX Paleologos, the last emperor of the Byzantine Empire, was killed.

Several years ago, I learned from a taxi driver (taxi drivers are possibly the very best sources of information for everything) that Constantinople did not fall to the Ottoman Sultanate on May 13, 1453, but on Tuesday May 29, 1453, Black Tuesday. So why is Tuesday the 13th a day of superstition for the Greeks? One explanation is that the sum of the digits of the year 1453 is 13, but it is possible that this was contrived to rival the western Friday the 13th. In truth, however, the Greeks are very suspicious about all Tuesdays.

Constantinople had fallen once before, in April 1204, to the Fourth Crusade. Crusader armies had captured, looted, and destroyed parts of Constantinople. Alexios V, who had been emperor for three months when Constantinople fell, escaped to Thrace. Baldwin of Flanders was crowned Emperor Baldwin I of Constantinople in the Aghia Sophia Church, but as emperor of the new Latin Empire. Alexios V was the last Byzantine Emperor for the next fifty-seven years until Michael VIII Paleologos reclaimed the Empire in 1261.

Among the rich treasures that were plundered from Constantinople were the four bronze horses that had adorned the Hippodrome. Those four horses, known as the Quadriga of Saint Mark's, now adorn the Cathedral of Saint Mark's in Venice. When Elias and I were in Venice in 1972, I remember that I could not stop looking at them. They were magnificent.

Did I remember that they had been looted by the Venetians from Constantinople? Probably not. I found out later when I told my parents about them and my father made a face.

"They were stolen by the Venetians".

Although Constantinople was taken back in 1261, the Byzantine Empire was never the same again. It had neither the power nor the economic strength that had once defined it and, in its weakness, was ultimately vulnerable to the siege in 1453 by the Ottoman Sultanate.

Many people in my village have told me a legend about that beautiful Byzantine church in the village square, the Church of the Holy Apostles, and the Emperor Constantine. It is said that when Constantine's brother, Ioannis, died, Constantine was summering in Leontari. Ioannis was the Emperor of the Byzantine Empire and, when he died, Constantine would become emperor. It is also said that when Constantine heard the news about his brother's death, he walked to the church and prayed for the Lord's blessing. History says that Constantine was in Mystras when Ioannis died, but legend says differently.

Shortly after I bought my house in Leontari, the Archaeological Society closed the church down for ten years in order to renovate and restore it. Unfortunately, since the restoration, the only service that is held there is on the annual feast day of the Holy Apostles on June 30.

In 2012, the evening service of the feast day of the Holy Apostles was held for the first time in ten years. People came from everywhere to attend the service. As I stood inside the church with many other people, I looked out the side door at the olive trees and had the feeling that this is what it must have looked like one thousand years ago. I heard people murmuring, "This is where I got married." "This is where I baptized my children."

Four priests had come from the Patriarchate in Istanbul to perform the service at this church that had seen so much history. Perhaps Constantine had come here to pray after all.

In every war, in every revolution, in every resistance, we hear about the men and their heroism, their heroic actions. We rarely hear about the women. It's too bad, because everywhere, all over the world, women have played decisive roles in defending their countries and fighting for them. In Delacroix's iconic painting, *Liberty Leading the People,* Delacroix depicts Liberty as a woman. In the other of Delacroix's iconic paintings, *Greece on the Ruins of Missolonghi,* Greece is depicted as a woman.

The women of Greece are strong. They always have been. It doesn't matter whether they live in urban centers or whether they live in the countryside. They work hard, they are brave, they are practical, and they are stoic. They put their heads down and get things done.

I live in one of the central neighborhoods in Athens. It is racially, religiously, linguistically, and culturally diverse. Diagonally across the street from my building, there is a public primary school, Kindergarten through Grade 6. During recess breaks, I can hear the children playing and shouting happily – children of all races and religions, playing with each other, side by side.

The school, like all public schools in Athens, has a number. I don't remember the number of the school but the street on which the school is located is named for one of Greece's famous heroines, Lela Karagianni. I knew almost nothing about Lela Karagianni until I went to the island of Spetses in 2015. While I was there, I visited the home, now a museum, of one of Spetses' most famous residents, Bouboulina.

Bouboulina was a heroine of the War for Independence in 1821. She was born Laskarina Pinotsi in a prison in Constantinople when her pregnant mother went to visit Bouboulina's father there. When her husband died in prison, Bouboulina's mother went back to the island of Hydra with her young daughter and a few years later, Mrs. Pinotsi married her second husband, a sea captain from the island of Spetses.

Bouboulina grew up in Spetses, and married there twice. Both husbands were sea captains and both were killed by Algerian pirates. Her second husband, Dimitris Bouboulis, was a wealthy man and, when he died, he left a huge inheritance of ships, Spanish silver coins, and property to his wife and children.

Using her various connections, Bouboulina was inducted into the *Filiki Etaireia,* the underground organization that was planning the war for independence against the Turks. She was the only woman in the organization. She fought bravely against the Turks alongside other heroes of the revolution and spent all her money funding the revolution. In one of those ironies of life, she was killed in 1825 in a family argument.

Lela Karagianni was the great-great-great-great-granddaughter of Bouboulina. Karagianni was born in 1898 and, during World War II, she joined the Resistance. Her resistance cell was called *Bouboulina* and her home became the headquarters for the resistance cell. The missions of that cell were to help British soldiers trapped in Athens to escape to Cairo and to sabotage the Germans. Karagianni created a spy ring that collected information about the movement of German ships, stole drawings of airports, and gave out information about Greeks collaborating with the German occupiers.

She was arrested in the summer of 1944 and was brutally tortured by the Nazi SS but never gave any information about the activities in which she was involved. She was executed by the Nazis on September 8, 1944, just one month before the Germans left Greece, as part of their scorched earth policy.

The bravery of these two women, who are my two favorite Greek heroines, as well as the bravery of others who fought with them, leaves me breathless. I cannot help but think that it is no accident that people such as Bouboulina and Lela Karagianni gave their lives for their country.

And it is no accident. This tenacity, this ferociousness, can be traced back to the women of ancient Sparta. Those women set the gold standard for that female steely nerve, for that fierce feminine determination.

Personally, I am in awe of the Greeks' history, ancient and modern. I am in awe of the Parthenon. I am in awe of the Spartans and their determination to defend themselves and Greece. I am in awe of the Greeks' heroism in World War II. I never tire of learning something new about Greek history and there is always something to learn. And always, I can connect the dots.

The Battle of Marathon. The Battle of Salamis. The Greco-Persian wars in which the Greeks defeated the Persians two and a half thousand years ago. The wars that have inspired legends and that still, to this day, capture the imagination of all who read about them.

Many historians maintain that the battles of Marathon and Salamis are among the most significant battles in the history of Europe and the Mediterranean. According to the historians, the Greeks' victories allowed them to develop their civilization which then became the blueprint for other western civilizations and democracies.

Hundreds of books have been written about these battles. Greek children learn about these battles in grade school. Foreign students learn about them in their classics and history classes. But all of us know about them from the history and the legends that surround them.

In 490 BC, when Darius I of Persia invaded Greece, Athens sent a messenger to Sparta to ask the Spartans for help but the Spartans were celebrating a religious festival and would not be able to help the Athenians for another ten days. Herodotus, the ancient Greek historian, has said that the runner to Sparta was probably Pheidippides. This is the runner of legend who was the inspiration for one of the greatest athletic events in the world, the Marathon.

The Athenians and their allies selected Marathon for the battle because the terrain of the battlefield would be difficult for the Persian cavalry. And in fact, the Athenians did defeat the Persians. But the Persians, undeterred, sailed to Athens because they thought that Athens was undefended. The Athenians had anticipated this move and marched as quickly as they could to Athens where they routed the Persians who retreated to Persia.

This is where history and legend merge. Legend says that the same runner who went to Sparta then returned and ran to Athens to tell the Athenians that the Greeks had won the battle at Marathon and to warn them that the Persians were sailing to Athens. In fact, it was most likely the Athenian army that marched to Athens after the battle, causing the Persian ships to turn away when they saw the Athenians. But the legend of the Marathon runner has remained.

Ten years later, in 480 BC, King Xerxes I, son of Darius I, sent the Persian fleet to Greece to engage in a naval battle with Athens and its allies. A small force of Greeks was sent to block the Pass of Thermopylae while the Athenians and their allies engaged the Persians in a naval battle in Artemesium, near Euboea. The defenders at the Pass of Thermopylae were all killed and the Athenian navy suffered heavy losses at Artemesium. However, despite these losses, the Athenians went on to defeat the Persians in a decisive victory at Salamis. That victory came at a heavy cost.

King Leonidas I of Sparta and his band of 300 Spartans who were sent to block the Pass of Thermopylae to the Persians had been joined by an army of seven thousand allies. According to ancient historians, the Greeks were overwhelmingly outnumbered but the Greeks held off the Persians for seven days, the last three of which were in battle.

After the second day of battle, a Greek villager betrayed the Greeks and showed the Persians a small path that the shepherds used. The Persians used this path to move behind the Greek lines. When Leonidas realized that his army was being outflanked, he dismissed his allies but remained with his band of 300 at the rear of the Pass to guard it and to allow the allies to retreat safely although various histories say that about 1,500 allies stayed to fight with the Spartans.

As the ancient Greek historians have related, King Leonidas sealed his fate and that of his soldiers when King Xerxes I demanded that the Spartans and their allies lay down their weapons and hand them over. According to the historian Plutarch, the demand from Xerxes I was delivered, in writing, to Leonidas on the night before the battle. King Leonidas' response, also in writing, was simple and direct:

"Μολών λαβέ" (Molon lave). "Come and get them."

The rest is history.

- 11 -

My Athens

"Let there be light! Said Liberty, And like sunrise from the sea, Athens arose!"

Percy Bysshe Shelley

In the summer of 2020, with Covid raging all around us, Stefan and I went to see a Greek movie at a summer cinema. If you live in Greece, you have definitely been to an outdoor cinema. If you don't live in Greece, you are most likely not familiar with the concept of the summer cinema.

The movie theater in the summertime is usually in an empty lot in the middle of the city, between two apartment buildings, where the lot has been cleared, plants and flowers have been placed around the lot, and tables and chairs have been set out to accommodate the movie aficionados. The screen is in the front of the lot, and the sound is loud enough for the neighbors within a three-block radius to hear the movies every night. It might not sound enticing but it is. I have always said that I can forgive Greece and Athens for all their sins just because I can go to the movies outdoors.

Forty and fifty years ago, the outdoor cinema was a way to cool off on a hot evening. There were no air conditioners then so families would go to the movies. If the movie theater happened to be on a rooftop, then a cool breeze could almost sweep you away.

The movie that Stefan and I saw in 2020 was a beautiful film about a Greek woman who wrote rebetika songs (more about rebetika music later), but who also had an addiction. She played poker with the truck drivers in the truck stops. She wrote, and then sold, the lyrics to the songs because she needed money to get into the games. Once, she even sold her husband's police uniform to get into a game.

The movie itself is not the only attraction of summer cinema. It's the entire atmosphere, sitting in slightly uncomfortable plastic chairs until your butt hurts, eating nacho chips and drinking beer or coke. It's Athens at its absolute best.

In my opinion, Athens is the most underrated city in Europe. The Athenians are always complaining about it. The Greeks who do not live in Athens are intimidated by it. Tourists use Athens as a gateway to go to the islands. Big mistake. This seems to be changing, however, and Athens has become a trendy European city to visit, even for a weekend getaway, no matter the season.

For the record, and just so there are absolutely no doubts in anyone's mind about this subject, I love Athens. I really love

Athens. It is one of those cities that are always on. It is exciting and vibrant with so much happening day and night, night and day. True, there are some areas that I might avoid even during the day, but I feel comfortable and safe here. I appreciate the city's beauty and history. I love its energy and everything that it has to offer. I love its urbanity and sophistication.

Athens basks in the light of Attica. There is beautiful light all over Greece but the light of Attica is special, different. It illuminates. It blazes. It radiates. The Attica light is incandescent and lustrous, intense and white. It is splendid, abundant, and glorious. It shimmers off the surface of the sea, creating refracting images that can be seen from miles away.

As with any big international city worth its salt, the best way to get an overall view of Athens is to go to one or to both of the city's highest points - the Acropolis (Acropolis means *top of the city*) and Lycabettus Hill- where one has an aerial view of the city. From the Acropolis, there is a clear view straight to Piraeus and the sea beyond and it is easy to understand why the ancient Greeks chose this site on which to build the Parthenon. The Acropolis was the perfect fortress as well as the perfect lookout for enemy attacks.

Lycabettus is a higher point than the Acropolis and again there is a view straight down to the sea. There is a café as well as a restaurant close to the top. The Saint George Church is at the very top. As you sip your coffee or enjoy a meal, you can watch the magic of the city as it gradually descends into darkness in a brilliant sunset and then lights up electrically. And on a night when there is a full moon, the view is incomparable.

Athens is a multi-faceted city, a city of layers, literally. Wherever one digs, something old is found and a different aspect of civilization is discovered. When I first moved to Greece, I remember one particular spot, near my neighborhood, where an ancient ruin stood right in the middle of a street and all vehicular traffic was required to go around the ruin. The ruin was a remnant of the Hadrian aqueduct from the Roman period.

During a fairly recent construction phase, new roads were built. The aqueduct no longer sits in the middle of the street requiring traffic to go around it. That would have been a nightmare. I have looked for the ruin but cannot find it. I assume that it is still there but it is probably tucked under an overpass that was most probably designed to accommodate it.

The layers are one of the reasons, although not the only reason, that construction progresses slowly, not only in Athens but all over Greece. No one ever knows what antiquities will be unearthed. One of the first attempts at constructing a metro system in Athens used a top-down approach. This meant digging a hole in the street and drilling down. In the late 70s, the first digging site for the proposed metro was in *Plateia Kotzia* (Kotzia Square) where the old Athens City Hall is. I used to take the boys to *Plateia Kotzia* when they were little because it was a fun place to be. There was always some kind of street performance going on and the boys could have a sweet treat before we headed home on the trolley.

The hole was drilled after we left Athens in 1979 to go to the States for a year and, when we returned to Greece, I took the boys there without knowing what had been going on. I was horrified to see that ugly hole that no one seemed to be in too much of a hurry to cover up. Antiquities, lots of them, had been uncovered in that hole and, according to Greek law, the minute anyone's shovel hits an ancient artifact, construction has to stop - immediately.

Several years later, a second, and fortunately successful, attempt was made at building the Athens metro. The same sophisticated construction machinery and techniques that had been used to build the tunnel under the English Channel were used to build the metro. The theory was that if the construction consortium drilled down far enough, it would drill through all the layers and bypass most of the antiquities in those layers.

That was a logical approach for the rails and tunnels underground, but the only way to build the metro stations was to dig down from the top. This time, the authorities' approach to dealing with the antiquities that were discovered *en route* was creative and ingenious.

The summer that the Syntagma Square metro station was under construction, it was hot, very hot. A tent had been erected at the construction site and, every time I went by, I saw archaeologists, mostly young men and women, sweating under the tent, with hats on to prevent sunstroke and cotton scarves around their necks to prevent sunburn. They were all bent over artifacts and antiquities, brushing them very carefully and very seriously to remove the dirt.

The Syntagma Square metro station has become a mini-museum for the antiquities and artifacts that were unearthed while the station was under construction. It is a museum that tourists and Greeks see every day. Graves, steles (headstones) and human bones were also found nearby and are displayed in the station. Outside the station and a little further down from it, sites of ancient layers that were uncovered have been left as they were discovered. Only now they have thick layers of tempered glass over them, glass that cannot be broken or shattered and that protects the ancient layers from the elements and from looting.

When my niece Jamie visited Athens a few years ago I took her to the Acropolis Museum so that I could show her around and show off the museum. As she stood at one of the windows looking at the jumble of buildings in the neighborhood, she quietly murmured,

"Athens is so beautiful!"

I looked in the direction that Jamie was looking. The view was somewhat obscured by the window shades but, still, I could see the apartment buildings close together, most of them off-white, some of them gray from the passage of time. I could have been looking at the same crowded jumble anywhere in the Middle East except for the grayness of some of the buildings.

I remembering saying to her that beautiful is not a word that I would use to describe Athens, although there certainly are parts of the city that are beautiful. But other words for Athens do come to mind. Vibrant and alive. Old yet contemporary. Fun. Accessible. Complex but straightforward. There are always people walking around, at all hours, and there is always something to do, something to explore, something to discover. Even in the middle of a horrendous financial crisis that beat us all down day after day, Athens rocked.

Athens is also gritty and dirty. It is crowded and noisy. Athenians can be rude, and they are, a lot of the time.

There is nothing pretentious about Athens. It is what it is. Take it or leave it.

Athenians, however, are also welcoming, polite, and helpful. And despite the fact that they complain about Athens, Athenians love their city and are proud of it. They love showing it off to everyone. If you ask Athenians for help (and most Athenians speak English and other languages, too), they will go out of their way to help you in any way they can.

Athens is an inclusive city. Some neighborhoods are pricy, such as Kolonaki in the city center but, for the most part, Athens is still an affordable city. If someone wants a pricier or fancier neighborhood, then that person will usually move to one of the more exclusive northern or southern suburbs.

Athens doesn't have the overwhelming skyscrapers that many big cities have, blocking out the sun and the views, although they are beginning to mushroom in the suburbs by the sea and on the roads to the northern suburbs. Many years ago, before I moved to Greece, a law was passed prohibiting the construction of buildings that were higher than the Acropolis so that the Acropolis and the Parthenon would always be visible, wherever one was in Athens. This law actually specified the number of floors - six, I think - but as with many laws, this particular one fell through the cracks. People were aware of the restrictions but some owners and builders found ways to get around them and there are now some tall buildings although nothing like the skyscrapers that we see elsewhere in the world. These buildings do stick out like sore thumbs, however, and are more an annoyance than anything else, especially if they are blocking the view of the

Acropolis, as in "what is that building doing here".

One of the first buildings that benefited from that particular law falling through the cracks was the Athens Hilton hotel. This was in the late 50s. The Hilton was a breath of fresh air for Athens, with its modern architecture, its sexy, sleek, curvy design, and its seven stories. It was a sharp contrast to the older neo-classical and art deco buildings and the new cement apartment and office buildings that had started to go up in the 50s. It quickly became the place to see and be seen. If you were meeting someone, it was always at the Hilton which also became a point of reference for the geography of Athens. Whenever someone was asked where he or she lived, the answer was always "behind the Hilton". This prompted one of my parents' wise-cracking friends to comment that the Hilton must have the biggest ass in Athens because everybody lives behind it!

Athens is a "feet on the ground" city and not a "head in the clouds" city. It is an outdoors city, a walking city, a democratic city, a city for everyone. It is a city of neighborhoods, where everyone knows everyone else, where everyone talks to everyone else, where the kids still play in the streets and sit on the stoops of their own buildings and other buildings, although not as much as when my kids were growing up. It's a city where almost all apartments have balconies so parents can go out and check on their kids from two, three, or four stories up.

When Stefan and Costis were growing up, they went to the neighborhood public schools together with the other children in the neighborhood. I was friends with the parents. The kids all knew each other and those friendships have lasted through all these years. The parents knew each other, too, and if someone needed help, any kind of help, the neighborhood was always there for support.

A few years ago, one of the young women who had grown up with my kids got married. She invited the old neighborhood even though many of us had moved away from that street where we had all lived when the children were young. She seated all of us together at the same tables – the parents at one table, and our forty- and fifty-year-old kids at another table. I still smile whenever I think about it. It was one of the happiest events that I have ever attended.

Athens is a capital city, a European capital city. Like all other European capital cities, Athens is the place where domestic policy is defined and international diplomacy takes place. Parliament is in Athens. The Prime Minister's residence is in Athens. All the embassies are in Athens. And the pomp and circumstance surrounding diplomatic and official visits from all over the world happens in Athens.

Many world leaders and their ministers have visited Greece during the years that I have been here. They have all made the requisite visit to the Tomb of the Unknown Soldier in Syntagma Square to pay their respects and to lay a wreath at the tomb.

I have seen three sitting US Presidents visit Greece – President George H.W. Bush in 1991, President Bill Clinton in 1999, and President Barack Obama in 2016. (President Dwight D. Eisenhower, the first sitting president to visit Greece, came in 1959, before my time.)

This, of course, comes with a price. Washington DC is

a city that is dedicated to the business and pomp of politics, something that other major American cities rarely see. Athens is not dedicated exclusively to politics and neither are the other European capital cities. This means that although life supposedly goes on as usual, when any President or Prime Minister or high-ranking minister visits Greece, nothing moves in Athens. Literally. I cannot even begin to describe what the traffic is like. It's best to be out of the city during some of the more high-profile visits.

For me, one of the most memorable visits was when Yassir Arafat, the head of the PLO (the Palestine Liberation Organization) came to Greece in the early 80s at the invitation of the then Prime Minister, Andreas Papandreou. Arafat stayed at the Grand Bretagne Hotel in Syntagma Square. At the time, I was working for a Greek multinational company and the office in which I sat looked out onto the bottom part of Syntagma Square. My back was to the window.

There were five or six other women in the office. We were all looking out the window, exclaiming how everything had simply stopped so that Arafat's motorcade could come to Syntagma. And then we looked at the buildings that ringed the square. There were military sharp-shooters on the roofs of every building. The government wasn't taking any chances. It was bone-chilling, though, to see twenty or thirty sharp-shooters, wondering what the chances were that a stray bullet could find its way into our office.

There are several museums in Athens, some well-known

and some not so well-known and a few not known at all. When I first came to Greece, I was puzzled by the fact that I would see only Greek antiquities in the museums. Other museums, worldwide, had collections of paintings, artifacts, and sculptures from all over the world. It took a while for me to understand that Greece displayed only what belonged to it and what came from it and not from anywhere else. I also understood, eventually, that Greece did not have the financial wherewithal to acquire paintings or sculptures or artifacts from other countries.

The Acropolis Museum, which opened in June of 2009, is probably the best-known of all the museums in Athens and in Greece. It is included in a list of the ten best museums in the world. The Acropolis Museum is in good company; the other museums occupying a coveted slot in that list are the Smithsonian in Washington DC, the Louvre in Paris, the Hermitage in Saint Petersburg, the British Museum in London, the Prado in Madrid, the Metropolitan Museum of Art in New York, the Vatican Museums, the Uffizi in Florence and the Rijksmuseum in Amsterdam. Ten. The top ten. As I said, the Acropolis Museum is in good company. It is interesting to note that two of the three top attractions at the Louvre are Greek – the Venus de Milo and the Winged Victory of Samothrace. (The third top attraction is the Mona Lisa.) As for the British Museum, the Parthenon Marbles that were plundered by Lord Elgin are front and center, in a room that has its own alarm system and its own climate control system. At least they are well taken care of.

Before the Acropolis Museum was built, some of the marbles from the Parthenon were housed in a tiny building on the Acropolis just behind the Parthenon. It was one nondescript room and it was easy to miss. There was room for only a very small number of exhibits. The new museum was built to house the marbles and friezes from the Parthenon, the ones that were still there, and to provide a compelling argument for the British Museum to return to Greece the Parthenon Marbles that it has curated for the last two hundred years. The Acropolis Museum is stunning and has one subject only – the marbles and artifacts from the Parthenon and from the area around the Acropolis.

The Parthenon itself has been denuded. Even from afar I can see the bareness of this beautiful temple. It continues, however, to project a serene command of the Athenian landscape.

The new museum, on the other hand, is the perfect place for the marbles to be. It is also the perfect complement to the Parthenon itself. It is across the street from the Acropolis and its measurements reflect the measurements of the Parthenon as does the placing in the museum of the marbles themselves.

The Acropolis Museum is also an outstanding example of the layers that I have mentioned. As construction began on the museum, thousands of artifacts were unearthed, both on and near the construction site, as well as from excavations on and around the Acropolis. Layers of the ancient city of Athens were also uncovered since this is the area where ancient Athens flourished.

The artifacts from the slopes of the Acropolis are displayed on the first level of the museum. The layers, which show ancient Athenian dwellings, have been converted into mini-archaeological sites and are covered with tempered glass. They are on display both inside and outside the museum.

I love this museum and have visited it more than forty or fifty times to show it off to friends and family visiting from abroad. I love it because of what it stands for and for what it means. I love it for its perfection, its architecture, its display of the ancient city. I love the care that has been taken to explain, in Greek and in English, each display, in detail. I love it for the promise it holds to bring the Parthenon marbles back to Greece.

Most of all, I love the Caryatids. Five of the six original Caryatids are displayed in the same order that they were in the Erechtheion. There is a spot for the sixth original Caryatid with a sign indicating that the other five are waiting for her to come home.

The Acropolis Museum is the brightest jewel in Athens' crown. Another jewel is the National Archaeological Museum (NAM). The NAM was founded a little more than one hundred and fifty years ago to house and to protect antiquities from all over Greece and from all different eras. It is somewhat overlooked because of the Acropolis Museum and shines a little less brightly. It is, however, a magnificent museum in its own right. I do not want to compare the two as this wouldn't be fair to either of the museums. They are each a star in their own niche and category.

In September 1999, an earthquake in Athens caused structural damage to the NAM. A decision to repair the damage and to renovate the museum was made and the museum closed to the public on October 1, 2002. For the next five months, more than 20,000 exhibits were removed from the exhibition halls and many more from the storage areas. They were all carefully numbered, catalogued, boxed, and securely stored.

Once the damage from the earthquake had been addressed, attention was given to the exhibition halls. Before the renovation and restoration, as many exhibits as possible had been displayed. A decision was made to show them instead with as much space as possible between each one so that visitors could admire each without being distracted by another. The result was stunning.

My first visit to the museum, after many years and after the restoration, was an eye-opener. I had gone with friends one of whom is a certified guide. The visit was pure joy. The exhibition halls were now full of light. The exhibits themselves had room to breathe, and our friend's narrative about each exhibit was perfect. It was on that visit that I truly noticed the Artemesium jockey, a beautiful bronze sculpture of a young and diminutive boy riding a horse that looks as if it is flying.

A few years ago, as I was reading the Sunday newspaper, I read about a concert of chamber music that was going to be held at the NAM and I made plans to go. It was a cold December evening but the hall where the concert was being performed was full. Some stuffed-shirt politicians arrived late, about a half-hour after the concert was scheduled to begin, and delivered their pompous speeches to a bored audience (bored because of the speeches). When the last, maybe fifth or sixth, stuffed shirt got up to pontificate, someone said, loud enough for all of us to hear,

"… and the music??"

The last politician finished his speech and the concert finally began. Everyone visibly relaxed and, with beatific smiles on their faces, closed their eyes and enjoyed the melodic music.

Athens has many other treasures, as well. Some are hidden away and if you don't know about them, you might never find them. One of those treasures is the garden behind the Numismatic Museum on Panepistimiou (University) Avenue, one of the major avenues in Athens. The museum building was once the residence of Heinrich and Sophia Schliemann. Heinrich Schliemann was the German archaeologist who led the excavations of the site that is now presumed to have been Troy. His excavations lend credence to the idea that Homer's Iliad and Odyssey may actually reflect historical events. I have never been inside the museum itself but have been at least three times to the lovely garden and café behind the museum. Once you are in the garden, with its beautiful greenery and graceful statues, it is easy to forget that you are in the center of bustling Athens.

Many other delightful museums dot the Athenian landscape. The Byzantine and Christian Museum is in an Italianate-style mansion and displays beautiful icons, fabrics, and manuscripts from the 3rd century to the late medieval era. The Benaki Museum was founded by the Benakis family to display their collections of Islamic and Byzantine objects and Chinese ceramics. It is now known as the Benaki Museum of Greek Culture and houses its collection of Greek art and Greek costumes, and Chinese ceramics, too. A new Benaki

Museum of Islamic Art was opened to display the Islamic collection.

The Museum of Cycladic Art is a small jewel tucked into a side street near the Benaki Museum. It houses Cycladic sculptures and artifacts from the Aegean and from Cyprus. The War Museum has a collection of military airplanes which appeals to little boys. The Hellenic Children's Museum which first opened in the Plaka has now moved to more spacious facilities. It provides a safe and creative environment for children to play together and to learn about themselves and the world that they live in.

The newest addition to the museum scene in Athens is the National Museum of Contemporary Art. It is in the building that was once the brewery for the famous Fix beer. The brewery had been abandoned for several years but, a few years ago, was renovated and converted into a museum. The museum is focused on collecting and exhibiting Greek and international contemporary art.

The National Gallery of Art was a discordant note for several years. It is a modern structure that was designed after World War II to showcase 19th and 20th century Greek artists and to host exhibitions from abroad. I remember one exhibition of Impressionist Art from the Metropolitan Museum of Art that drew thousands of people to the museum, including schoolchildren. A few years ago, the government decided to renovate the building and to add another floor. There were several delays and the museum had a look of abandonment about it for a long time. Fortunately, the Ministry of Culture put the project back on track and the museum is now open.

❧

Athens is a museum in and of itself. Wherever one walks, especially around the Acropolis, there are ancient Greek, Roman, and Byzantine monuments. The city has a heady mix of architecture and stunning Byzantine churches, and stories to go with everything.

Athens also has wonderful tour guides. They are the ones who know the history of everything and tell the most amazing stories. I have been on several guided tours, but two stand out in my mind. The first was a tour of the Byzantine churches in the Plaka and it took place during an Easter week, on Holy Tuesday. I remember how much we walked on that tour, four hours at least, and how much my feet hurt! And I remember that the guide was carrying a huge book with her, *Byzantine Athens*.

We saw seven stunningly beautiful churches that afternoon and evening. There were one or two that I didn't even know about. Maybe I had passed them on my way to somewhere else but I had never realized that they were Byzantine or understood their significance. Because it was Holy Tuesday, most of the churches were conducting the service for that evening so, if we entered a church, we did so very respectfully and quietly. The tour guide would tell us about what we had seen after we had exited.

One of the churches that we did go into was the Russian Orthodox Church which was originally a Byzantine church, built in 1041 AD or maybe even ten years earlier. In the 1850s, Tsar Nicholas of Russia made a proposal to purchase it from Greece so that Russian Orthodox services could be held for the Russian expatriates living in Athens. It is a beautiful church with impressive icons.

Another of the churches that we visited, but saw only from the outside, was the Saint Eleutherios Church, also known as the Little Metropolis. It is behind the Metropolitan Cathedral of Athens, the Great Metropolis. I had never known that this small church was from the Byzantine era because many of the architectural details that identify a church as Byzantine were not there. But again, like the other churches that we saw, this one is breathtakingly beautiful. It is like a small jewel box. I couldn't stop looking at it because its beauty was so striking.

The second tour that I remember vividly took place on the south and south-west slopes of the Acropolis. The Herod Atticus theater is on the south-west slope and the ruins of the Asklepieion of Athens, an ancient center for healing and well-being, and the Theater Dionysus are on the south slope. About fifty participants had signed up and the two tour guides, one man and one woman, divided us into two groups. The woman got my group.

We began the tour on the south-west slope in front of the Herod Atticus theater. Most of us were sitting on the low stone walls in front of the theatre, with slightly bored expressions. I guess that we were probably expecting names and dates, something perhaps not very interesting but informative and educational and that's why we were there. What we got instead was a tale of wealth and power, domestic violence and murder, tax evasion and palace intrigue, with a little bit of incest mixed in for good measure. And all of this took place in ancient Greece and in ancient Rome. We were spellbound.

The Odeon of Herod Atticus, also known as the Herodion, was built in 161 AD by Herodes Atticus. It is a stunning example of Roman architecture. It has been described as "the world's most spectacular theatre" and "the second-best theatre in the world to watch live performances", by various web sites.[xix] Originally, the theater was covered by a roof although I have difficulty imagining that. It was destroyed in 267 AD by the Herulians and was restored, without the roof, in 1951.

The Herodion is one of the venues for the annual Athens and Epidauras Festival.[xx] I have seen so many performances at the Herodion that it is impossible to remember them all. Some, but certainly not all, of the highlights are Nana Mouskouri, Yannis, the opera Carmen with Agnes Baltsa in the title role, Mikhail Baryshnikov, a night of Beethoven symphonies only and a night of Tchaikovsky symphonies only. The first summer that Elias and I lived here, I think we came to this theatre every week.

I took Stefan to see the Bolshoi Ballet perform Swan Lake one summer evening when he was eighteen years old. I had been very diligent about introducing the boys to theater, classical music, and opera but I had never taken them to the

---

[xix] The Minack Theatre in England has been ranked as the best theatre in the world for live performances.

[xx] The other venues are the Ancient Theatre of Epidaurus, the Little Theatre of Ancient Epidaurus, and Peiraios 260

ballet. We got to the theater later than we should have and we had to sit way up at the top, on the stone walls behind the last row of the theater's marble benches. The theater has a capacity of 5,000 and every seat was taken. I was disappointed that we were not able to find someplace closer to the stage but, in the end, it turned out to be the perfect place to see the performance. At some point, I heard Stefan say softly,

"This is the most beautiful thing I have ever seen".

The Herodion is also the place to see people because everyone goes there. It's very rare that a performance will not be sold out. The boys were ten and seven when I took them to see Carmen with Agnes Baltsa and the Swiss National Opera. As we walked into the theatre, it was full of people and blazing with light. We walked past Constantine Karamanlis, the former Prime Minister of Greece, and by Constantine Mitsotakis who later became the Prime Minister and whose son is the current Prime Minister. We saw Melina Mercouri. The boys were duly impressed. So was I.

We squeezed ourselves into our row (Elias was with us, too) and I told the boys the first half of the story. During the intermission, I told them the second half of the story. They were enthralled.

Herodes Atticus was a Greek. Most Greeks think that he was Roman but he was not. He was Greek and lived in Rome as did his father who was a Roman senator. Herodes himself was appointed Consul. His parents were related as uncle and niece (this is the incest part).

When he was forty years old, he married a young Roman woman, Aspasia Annia Regilla. She was fourteen years old. They had five children. When Regilla was pregnant with their sixth child, Herodes apparently ordered one of his freedmen to kill her which he did by thrusting a pole into her abdomen. Regilla died and the child died, too, either with its mother or a few months later. A book has been written about this but there are not too many facts to go on.[xxi]

Herodes Atticus never married again but instead commemorated his dead wife with several public works, one of which was the Odeon of Herod Atticus. Here, another rumor inserts itself, – that Herodes' father had evaded taxes in Greece and had buried his money on his property in Marathon (yes, that Marathon), outside of Athens. Herodes found the money and dug it up although it isn't clear if he knew about the money or if he discovered it accidentally. However, because it was money that hadn't been declared, as the rumor says, the only way he could use the money without the government confiscating it was to build public works that would benefit Athens and its residents. As the Herodion does, even to this day.

Athens is not a city of ruins, museums, and monuments only. It has so much more to offer including a beautiful public garden right next to Parliament, great shopping, many bookstores, a first-class food scene, theater and concerts, a lively night life, and world-class athletic events. It also has accessible beaches,

---

[xxi] Sarah B. Pomeroy, *The Murder of Regilla: A Case of Domestic Violence,* Harvard University Press, 2009, Cambridge, Massachusetts / London, England

what I call city beaches, and the Athens Riviera.

The beaches need no introduction. They are everywhere – a short walk or drive or bus ride away. The municipal beaches are mostly organized beaches, but there are also small coves or a short length of shoreline for taking a swim. Summer without swimming is unthinkable even in Athens, or especially in Athens.

The Athens Riviera, on the other hand, is a surprise for those who do not know it or who have not experienced it. It begins in Piraeus, goes through the southern suburbs along the coast, and stretches to Cape Sounion where the Temple of Poseidon is located.

Cape Sounion is another surprise, an archaeological site with a temple, wonderful views of the sea, and beautiful sunsets. It was from the promontory at Cape Sounion that Aegeus, the king of Athens, threw himself into the sea and drowned because he thought that his son Theseus had died. Theseus had gone to Crete to slay the Minotaur and had agreed with his father to change the sails from black to white if he was coming back to Athens alive. He forgot to change the sails and when Aegeus saw the black sails on the horizon, he despaired and jumped off the cliff to his death, thus giving the Aegean Sea his name.

In April 2018, Athens became the World Book Center for one year. The nomination of a city to fill this role is a UNESCO initiative and it takes place every year. Other cities that have been honored with this title include Helsinki, New Delhi, and Buenos Aires.

The Greeks will tell you that the Greeks don't read and then, in the next breath, the Greeks will tell you that the Greeks read a lot. I am of the second opinion. Before the online sites became the rage for buying books (and yes, I am guilty of that, too), Athens was full of bookstores. There were bookstores that sold books in Greek only, books in English only, books in French only, and books in German only, and books in other languages, too. Often, I would see well-known people who I recognized, mostly politicians, browsing through the shelves.

Some bookstores have closed now. The online competition was simply too much for the small businesses, most if not all family-owned. And yet, I insist that the Greeks read a lot. There are still several bookstores in Athens and many of them are close to the downtown campus of the University of Athens.

The bookstores are being creative and innovative and are supplementing their book-selling activities with other activities. Some bookstores have readings in their stores, where authors read passages from their new books. Others provide courses in writing, - fiction, non-fiction, children's books, and poetry. Still others offer courses in editing and proof reading. All this activity indicates that Greeks are not only reading but are interested in writing, too.

Just a few weeks before Athens officially became the World Book Center for 2018, there was a delightful event, the first event in preparation for the opening. One of the major Greek banks did a presentation at the Museum of Cycladic Art on a book that it had designed and written together with a prominent archaeologist. The book was about money in ancient Greece. The presentation and the exhibition were fabulous, with exhibits on loan from the Louvre and the British Museum. The exhibits demonstrated how the ancient Greeks used coins in their commerce and how they developed their banking system so that Greeks could make deposits or take out loans. It was a wonderful mixture of museum and books.

When I first came to Greece to live, Athens had a shopping culture but shopping was not the activity that it was in the States. Most people shopped in their neighborhoods, partly because they could not afford the more expensive stores in downtown Athens and partly because the economy did not encourage shopping so people shopped only for what they needed.

That scene has changed. Athens has shopping streets with beautiful items to buy, touristy items, fun items, and just about anything else that one can imagine. The new malls, in classic US style, have begun to spring up around Athens, mostly in the suburbs, although there are a couple of malls in city neighborhoods. I prefer shopping downtown, outdoors, and in the different Athenian neighborhoods. I also prefer the smaller stores to the big department stores.

One of my favorite shopping streets is Ermou Street, off Syntagma Square. It is a cobblestoned street, with no cars allowed, that is always crowded with people, especially on Saturdays and holidays and whenever the weather is fabulous. There is usually a street performance going on there and, when the weather permits, the cafes and restaurants are filled to overflowing.

I met some friends downtown one Saturday, three or

four years ago. It was a couple of weeks before Easter and we were walking towards an area that had become trendy to have something to eat. There were literally hundreds of people in the street, maybe thousands.

"What are all these people doing here?" my friend Despina asked. Despina lives in a suburb and prefers the malls because she can take her young daughters there.

"It's a beautiful day today and people are out enjoying the weather and having a good time," I replied. And the people were indeed having a wonderful time, just walking around and browsing.

I also like to shop in my own neighborhood. It has everything I need and I know most of the shop owners so when I am in a store, I usually linger to chat with the owner and whoever else is working there. Not a very efficient way to shop but it is fun.

On Saturdays, I go to my knitting class downtown. Athens has this, too - lessons on just about everything you can imagine. You just have to search the lessons out. My knitting class is in the historic center of Athens which is very near to Ermou Street. The area is a jumble of narrow and crooked streets with lots of stores, including several stores with yarns and needles for knitting and crocheting and embroidery.

This jumble of streets, just wide enough for one car, is known as the Historic Triangle. Because this area has so many small stores and so many bargains, it is always crowded with shoppers. It is organized the way a Turkish bazaar is organized and it is possible that the Historic Triangle is a leftover from the Ottoman era. Most of the stores with knitting and embroidery supplies are clustered together, as are stores with linens and towels or stores with spices and dried fruits or stores with lamp shades that can be made to order.

One Saturday, on a cold, blustery and drizzly day, I needed one of those big safety pins that are for knitting projects so that I could transfer my sweater-in-progress to the safety pin and use the needles to knit the back of the sweater. The store where I take my lessons didn't have any of those safety pins that day, so I asked the owner,

"Sifi, I really need that safety pin. Is it okay with you if I go across the street and see if they have any?"

What could Sifis say? He said "Of course."

I grabbed my purse and, without putting on my coat, went out into the cold, crossed the narrow street and then went into the store. There, around a big wooden table, sat about fifteen women working on their knitting projects. I smiled a big smile and thought how nice that this is available and women are working on their knitting projects, chatting with each other, and drinking coffee on a cold Saturday morning. It really doesn't get any better than that.

As in all other European capital cities, the food scene and the nightlife in Athens are outstanding. Greece's cuisine has come a long way from the ubiquitous Greek salad of the 60s and 70s. Many restaurants in the big cities and on several islands now have chefs who serve sophisticated dishes with Greek produce. The wine bars focus on Greek wines, but also sell spirits from all over the world. Many bars have won European awards for their innovative cocktails.

The city is full of bakeries with the freshest bread and the most tempting pastries. The displays in the fruit and vegetable stores are works of art and the fruits and vegetables themselves come from greenhouses near Athens. Greek olive oil, considered to be among the best in the world, is *de rigueur* in homes and in restaurants.

The street food is another hallmark of the Athens food scene. When I first came to Athens, one of the more special treats was a plate of *loukoumades*, dough that is deep-fried in oil and served with honey and sprinkled with cinnamon and chopped nuts. *Loukoumades* are still a special treat, but there are so many other foods that all Greeks enjoy as a quick snack – *souvlakia* (shaved roasted meat wrapped in a pita), *tiropita* (cheese pie) and *spanakopita* (spinach pie), small fried fish in a paper cone and, of course, the ever-present *koulouri Thessalonikis,* (Greece's answer to the bagel), a round ring of bread topped with sesame seeds, soft and chewy or crisp and crunchy, depending on one's preference. And this is just a sample of what is available. Let your nose and your eyes guide you.

And finally, the nightlife in Athens. Several years ago, when my sons were teenagers, the government made an earnest attempt to curtail Athenian nightlife – the bars, the clubs[xxii], and the noise. The reasoning was that people stayed out all night and then were too tired to work the next day. They would go to work but they had no energy to do any work.

[xxii] Some clubs are known as the *bouzoukia*, nightclubs where Greek popular music is performed live, often until 6, 7, or 8 in the morning.

The attempt fell flat. Hundreds, and maybe thousands, of people, including at least one of my sons, just outright rebelled and, for a few nights, showed up in Syntagma Square in droves to protest the new ruling. The ruling was shelved. It never would have worked anyway.

Today, the nightlife is as lively as ever and whoever wants to can have a good time and stay out till 6 am or even later if they can. What they do at work the next day is between them and their employers.

In 2004, Greece had a banner year in sports events. First, the Greek National Soccer team, with their German coach, Otto Rehagel, won the European soccer championship in July, taking the world by surprise. The day that the team came back to Greece from their triumphant win against Portugal (for the *second* time in those championship games), my company sent us all home early because, even at 2 pm, the streets were already lined with the thousands of Greeks who were waiting to greet their heroes.

When I got home, I watched the team's return on television. All along the route that the buses took from the airport into the center of Athens, fans were reaching out to touch the buses, with tears streaming down their faces, shouting "Thank you, thank you".

Then, in August, the 2004 Athens Olympics took place. This was the event that really took the world by surprise. Nobody expected Greece to put on the games that they did

- with panache, with almost perfect organization, and with imagination.

The mood in Athens was euphoric. Everyone walked around with huge grins. And if you were wearing a volunteer's uniform and came across another volunteer, there was an instantaneous sense of community.

I applied to be a volunteer for the Athens 2004 Games and was interviewed three times before I was accepted. When I told some colleagues that I had applied to become a volunteer, they jokingly asked,

"But why?" They thought it was silly and pointless. And my answer was *"Gia tin Ellada re gamoto!"* (For Greece, dammit!)[xxiii]

Half an hour later, ten colleagues had sent their applications to become volunteers, too.

Greece had 52,000 volunteers for the Olympic Games and more than 150,000 applications. During the opening ceremony, I sat next to a journalist from Atlanta. She told me that without volunteers it's almost impossible for any city to put on the Games because they simply become unaffordable.

August 2004 was a month of surprises, a month that made all Greeks proud. The government announced that it was designating lanes for Olympic vehicles only and, much to everyone's astonishment, all drivers respected this. The volunteers who drove the buses from the center of Athens

---

[xxiii] The famous quote of Voula Patoulidou who won the gold medal in the 1992 Olympics in Barcelona for the 100 meters hurdles.

to the various event venues spoke perfect English, also to everyone's astonishment. The camaraderie and the pride were so obvious on our faces. Nothing bothered us – well, almost nothing.

Earlier, while getting ready for the games, Greece got sharp criticism from the International Olympic Committee which accused Greece of not being prepared. They had a point and a new committee, chaired by the formidable Gianna Angelopoulos-Daskalaki, was set up and the committee raced ahead to finish the preparations. One of my friends had been hired for the marketing team. I asked her one day if we were indeed going to be ready and she said,

"Joan, when I say that we will be ready, we will be ready."

The biggest negative publicity came from the European countries which were trying to find, in any way possible, something for which they could berate and belittle the Greeks. The biggest offenders were the British who actually spied on the stadium preparations to report back to the UK that the Greeks were hopeless.

Then a group of planespotters came to Greece on a tour. They went to a military installation in Kalamata in Southern Greece that had huge signs, in English, which said that NO PHOTOGRAPHS ARE ALLOWED and that TRESPASSERS WILL BE ARRESTED. The planespotters ignored the signs, took the pictures, got arrested and served five months. They had been fairly warned.

The arrests created an enormous furor in the UK and in the rest of Europe, as in "how could the Greeks do this to us", and "planespotting is just a hobby". Of course, if any

Greeks had gone to a foreign country to planespot and took photographs at a military installation, the results would have been the same.

The opening ceremony for the Games was brilliant. I had seen a dry run the week before when all the volunteers were getting their bearings in the stadium. But it had nothing on the real thing. The ceremony started off with the emcee, Nikos Aliagas, a Greek-French journalist, hammering away with a hardhat on. It turned the tables on the critics and set the stage for what was to come.

For the first time in modern Olympic Games history, the host country did not put on a ceremony with folk costumes, folk dances, and folk songs. Instead, Greece showcased its glorious history from the beginning to the present. It was impressive and easy to understand.

When the history procession had passed through the stadium, the Parade of the Nations began and the athletes came out to parade around the stadium, with the countries in alphabetical order. In all Olympic Games, Greece always comes out first because the Games started here. But protocol states that the host country comes out last so, this time, Greece came out last. As the Greek athletes entered the stadium, the crowd stood up and roared. Greece's moment had arrived.

The closing ceremony was brilliant, too, but it was also funny and fun. It had great music and very amusing sketches. I didn't go to the closing ceremony because the next morning I had to get up at 4 am to be at the airport extra early for an 8 am flight to London for business.

As I stepped into the airport, a young woman approached me and asked if I needed any help. She was a volunteer and I thanked her kindly and told her I had done this trip several times so I knew where to go. However, I wanted to reassure her so I showed her my ticket and my passport and went through all the steps that I needed to do in order to get on the plane. She was reassured and I passed through.

The plane was full of Olympic athletes and I kept praising myself silently for making the reservation early. We landed at Heathrow and, as I made my way through the airport, the headlines on all the British newspapers were blaring "WE'RE SORRY, GREECE."

I took the Tube to get to the office building and when I entered the office, my British colleagues all stood up to congratulate me, clapping.

In 2012, London hosted the Olympic Games. They copied the concept of history through the years and the centuries without one nod to Greece for its innovative ideas. But by 2012, Greece's magical aura from the summer of 2004 had worn off and evaporated. We were in the middle of a horrible financial crisis. Greece had become invisible again.

"He's running in full armory and he feels his wounds burning, but he doesn't stop. The pulse commands the pace and the heart dictates the will. The purpose gives him wings to run against the sun, all the way into the city, into the Assembly and breathlessly

cry out: 'We won!' The famous last words of the first Marathon runner." [xxiv]

The narrative above is the stuff of legends and this legend is one of the best. Apparently, none of the ancient historians wrote about this event so it may not have happened, ever. All legends, however, begin somewhere so there must have been some event that inspired this particular one.

Athens is home to the Marathon – The Athens Marathon the Authentic – because, if we believe the legend, this is where it all began. Athens' most famous event commemorates the endurance of the runner Pheidippides who, it is said, ran from Marathon to Sparta, in two days, to request assistance from the Spartans in the war against the Persians. Then, when the Greeks won the battle of Marathon, Pheidippides supposedly ran to Athens to announce "We won!" to the Assembly whereupon he collapsed from the exertion and died. According to the legend.

The modern Marathon in Greece began in 1896 with the first modern-day Olympics. Another event inspired by the legend is the Spartathlon that was established in 1984. It is an ultra-marathon race that takes place every year in September, 250 grueling kilometers, from Athens to Sparta, over the bridge that spans the Corinth Canal. Runners have thirty-six hours to finish the race. Most do, maybe some do not. And just as in

---

[xxiv] http://www.thisisathens.org/never-ending-stories-landing/neverending-detail/?id=15&langid=1

the Athens Marathon the Authentic, what matters is that you finish the race, not the place in which you finish.

In November 2014, I ran the 5 K road race, one of the events in the annual Athens Marathon. That year, more than 40,000 people ran in one of the marathon events and they came from all over the world. I did the 5K to honor the memory of my son Costis who had passed away in 2011. Costis had been a marathon runner and had done several marathons in Europe although he had never done the marathon in Greece. I told my friends what I planned to do and several of them joined me. Seventeen of us ran together in Athens on that November day in 2014.

It was an amazing event, as I am sure that marathons are all over the world. It was fun. It was a celebration. While we were waiting for the 5K to begin, one of my friends overheard some women near us chatting in French. Their husbands were running the full marathon so the women had decided that, since they were coming to Athens anyway, they would run the 5K.

I ran the 5K again, just one more time, in November 2016. The rush was the same. It was fun and it was a celebration. It was part of the legend that Greece celebrates every year, the one that inspires us all to achieve and to do our best.

- 12 -

The Storytellers

"I was born a Greek and I will die a Greek."

Melina Mercouri

The Greeks have a very long tradition of storytelling, from the time of ancient Greece. Critics and skeptics will be the first to object saying that the modern Greeks are not direct descendants of the ancient Greek storytellers so the tradition doesn't extend to them. It doesn't matter. Even if today's Greeks are not direct descendants of the ancient Greeks, modern Greeks inhabit what used to be ancient Greece. The legacy was here for them to take or not. They took it and they ran with it.

Aesop was one of the greatest storytellers of all and his fables are known throughout the world. Like all other stories that have been handed down over thousands of years, Aesop's fables began in the oral tradition. A few hundred years later, they were collected and then recorded. Thus, Aesop's Fables could very well be considered the first self-help book on how to live a fuller and more ethical life.

Homer, Sophocles, Euripides, Aeschylus and Aristophanes are also famous and well-known all over the world. They are taught in Greek schools, from primary school through university, as well as in schools and universities abroad. The Greek theaters, both in winter and in summer, resonate with productions of *Medea, Lysistrates, Oedipus Rex* and the *Odyssey* (among others), for children and for adults.

Storytelling, however, is not limited to the greats, or to the ones who have become great over thousands of years. Storytelling is everywhere. It is the folk songs and the demotic songs from the different regions of Greece. It is the rebetika songs that came to Greece, one hundred years ago, with the refugees from the Smyrna catastrophe. It is the grandmother telling her three-year-old grandson a story, improvising as she goes.

The tradition of storytelling in Greece continues to this day. For a small country, Greece has enjoyed more than its fair share of awards. And many Greek luminaries have enjoyed, and continue to enjoy, international recognition. The poets George Seferis and Odysseas Elytis both won the Nobel Prize for Literature, Seferis in 1963 and Elytis in 1979. Many other Greek poets and novelists are renowned in the world of literature, including the poets Constantine Cavafis (born in Egypt) and Yannis Ritsos, and the novelist Nikos Kazantzakis who was nominated for the Nobel Prize in nine different years. Kazantzakis is most well-known for his books *The Life and Times of Alexis Zorbas* and *The Last Temptation of Christ.*

There are the filmmakers, Theo Angelopoulos whose films include *Alexander the Great* and *Ulysses' Gaze,* and Michael Cacoyannis whose films include *Zorba the Greek* (adapted from Kazantzakis' novel) with Anthony Quinn and the Greek actress Irene Papas, and *Stella* with Melina Mercouri.

The musicians are storytellers. There is Mikis Theodorakis who wrote the music for *Zorba the Greek.* There are the musicians who wrote the music and the lyrics for the songs known as *rebetika* or Songs of the Underground, songs that tell stories of poverty, disease, and death, drugs and jail, and finally being alone and lonely in a foreign country. Rebetika songs, which came from Smyrna, were banned in Greece during the war and during the dictatorship but they flourished anyway. This is probably how they became known as the Songs of the Underground. And there is, of course, Nana Mouskouri, the international singer who lives in Paris now. Everyone knows Mouskouri.

The artists are storytellers. Spyros Vassiliou's paintings capture the essence of Athens and of Greece, as do the paintings of George Sikeliotis. Nikolaos Gyzis, who painted *The Secret School* in 1895 – 1896, depicts one of the several secret schools that supposedly functioned during the occupation of Greece by the Ottoman Empire. Many say that the secret schools are a myth and did not actually exist during the Ottoman Empire. But whenever I would stand in front of this beautiful and lyrical painting at the National Gallery of Art, it would tell me the story of why the Greek language and the Greek Orthodox religion persisted during four hundred years of occupation, and survived.

A few months ago, while I was writing this chapter, I read that we all walk by a thousand story ideas every day, but most of us do not recognize what we see as a story. Still, it is my firm belief that everyone has a story to tell and that if you give people a chance, they will tell you stories that will break your heart or lift your spirits or inspire you or make you laugh for days and even in the middle of the night. The Greeks see these story ideas and take them to the next level. Their stories are just like the ancient Greek plays – funny, heartbreaking, tragic, solemn, dreadful. I have listened to these stories for the past fifty years and they have helped me to understand the Greeks and their culture. Their stories are a window to the drama and comedy of everyday life.

The Greeks have several ways to tell their stories. They talk. They write. They act. They emote. They sing. They dance. They paint. They sculpt. They build. And always, they use their hands. Greeks cannot talk unless they are moving their hands at the same time. Sometimes their stories are serious. Sometimes they are drop-dead funny. In fact, I think that the Greeks may have the best sense of humor of any ethnic group that I have met.

When the Greeks talk, their conversation is sprinkled with anecdotes, jokes, and a lot of slang – all done in their unique fast staccato pace. When the Greeks write, they tend to be more serious, especially in books and in newspaper or magazine articles. Their comedy television series, however, are a work of art and a forte of Greek actors and screenwriters. The dramatic series I can do without – there's too much drama and most of the time without a viable plot. But the comedies – ah, the comedies. I can watch the re-runs of my favorites over and over again. The comedies don't need strong or believable plots. They just need episodes that are propelled only by the jokes and the dead-pan expressions of the actors.

The comedy series are a little like the ancient Greek play *Lysistrates* that Aristophanes wrote and performed. I mean, come on, did anyone really believe that all the women in ancient Athens would withhold sex from their husbands until the men stopped fighting wars? Of course not, but the silliness of the proposition and the implausible plot as well as the slapstick humor of the anecdotes and jokes made this play a favorite with the ancient Athenians. It is still a favorite today.

The acting in the comedy television series is superb and sublime, better than the acting in a comedy on stage which can be more slapstick and sometimes vulgar. On television, the writers, producers and actors need to be a little more careful with their language so they can get past the censors. And they usually succeed. Hilariously.

When I first came to Greece, television was new to the Greeks and there were only two television channels – ERT, the Hellenic Radio and Television public channel, and YENED, the armed forces channel. They operated only a few hours a day which was a marked contrast to the way television worked in the US, even in the 70s. Greece was still governed by a military dictatorship and both channels were heavily censored. The news was boring and predictable, delivered according to the scripts written by the colonels. There was really nothing to take people's minds off the sheer drudgery of everyday life.

But then, a few comedy series appeared on the two channels and, unsophisticated as they were, they were very funny in how they depicted Greek life in Athens and in the countryside. They were stories that made everyone's lives a little more bearable. These stories are how I learned to appreciate Greek humor.

Often, Greek movies were shown on television. The movies were mostly romantic comedies, stories that were funny and bore little resemblance to reality. Greece also had its very own national movie star, Aliki Vougiouklaki. All Greeks were in love with her and followed her life in the gossip columns with great interest. Her movies were innocent and sweet and full of smart-ass sassy quips and comebacks. And in addition to appreciating Greek humor, I also learned Greek from watching these movies.

When the dictatorship fell, television moved a step up. The first indication that something had changed was in the news. The journalists were different and were able to comment freely on the new political environment in Greece. The politicians in the new government, headed by Constantine Karamanlis, were intelligent and educated men and comfortable in front of television cameras. They were different from the colonels of that time who delivered their speeches woodenly. And the new journalists now had a different story to tell as well as a different way to tell the story.

One evening, George Mavros who was in the new government in the dual role of Vice-President of the Government and Foreign Minister was giving an interview to a foreign reporter. Mr. Mavros was speaking in fluent English and next to him was a Greek woman translating into Greek. At one point in the interview, Mr. Mavros and the reporter were discussing the recent invasion of Cyprus by Turkey. Mr. Mavros used the word "invasion" in English but the translator used the Greek word for "attack". Mr. Mavros spun around to look at the translator and, with one word only, gave her the correct Greek word for "invasion". It was one of those moments when it was impossible to not understand that change had indeed come to Greece and to the Greek media.

In this grand tradition of storytelling there was one trio that stood out. Melina Mercouri. Manos Hadjidakis. Jules Dassin. Each component of the trio was exceptionally strong on its own but, individually, the components would not have accomplished what they accomplished together in 1960. Together, they put Greece on the map.

Never on Sunday, the movie and the song, came flying out of post-war Greece and took the world by storm. Manos Hadjidakis' beautiful and memorable theme song won the Academy Award for best song. Melina Mercouri won the Best Actress award at the Cannes Film Festival that year for her role in the movie. And Jules Dassin was nominated for two Academy Awards for writing and for directing the movie.

Melina Mercouri was Greek through and through, and proud of it. She was fierce and she was ferocious. And she was fearless. She was also the consummate storyteller. Whether she was on the screen or on the stage, her role became a second skin and that is how she communicated her story to the audience.

Never on Sunday was the first movie in which I saw her. I was only fifteen years old when the movie came out and I remember being so impressed by her strong personality and her confidence. The movie's storyline revolved around Ilya, the good-hearted prostitute who never worked on Sundays. Instead, on Sundays, she immersed herself in Greece's ancient history.

In 1960, most, if not all, Greek-Americans were a little embarrassed by the story (how would they explain it to their children?), but the story was endearing and, eventually, it won everyone over. And it gave the world a glimpse into Greece's culture and music.

In the movie, Ilya meets an American tourist named Homer, played by Jules Dassin, the man who would become Mercouri's husband in 1966. Homer wants to reform Ilya and to educate her by teaching her Greek history but Ilya not only resists his attempts to put her on the right path, she also persists in interpreting Greek history and Greek drama in her own way.

Almost fifteen years later, I was married and living in Greece. One November Friday evening in 1974, Elias had gone out with his colleagues. It was boys' night out, just one year after the Polytechnic uprising that had led to the fall of Greece's dictatorship.

Our baby son, Stefan, was sleeping and I had turned on the television. One of the two Greek channels was airing a Greek movie; I had come in at the beginning. I slowly realized that the star of the movie was Melina Mercouri and, as the plot unfolded, I became mesmerized.

When Elias came home, I told him excitedly about the movie that I had seen with Melina, and he said,

"Oh, you saw *Stella*."

Stella, which was filmed in 1955, was Mercouri's movie debut and it was stunning. The movie was directed by Michael Cacoyannis and the music was composed by Manos Hadjidakis and by Vassilis Tsitsanis, the famous rebetika musician, songwriter, and storyteller.

Stella was a feminist movie, perhaps one of the first to be seen in Greece. It depicted the conservative Greek society of the 1950s, a society in which a strong and independent woman, especially one who sings rebetika songs in a nightclub, is shunned. The role fit Mercouri like a glove.

Giorgos Foundas, who was also in *Never on Sunday*, starred opposite Mercouri. He played the role of Miltos, a Greek soccer player on the Olympiakos team who falls hopelessly in love with Stella. Miltos wants to marry Stella and Stella reluctantly agrees although she doesn't want to get married, not because she doesn't love Miltos but because she doesn't believe in marriage. When Stella, true to her beliefs, doesn't show up at the church on their wedding day, Miltos goes out to find her. When he does find her, Stella is waiting for him, expecting him. She knows what her fate is and is calm and accepting even while he pleads with her to leave.

"Stella, fyge. Kratao mahairi." (Stella, leave. I have a knife!)

The movie *Stella* was banned during the dictatorship as were all Mercouri's movies. When the dictatorship fell, the ban was lifted and from that first time that I saw the movie in 1974, *Stella* was on television at least once a year. Each time it was aired, I set aside that time for myself and watched it – every time. After a while, I knew all the dialogue in the movie by heart.

Mercouri was in New York, starring in the Broadway production *Ilya Darling,* a theater adaptation of *Never on Sunday*, when, on April 21, 1967, a group of colonels closed Greece down for a week and imposed a dictatorship on the country, a dictatorship that lasted for seven years. Mercouri did not come back to Greece. Instead, she went to Paris and to London. She became a political activist and began a struggle against the military junta, travelling all over the world to inform the public, hoping to isolate the colonels but instead infuriating them so much that they revoked her Greek citizenship and confiscated her property in Greece. It was then that she said,

"I was born a Greek, and I will die a Greek."

Melina was unbowed. She continued her fight all over the world and, when the junta fell in July 1974, she returned to Greece, triumphantly. She became the first female Minister of Culture in the socialist government of Andreas Papandreou and, in this position, was an outspoken and passionate advocate for the return of the Parthenon Marbles to Greece. She held an international competition for the construction of the Acropolis Museum so that the marbles would have a proper place to return to. She introduced free access to museums and archaeological sites for Greek citizens. She supported the construction of the Museum of Byzantine Culture in Thessaloniki. It was she who commissioned a study for the integration of all the archaeological sites in Athens. And she did so much more.

Melina was bright, smart, and powerful and, like all bright, smart, and powerful women, she got under people's skin and on their nerves. In *Never on Sunday,* she wore a black dress that became as iconic as the black dress that Audrey Hepburn wore in *Breakfast at Tiffany's.*

There was nothing girly or breathless about Mercouri. She was passionate and larger than life - in her movies, in her plays, and in her life. Wherever she was, whether it was on the screen or on the stage, or out for dinner with her friends, she dominated her environment.

I was fortunate to see Mercouri in two plays in Athens – the Greek production of Berthold Brecht's *The Threepenny Opera* and Euripides' ancient Greek tragedy, *Medea*. Elias and I saw *The Threepenny Opera* the night before we left for Boston with Stefan, in December 1975, to celebrate Christmas with my family. Melina was expansive and energetic and all eyes were on her. In the early 80s, when she starred in *Medea* in the outdoor theatre on Lycabettus, her performance was again electrifying. Even though I could not understand all the Greek, it was impossible not to understand that Medea was hell-bent on murdering her own children to take revenge on her cheating husband, Jason.

Whenever Mercouri was photographed, there was a cigarette

dangling from her mouth. If it was not dangling from her mouth, it was in her one of her hands with which she was always gesturing expressively. Greece - its politics and culture - and the stage were her life. She herself was always so alive.

But she got sick, with lung cancer, and went to the United States for treatment, accompanied by her husband, Jules Dassin. She died on March 6, 1994 at the Memorial Sloan Kettering Cancer Center in New York.

Two days later, on Tuesday, March 8, her remains were returned to Greece. When the Olympic plane carrying her coffin entered Greek airspace, four Greek fighter planes flew up to meet the jumbo jet and escorted it, and Melina, to the airport. As her coffin, draped in the Greek flag, emerged from the plane, Melina Mercouri was greeted with the Greek national anthem and honors reserved for heads of state.

The cortege of cars that had met the plane drove from the airport, flanked by twenty-five police motorcycles, to the center of Athens via Syngrou Avenue. The street was closed to traffic to allow the cortege to move slowly, allowing mourners to pay their respects. Thousands of people lined the streets and others thronged at the windows of office buildings, including me. As the cortege drove by, people threw flowers on her coffin.

The cortege made its way to the Metropolitan Cathedral of Athens where Mercouri's body would lie in state but first it passed by the Ministry of Culture where the employees who worked there were gathered at the windows of the Ministry to honor their Melina in their own way. Loudspeakers played the song *Never on Sunday* and flowers and rose petals showered down on the hearse. There was not a dry eye anywhere. Melina was, once again, telling her story.

- 13 -

1988 – 2011 Following my Dreams

"You can get what you want or you can just get old."

Billy Joel

I can still remember where I was sitting, with the boys who were toddlers running around me, when I read the article in *Time* magazine about the small liberal arts college in Boston that had started an MBA program. The college was Simmons College, now Simmons University. Dr. Margaret Henning and Dr. Anne Jardim, both graduates of Harvard Business School, had designed an MBA program for women and had teamed up with Simmons to establish the Simmons College Graduate School of Management.

The MBA program at Simmons, with Dr. Henning and Dr. Jardim as deans, began its first class in 1973. I don't remember when the article appeared in *Time* but it must have been sometime in the late 70s. *Time's* article gave the program high praise and, for that reason, the article got my attention. The idea of a women-only business school was revolutionary. The deans' rationale was that the environment at a women-only business school would be less aggressive than the male-dominated environment at all the other business schools and would give women a chance to be heard without being continuously interrupted by the men.

The thought that I might possibly be able to go to graduate school took hold in my mind. It wasn't the *women-only* that got my attention. It was the fact that it was a one-year program, intense but doable. And it was the Simmons MBA's admission policy that the applicants had to have at least five years' work experience, any experience, and they had to be at least twenty-five or twenty-six years old. There was only one problem. Simmons was in Boston and I was in Athens. If I really wanted to do this, I would have to figure out the logistics down to the last detail.

I was married and my husband had an academic and research career that couldn't be interrupted. And I was also the mother of two very young pre-school children. And to top that off, I had only four years' teaching experience in the States and four years' part-time working experience in Greece.

I had been working for a study abroad program as the assistant to the director of the program. It was a part-time job but it was fun. I enjoyed it and I met so many students from the United States and professors and instructors from Greece. After Costis was born in 1977, however, I resigned so that I could focus on bringing up the boys. I hadn't realized how much work it was to bring up two toddlers. But I was out of the work force and I missed it, even the ten hours a week. However, as they say in the States,

"Where there's a will, there's a way".

Still, the MBA went to the back burner and stayed there for a few years.

When my husband and I separated in 1981, I moved into my own apartment with the children and found a job. It was an exciting time for me. The job was at Motor Oil Hellas, one of the most prestigious Greek multinational companies, and it was a good job.

The years rolled by at Motor Oil with one year off to teach at TASIS (The American School in Switzerland). I began thinking about the Simmons MBA program again. Finally, in 1987, I started formulating a plan to go to business school but decided first to investigate business schools in other countries, including Greece.

As I considered all my options, I made a list of pros and cons for each option. The first possibilities to be eliminated were the MBA programs in Greece. There weren't many at that time and there were none in English. If I went to a business school in Greece, even if the program was in English, I would have to continue working in order to pay the bills which meant that I would have to go to school part-time because I couldn't work full-time and go to school full-time. The boys would need a major amount of my attention and I would need a lot of help. Finally, the problem solved itself. I knew that I couldn't do an MBA in Greek because my Greek wasn't good enough and I didn't want to end up last in the class.

Another option that I considered, and then rejected, was a business school in Europe, ideally a business school with an MBA program in English. There was the UK of course. There was also INSEAD, the business school in France. But the prospect of being alone in another country without a support network was something that I didn't relish.

That left the US. And for the same reason that I didn't want to go one of the European business schools, I wanted to stay in the Boston area where I did have a built-in support system. Again, I carefully considered my criteria and I kept coming back to Simmons. It was a one-year program and, therefore, not only would I be back in Greece in a year's time but, at least in the 80s, the one-year program was less expensive than the two-year programs. I'm glad, though, that I considered other schools and understood the reasons why I had eliminated the other options. I think, however, that it was a foregone conclusion that I would decide to go to Simmons because it had been in my subconscious for fifteen years.

So, Simmons it was. I began all the paperwork and the preparations. I sent in my application. I took the GMAT. Elias and I decided that the boys would stay in Greece that year with him so that we wouldn't interrupt the flow of their schooling. My parents told me that I was welcome to stay with them in Lynn while I was in business school. It would be a huge move and a major change in my life but I would have regretted it if I hadn't gone ahead with my plans.

In the spring of 1988, I got an answer. I had been accepted but Simmons wanted me to take an algebra class. It was basic algebra – how hard could it be. I found a class, in

English, at the downtown branch of Deree College and went to the class. The algebra was a little harder than I thought it would be. On the first test that we took, my grade was a 6. (We were graded on a scale of 1 to 10). I went home and told Costis, who was eleven years old at the time. He made a grimace which indicated that he was not at all pleased.

A week later, we had another test and I got an 8. Costis looked a little relieved that I had improved but he was still not pleased. But a few days later, when I came home with a grade of 10 on the last test of the algebra class, he was thrilled. He flung his arms around my neck and said,

"Oh, Mummy, I'm so proud of you!"

It was worth it to take the class, just for that.

I resigned from my job and packed my things, getting ready for the move. The boys began moving their belongings to their father's house and, in July, Stefan, Costis and I flew to the US. Stefan and Costis went to spend part of their summer vacation there, as they always did, and to see my parents and the rest of the family. I was going to get an MBA. I was going to do a *gap year*.[xxv]

The year was intense, very intense, August to August. And I learned that a master's degree is very different from a bachelor's degree. But there was a measure of freedom in the

---

[xxv] A gap year, in the US, is a year that a student takes after graduating from high school and before starting university or after finishing university and before starting work. The purpose of the gap year is for the student to acquire life experiences and / or to engage in educational or developmental activities.

class that I had not really experienced before. Maybe I had been out of school too long. But I truly enjoyed being in the classroom again, figuring things out collectively with the rest of the class, made up of seventy women, and working on various projects with different teams.

In August 1989, the class graduated. We were all exhausted but exhilarated, too. My father had teased me that graduation was on a working day and he and my mother would not be able to attend.

"That's okay," I said. "The only two people in the world who have to be there are Stefan and Costis."

But in the end, everyone was there - Stefan and Costis, my parents, my brothers and my sisters-in-law. I graduated with honors and this impressed my family but, most of all, it made an impression on Stefan and Costis – that their mother, at the age of forty-four, had received her master's degree. The boys and I had been on opposite sides of the Atlantic for a little more than a year. Graduating with honors made our sacrifices worthwhile.

Five months later, I began my first post-MBA job at Mobil Oil Hellas, an American multinational in the petroleum industry. I realized once again how important it is to be in the labor market – to be working, to becoming familiar to people, to becoming familiar with and understanding the requirements and protocols of the work environment.

Working at an American multinational was another dream that I had had when I started thinking about doing an

MBA - a multinational where I could travel, where the work would be challenging and would give me an opportunity to soak up knowledge. I envied the people I knew who were working for multinationals and were traveling a lot for business.

Working at Mobil was like getting a second MBA. I learned to be disciplined in my work. I learned to get along with people, to work on a team and to manage a team. All multinationals, but especially American multinationals, are very complex organizations with distinct identities and personalities and with defined hierarchies depending, of course, on the industry. Multinationals require careful navigation around the management and around the policies and procedures. I was fortunate to go through a number of positions in the company, acquiring an understanding of how the company worked and who the people were.

After I had been at the company for almost two years, I was asked by the Managing Director of the company in Greece to join a pan-European project that was being run out of London with employees from all over the world. The time frame was for six months but when that time was up, the project team in London asked me to stay on for another six months, which I did.

The one year in London was a bonus, one that I had not expected but which again gave me the opportunity to meet people and to network. When I was a teenager taking high school French in Lynn, I started daydreaming about Europe. It was the fashion then, and still is, to do a study year abroad in Europe. My dream was to study abroad for a year in Paris, and then extend the time for another one or two years to spend time in London (after I had graduated from university) and then in Rome. In the end, as I tell my friends, I overshot my target by about two thousand miles (moving to Greece instead) and by several years. The London year in 1991 was my study year abroad about thirty years late.

The London year was also the second time in fewer than four years that I was living outside of Greece. I had been in Boston for one year while I studied at Simmons and now I was in London for one year working for my company. I was ambivalent about those two years. Yes, I was happy to be there but, at the same time, it felt really good to be back in Athens and to be back in Greece, generally. I cried when I left Boston and I cried when I left London, right before Christmas, after the one year there but I was happy to be back with the boys and to spend the holidays with them. But where was I exactly? I didn't know. When I went to Boston and then to London, I felt each time as though I was leaving on an adventure, almost as though I was escaping. But when I came back to Greece both times, it was good to come back to familiarity even though Greece, at that time, did not have the glamour that Boston or London did. But Greece was familiar and that was enough for me.

I stayed at Mobil for seven years and then it was time to move on. My next move was to Oracle, another American multinational but this time in the high-tech industry. And this time I planted roots. This time it became a career with the components that I was looking for – a continuous learning curve, a lot of business travel, a less conservative industry with a flatter hierarchy, and super-smart colleagues. This time, I got it all.

All in all, I stayed fifteen and a half years at Oracle. For the first seven and a half years I worked at the Greek office. In 2004, I was asked if I would be interested in a position in the Europe Middle East Africa region (known as EMEA) and I said yes. The learning curve, after seven and a half years in the Greek office, had flattened. This changed when I moved to EMEA. My desk and chair were still in Greece but my team and my assignments were not.

In the EMEA region, I worked on much larger deals and with much larger customers. My team was from the western European countries. Our home base was Belgium where my manager was from. So, in addition to the changes in the work that I was doing, I also began traveling – a lot.

About two years before I was offered the job with EMEA, my parents passed away - my mother in December 2002 and my father in September 2003. While they were alive, almost all my trips were to Boston. The axis was Athens – Boston – Athens, with Boston being home and Athens being Athens, the place where I lived.

After my parents died, I still went to Boston although not as often, but now that I was traveling for EMEA, the departure and destination axis changed. Now the axis was Athens – Destination x - Athens, with Destination x being a business trip city and Athens being home. The change in my mental perception of Athens, and of Greece generally, surprised even me once I started thinking of Athens as home.

For the first time, I really did feel that I was coming home whenever I returned to Greece from a business trip. As we would fly over Greece, I would find myself looking out the small airplane window to identify landmarks and locations that I recognized. As we neared Athens and I saw the stark and spare but beautiful landscape of Attica and the sparkling Mediterranean Sea, I knew I was home and it felt good to be back. I realized that what the web site *Growing Up Greek Style* had posted on Facebook, two or three years earlier, was indeed true:

"Happiness is looking down on Greece from your plane window."

Recently, my son Stefan and I were discussing business travel which has been severely curtailed because of the Covid pandemic. I traveled a lot for Oracle, mostly to Europe but also to South Africa, the Emirates, Russia, and twice to corporate headquarters in the US. I cannot begin to imagine what it is like to do these meetings remotely, all the time.

I am grateful for the travel that I did. Traveling for the company gave me the opportunity to see the world. It also gave me the chance to work with some of the smartest people, ever. It was a privilege to be part of that team. And I have to admit that I always got a rush of adrenaline whenever I spoke to and networked with executives of some of the largest and most well-known companies in the world. I got a rush of adrenaline whenever I delivered presentations to these companies or at conferences. I understand that maybe the world needed to take a break from the frenzy of traveling but there are times when I wonder if business travel will, or should, come back to what it was before Covid.

As I look back on my work experience in Greece, I am also grateful for the experience that I acquired from the first two companies that I worked for in Athens. At Motor Oil Hellas I met everyone who was anyone – people who I would read about in the newspapers and magazines and see on television. It was networking at its best, and glamorous, too.

At Mobil Oil Hellas, I saw corporate America, with its hierarchy and its policies and procedures, at its best. I couldn't have asked for more.

I continued to work at Oracle and continued to thoroughly enjoy it. It didn't matter that I worked crazy hours and long weeks and weekends. I simply enjoyed and loved the challenges. At some point, my work on the team changed and I moved from sales to business operations and didn't have the same travel schedule as I did when I was in sales. I missed meeting with customers and delivering presentations but now I had a different customer base, my colleagues. And I was still on the same team, a huge advantage for me. I started making plans to work there until I was seventy years old, but life had other plans for me.

- 14 -

Everywhere but Athens

"Happy is the man, I thought, who, before dying, has the good fortune to sail the Aegean Sea."

Nikos Kazantzakis

In 2019, I became one of those people who have had the good fortune to sail the Aegean Sea. My cousins Nicky and Gayle came to Greece with a small part of their beautiful family – son and daughter-in-law Greg and Lori, and grandchildren Adrienne and Nick. Their plan was to see as much of Greece as they could in two and a half weeks. As part of that plan, they rented a private yacht to sail the Aegean for five days and then sent me an email inviting me to join them! I wrote back and said,

"Yes, and thank you so much for asking me to join you, I would love to."

Our trip began in Rafina, a port town outside of Athens, where we took a ferry boat to Mykonos. When we arrived in Mykonos, we walked to the yacht where we met the skipper, Patrik, and his wife, Abbi, who was Patrik's first mate.

I hadn't been to Mykonos for fifty years, since my honeymoon in 1969. I remember that even in 1969 it was crowded with tourists but it did not yet have the veneer of worldly sophistication that it has now.

We unpacked our clothes and then set out to walk around a bit and find a place to eat. We went back to the yacht after dinner to sleep. It was a delightful Day One.

After breakfast in Mykonos the next morning, we sailed to Paros. It was fabulous, sitting on the deck with my family and sailing the Aegean. In Paros, we went to the beach in an area called Piso Livadi which had been a honeymoon destination fifty years earlier.

In Naxos, we berthed in a tiny and quiet village where there were only a small dock and a restaurant high up on a hill. The restaurant overlooked the dock and the sea. I remember that it was so quiet on the yacht that evening. Another yacht had settled into the berth next to ours but still everything was so quiet. It was beautiful.

Our next destination was Schinoussa, a tiny island that is part of a group of equally tiny islands called the Koufonissia. We went swimming again, of course, then changed and went for a walk to see what was on the island and to have dinner at one of the tavernas. Swimming, eating, and talking were the major activities of our trip. What I remember most about Schinoussa, however, was seeing the Skopelitis, an old-style ferry boat, sail into the harbor. It brought back so many memories from 1969 when I had my initiation to the Greek islands. The ferry boats then were smaller, with mostly outside seating and very few, if any, amenities.

We were leaving very early the next morning to go to Ios which was our next, but not final, destination so Greg bought eggs to make breakfast on the yacht while we were sailing. At one point, he asked me to hold the bag with the eggs and, when I peeked in, I asked Greg how many eggs he had bought.

He replied, "There are nine of us so I bought eighteen."

The next morning, Patrik and Abbi set sailing while the rest of us were still sleeping. It was a bit of a distance to Ios and we had a deadline. Patrik was going to dock in Ios and then we were taking a ferry boat to Santorini to spend the day there. Santorini was our final destination and it was going to be a busy day.

As we woke up and got ready for our trip that day, Greg made a fabulous omelet and Abbi made good strong coffee. The nine of us had our breakfast on the deck and generally enjoyed the beautiful day made for sailing. Gayle, Lori, and I washed the dishes afterwards.

At Ios, we boarded the ferry to Santorini. There were so many people although I didn't realize how many there were until we got to Santorini and disembarked. There must have been a thousand passengers getting off. I was standing next to Greg's son Nick and took his hand.

"Don't let go of my hand, Nick, or you'll get lost and we won't find you until tomorrow morning."

Nick didn't let go.

In the late 60s, the *New York Times* published articles about two Greek islands, Mykonos and Santorini. The reader reaction to those two articles was like a jolt of electricity. Overnight, Mykonos and Santorini became the places to go to and the places to be seen. When Elias and I went to both islands, as part of the one-week cruise that we were on, Mykonos and Santorini were already on everyone's radar but they were nothing like what they are now.

Mykonos was the jet-setting island, (and still is), with the nude beaches and the all-night clubs. Santorini, on the other hand, was the place to go for breath-taking scenery and taking pictures (and still is). Santorini is also famous for its earthquakes. The last big one was in 1956 although there are small quakes, frequently, on the island.

Once we were off the ferry, we took the bus to Thira, the biggest town on the island, and then another bus to Oia, the second largest town on the island and a little more touristy than Thira. Oia was full of tourists that day and they were all taking pictures. It is said that the most beautiful sunset in the world is in Oia and that even the dogs find a place to sit in the evening to watch the sun go down.

At some point I turned to Greg and said "so many tourists".

To which Greg replied, "That's ok. We're tourists, too." And he was right.

Santorini is also a wedding destination island. I think that it may have been the first island in Greece to do weddings for foreigners and, because this was Santorini, foreign couples pounced on the idea and business boomed. The other islands quickly followed suit because there was so much business and Santorini could not keep up with the demand.

Several years ago, the daughter of good friends of mine in the States decided to get married in Greece. She and her fiancé selected Santorini for their destination wedding. They got married in a lovely church overlooking the sea in Thira. I watched the guests during the ceremony and when it was over, I said to them,

"How did I know that you are all Greek-Americans and that there is not a native Greek among you?"

They shrugged. "How did you know?"

"Because you didn't make a peep during the entire ceremony. If you had been Greeks, the priest would have stopped the ceremony every five minutes to tell you to *stop talking!*"

As we were walking around Thira, I recognized the church, pointed it out to Nicky, and told him the story about the wedding. He smiled. We finished our day at a lovely restaurant overlooking the caldera, a beautiful view. I toasted my family and thanked them for inviting me to join them on what I called the trip of a lifetime, because it truly was.

We took two buses to get first to Thira and then to the port where we took the last ferry out of Santorini for the evening. It was a Saturday night and there were maybe just another five or six people waiting for the ferry boat. Who would be leaving Santorini on a Saturday night anyway?

But all good things must come to an end. We got back to Ios around midnight and spent our last night on the yacht. The next day, I took the ferry boat to Piraeus, and Nicky and his family took a ferry to Crete where they continued their vacation and had an absolutely fabulous time.

What made this yacht trip so special for everyone? What were the priceless experiences? The best part for me was that I was with my family. Because I live in Greece and my family lives in the States, it had been a while since I had spent so much time with Nicky and Gayle.

For five days, I was barefoot, in shorts or a bathing suit and so was everyone else. There's so much freedom in that and we all loved it. During the day while we were sailing, we would just look at the water and enjoy the view, maybe read a book or engage in some desultory conversation.

The kids, Adrienne and Nick, loved it because they had the chance to dive off the yacht into the water, with their parents, and swim to shore in one instance and back to the yacht in another instance. They slept on the deck, under the stars, on two or three nights, which has to be one of the most spectacular experiences anyone can have. They were a joy to watch because they had this wonderful curiosity that smart kids have and explored their environment in every detail.

It was a different experience from what I was used to. It was quiet, peaceful, relaxing. It was a different pace of life and I would do it again, in a heartbeat.

The Greek islands are famous throughout the world. They are the jewels in Greece's crown. It used to be that the tourists, whenever they came to Greece, would land at Athens Airport (mostly), skip Athens and take the ferries directly to the

Greek islands. This has changed in the past few years with many tourists spending at least two or three days in Athens before going to the islands. However, truth be told, Athens is very hot in the summer and, for people who are not used to such intense heat, the city is almost impossible to endure. So, the tourists follow the locals and the locals flock to the islands.

Summer in Greece is not just summer. It is a ritual, with the sea and the sunshine foremost on everyone's minds and in everyone's plans whether the plans are for a holiday vacation, a weekend, an afternoon or an evening. Summer is summer and nothing interferes with it. Everyone has at least one favorite place that they want to visit and many times more than one favorite.

Summer starts early in Greece. By the end of April, at the absolute latest, Greeks have shed their coats and boots and scarves and gloves and are wearing their summer clothes. Summer ends late, as well, maybe in mid-October or even the end of October. During the summer, the heat and the sun are relentless but everyone seeks out both.

The biggest rite of summer, however, is getting on a ferry boat and going to an island. It's just not summer in Greece if you don't go to an island even if it's only for a weekend. The islands are beautiful and although it sounds a little unbelievable when you hear it, each island is different from the others but, as a whole, they offer something for everyone.

One of my friends, when her children were young, would go every summer for a week or so with her husband and their children to an island. This was forty-five years ago and Greece was still a poor country. My friends would book passage for the four of them on a ferry boat (the old-style ferries took hours to reach their destination) and when they got to the island that they had decided on for that year, they would rent a room where the four of them would sleep. The accommodations were not important to them. What was important was to take their towels and sit on the beach for hours at a time and swim, too, and to let the children run around.

Every summer, urban Greece would empty out, especially in August, and head for either the islands or the villages, or both. Anywhere except Athens. That ritual, or tradition, has not changed.

A few years ago, I went to the island of Aegina for a weekend. Aegina is the closest island to Athens and some people who live on the island commute, by ferry, to Athens for work. I went for the weekend with my colleague, Katia, who had been there many times. She is a competitive sailor and some of the races in which she participated took place in Aegina.

We had gone out for dinner and I had made the huge mistake of drinking retsina wine with my meal. A lot of people love retsina (with resin in it), but it doesn't sit well with me. The result was a nasty headache which woke me up at 3 am. It was obvious after about five minutes that the headache had no intention of going away without some help so I took a bottle of water and quietly went out to the veranda. I sat on a chair and put my feet up on the balcony rail. I leaned back in the chair, drank sips of water, and stared out into the darkness at the sea.

After about twenty minutes or so, I began to discern a distinct pattern of traffic on the water. Cargo ships and oil tankers were either going into the port of Piraeus or leaving it. There were smaller craft, although I could not identify what they were, but some may have been naval craft. And there were the fishermen who were taking their small fishing boats out at 3:30 am for their daily catch.

The sea. This is where a very large part of Greece's livelihood and economic activity takes place. Greece has the largest merchant marine in the world and controls more than 23 percent of the world's total merchant marine fleet. There are many shipowners in Greece, quite a large number of them. Some of them were celebrities in their time many years ago, including Aristotle Onassis and Stavros Niarchos. Although several shipowners are well-known in Greece, and in London, as well, where many of them live, most of them shy away from the publicity and the bright lights.

Greece also has a large population of fishermen although their number has diminished somewhat because of the international fishing restrictions and because the international fishing corporations have eclipsed the small, individual fishermen. There has also been an increase in fish farming. Most of the Greek fishermen come, of course, from the islands where fishing was a traditional occupation and provided the islanders with a living and food to eat.

The Greeks have another summer ritual whether they live

in Greece or they have migrated to other countries. They go back to their family homes, if they have a family home, in the villages in Greece for at least a month in the summer or, if they are lucky enough, they go for the entire summer.

The villages can be in the islands but many, if not most, are on the mainland. The Greek countryside is simply gorgeous and now that there are new roads, all built within the last twenty years or so, they are easy to get to from Athens and from other urban centers. It's also much easier and much quicker to get from one village to another and from one prefecture to another. The village can be on the seaside or it can be in the mountains. Whatever its location, it is a wonderful place to spend the summer. It is a perfect holiday.

The village holiday serves another purpose, as well. Because most parents with young children work, the parents send their children to the grandparents for the summer. How many adults have their happiest memories from spending summers with their grandmothers and grandfathers in the village! And if there is no ancestral home in the family, families will buy or rent one so that they can get away from the stifling heat in the city.

This is what I decided to do in 1994 – to buy myself a family home in a village. My father and his family had left their village in 1914 to go to the States and, since then, their family home had been sold so I didn't have an ancestral home, anywhere in Greece. But I did have family in a neighboring village, three second cousins whose grandmother was the sister of my paternal grandfather. I asked my oldest cousin, Makis, if he knew of a house that was for sale where he and his family lived.

He did, and thus I bought my very own beautiful family home, which at the time was a one-hundred-year-old stone house just a few years away from collapsing because it hadn't been lived in for almost fifty years. But I rescued it, although for several months whenever I went to the village, I would stand in front of the house and ask myself, "What was I thinking?"

My sons, however, were thrilled with my purchase, something that I did not expect. They went to their father and said,

"Look at this. We now have a house in a village, and from whom? From our mother, who was born in the US."

The village is Leontari, in the prefecture of Arcadia in the Peloponnese. It is a twenty-to-thirty-minute drive to Logganikos where my father was born, in the neighboring prefecture of Lakonia, so I am very close to my roots. I started renovating and restoring the house in December 2002 and, in June 2005, I moved in. The house and the village became a restorative for me. Since then, I spend at least a month there in the summers, sometimes longer. Every summer, this is where I recharge my batteries. The two sisters who run the bistro in the village square tell me that they know it's summer when I come to Leontari towards the middle to the end of July because, for them, I open the summer season.

One of the most beautiful features of the villages in the countryside, all over Greece, is the stone houses, many of which have been restored, as mine has, or have been maintained because families have lived there continuously through the generations. When I restored my house, I tried to bring it back, as much as I could, to its original design or to what it probably looked like when the stonemasons, who traveled all over the Peloponnese for their work, built these beautiful houses.

We gutted the inside of the house because it had rotted after fifty years of being empty. We rebuilt it according to what I wanted the house to be like inside, with modern comforts and conveniences including central heating. But outside, the civil engineer, who was managing the restoration, and I decided to use traditional materials and methods so that the house would blend in with the other houses in the village and with the environment. The walls of the house remained intact. We removed the dirty and faded pink stucco that had hidden the stones for so many years and the beauty of the house was revealed.

Leontari, when there is normal traffic, is about a two-and-a-half-hour drive from Athens. It is no longer the daunting trip that it used to be. New roads were built making Leontari close enough to be a doable trip. The first time that I went to Leontari in 1986, the trip took seven hours. I was going there to spend Easter with my cousin Makis, the one who found my beautiful stone house, and his family. There was heavy traffic from Athens going to the Peloponnese. All the traffic was on a two-lane highway, if you could call it that, on a winding mountain road with barely enough breakdown lane between the road and the steep drop down the mountain.

If it were still a daunting trip to Leontari, maybe I would hesitate to take the trip because a seven-hour trip is too long. But even if it were far away, the thought of being in Leontari is irresistible. It is a completely different experience from being in Athens during the summer and is worth the trip, however long it is. The whole village is out during the summer in the village square, across the street from the stunning eleven-hundred-year-old Byzantine church with the stunning history to match. The bistro in the village square is fantastic with wonderful food and lots of company. In the month of August, the square is overflowing with everyone who has come home for the month.

During the day, we go out for coffee in the morning, again to the village square, then go home for lunch, or perhaps someone has invited us for lunch, and after that we go home for the *de rigueur* summer afternoon nap. Then maybe it's a walk with friends, or a church service, and then back to the bistro for something to eat and drink in the evening until at least midnight and maybe even later. It's a fantastic life.

Leontari is in the mountains. It's not too high up but just high enough so that the evenings are lovely, a little cool sometimes but definitely not hot. The sea and the beaches are, at the most, a half an hour to forty-five minutes away, and again, wherever one goes, it's delightful.

Leontari, like all of the Peloponnese, is agricultural. One of my friends in the States once told me that the Peloponnese is called the *garden of Greece*. Olive trees are everywhere. The prefecture of Argos is known for its olive groves and for its citrus trees, as well. And the entire Peloponnese is known for its vineyards which produce excellent wines. It is not unusual to be sitting in the square and see a tractor rumbling slowly by.

The Public Power Corporation is the biggest industry

in the Peloponnese and has a large plant in the neighboring town of Megalopolis. Almost all the men who live in the vicinity of the PPC work there. It is also usual to see the PPC equipment rumble by although not as often as the tractors.

The Peloponnese is strikingly beautiful. Because of the new roads and the ease of driving around in the Peloponnese, it has begun to attract foreign tourists. Three or four years ago, I had gone to Leontari for two weeks in May to get the house ready for summer. My brother Tom and sister-in-law Debbie were coming from the States for a visit and I wanted to have all the annual cleaning and maintenance work done before their visit.

I was splashing the veranda with a hose when I heard a loud noise that sounded like a lot of traffic rolling into the village and, sure enough, as I looked in the direction of where the sound was coming from, I saw about twenty-five motorcycles driving in. I looked at them out of curiosity for a few seconds and then got back to my cleaning.

A few minutes later, I realized that I had run out of some cleaning supplies so I got my keys and wallet to walk three minutes to the mini-market. Next door to the mini-market, I saw the bikers sitting outside the Guest House, waiting to order something to drink. I asked them where they were from and what they were doing in our village. They told me that they were members of an international bikers' club and had come from all over the world. A father and his ten-year-old son were from South Africa. Others were from the US, Canada, Ireland, Germany, and China, and other countries that I can't remember now. I think that they had started from Kalamata at the very bottom of the Peloponnese and were working their way north. The trip had been planned by an organization for bikers on the Internet and their plan was to go through Greece and the countries that had made up the former Yugoslavia and then go into northern Europe. What an adventure, I thought, especially for that ten-year-old boy who was traveling with his dad!

In the summer of 2020, my son Stefan took me further south from Leontari to a town called Kardamyli, a beautiful town in Mani, a very wild and rugged area in the southern Peloponnese. The weekend excursion was a milestone birthday present.

Many of the people at the beaches that we went to in Kardamyli and in a neighboring village, Stoupa, were from Europe. Several of them have bought homes in the area and come back every summer. They love summer in Greece - the heat, the sun, the easy access to beaches. What is there not to love?

Stefan had suggested Kardamyli because he knew that I wanted to see the house of Patrick Leigh Fermor, a British travel writer who had lived in Greece with his wife after World War II. Leigh Fermor was considered the finest travel writer in Britain and of his generation. He had gone to Crete with the British Army during WWII to fight behind the lines with the Cretan Resistance. When the war was over, he wanted to settle in Crete. But as fate would have it, he travelled to the Peloponnese and was captivated by the untamed beauty of Kardamyli. He and his wife Joan built a house there which they bequeathed to the Benaki Museum upon their deaths. The house, which Stefan and I saw only from the outside, is a beautiful stone villa in a wild setting, just a few feet away from the sea. Because of the Covid pandemic, the museum had suspended its tours of the house. But just seeing the outside of the house and the setting itself was enough for me.

There are three major geological characteristics in Greece. Two are the sea and the mountains, usually together. When we first came to Greece, Elias and I would go to one of the many beaches just outside of Athens. I never got tired of sitting on the sand and looking at the mountains sloping into the sea. I see the same sight all over Greece, and it never fails to impress me, everywhere, but especially in Mani.

The third geological characteristic is the rocky terrain, or the rocks and stones. They also are everywhere. They are in the stone houses all over the countryside. They are in the rock formation in Meteora, where several monasteries are poised at the top of the formation. They are the pebbles on the beaches.

When my Demakes grandparents went back to Greece in 1908, they went to live in my grandfather's village. My grandmother looked around for a bit and then said,

"I knew that there were a lot of rocks in Logganikos but I have never seen so many rocks in one place."

My grandmother's own microscopic village was just twelve kilometers away and I am sure that the landscape was the same there as it was in Logganikos but it was the rocks that impressed her most in my grandfather's village.

Elias shared my grandmother's opinion. He agreed

that Greece was all rocks and stones and, to Elias, rocks and stones represented poverty. He did not like the stone houses that dot the Greek countryside. He thought that they were proof to the world that Greece was a poor country.

When he went to the States to study, one of the first things he did was to buy a used car. And the second thing he did was to drive from Washington DC, where he was studying, to Detroit, Michigan to see his father's sister and her family.

When he came back from Michigan, he wrote a letter to his father and said that for the entire time he was driving to Michigan and back he did not see any rocks or stones. God must have put them all in Greece. He may have had a point. Duncan JD Smith, the British travel writer, wrote an article about Mani and said that it deserved its reputation "as being the place where God grew stones."

Patrick Leigh Fermor, in his book about Mani[xxvi], tells a delightful story about a man from there who told him that when God created the world, He had stones and rocks left over and He dumped them all in Greece. The man went on to say that it was too bad that the rocks didn't have any market value so he could sell them and become a millionaire.

I guess it all depends from which perspective one looks at the issue. I think that the stone houses are beautiful and distinctive.

As one goes further south from Tripoli, Megalopolis, and

[xxvi]   Patrick Leigh Fermor, *Mani: Travels in the Southern Peloponnese,* Great Britain, John Murray Publishers, 1958.

Leontari, the landscape becomes wilder and more rugged. It's almost like entering a different country. This is the southern Peloponnese. This is Mani, home to the austere stone towers and the infamous vendettas.

One of my favorite places here is Kitries Beach. Kitries is a small cove where one street goes into and out of the cove. The view from the beach is the classic sea and mountains combination where the mountains slide into the sea. I can sit on the beach all day and imagine that this is what ancient Greece must have looked like, but without all the people.

Ancient Greece, however, did not have modern glitches. The first time that Elias, Stefan, and I went to Kitries, we were utterly enchanted by the setting. We had parked the car with the other cars in a makeshift parking lot. The beach had some umbrellas and lounge chairs but most people were sitting in one of the three tavernas lining the beach, sipping a coffee, and getting up every so often to go for a swim. The view of the formidable and forbidding Taygetos mountain range was mesmerizing.

At about 2 pm, everyone dried off and sat down in the tavernas for a delicious lunch of fresh fish, kalamari, perfectly fried potatoes, Greek salad, and whatever else was on the menu. At about 3 or 3:30 pm, lunch was over and, as if on a preordained signal, everyone got up, got all their belongings together, and went to their cars. It was an orderly departure and the cars lined up to make their way up the hill on the only road that goes into and out of Kitries.

But one car, at the beginning of the line, broke down which meant that none of the other cars could leave. There was at least a one-hour wait for a tow-truck to arrive, get to the disabled car, and either fix it or tow it away. Undeterred and unfazed, everyone got out of their cars, shutting off engines and leaving the cars as they were. We all went back to the tavernas for a few more coffees and some ice cream, surprising the staff who hadn't expected to see us again for a second round of eating and drinking!

Two other favorite places in Mani are Mystras and Monemvassia (Monemvassia means *only entrance* in Greek). As you look at Monemvassia from afar, it resembles the Rock of Gibraltar. There is a narrow causeway from the mainland to the entrance of the fort. All cars are parked outside the fort and once you are inside, you walk to wherever you want to go. Monemvassia is sparse and spare. It has relentless sunlight and a spectacular view of the sea. It is also one of the most impressive fortresses in the world.

Another fortress is in the striking archaeological site of Mystras with its many Byzantine churches. Mystras is a UNESCO World Heritage monument and has been restored to a quiet but imposing elegance, steeped in history and religion. It is in Mystras and Monemvassia that one acquires some understanding of the Byzantine history that influenced Greece's own history.

I have been three times to Mystras and three times to Monemvassia. Mystras is a tourist site but not one where visitors stay inside the fort or eat or shop. All accommodations and other activities are outside the fortress so the mystery, the awe and the deep respect for the site are maintained. In contrast, Monemvassia, even inside the fortress, is residential with churches which hold services and weddings. There are restaurants and shops, cafes and bars. The setting is magical even if there is loud music at night. And the tiny alleyways that take you through and around the fortress exude an aura of a mysterious medieval city.

There is so much more to see in the Peloponnese. It is where you will find Olympia, the site of the first Olympic Games in ancient Greece. It is not a hyped-up Olympic stadium with the glitz and glitter that we have learned to associate with the modern Olympic Games. Rather it is an archaeological site where competitive games were held every four years in classical Greece.

In 2004, Athens hosted the Olympic Games. Although most of the events took place in various locations in Athens, some of the competitive events took place in ancient Olympia and in the Panathenaic Stadium in Athens where the first modern Olympic Games were held.

The shot-put competition, both men's and women's, was held in Olympia at the restored Olympia stadium. The archery competition took place in the Panathenaic Stadium, and both the Women's and Men's Marathons finished in this stadium, as well. This was the only time that any country had used the sites of previous Olympic Games, an impressive first for Greece and one that other countries will probably not be able to replicate.

Olympia is also where the Olympic flame is lit every four years and is then taken by teams of runners to the country where the Games are being held that year.

The Peloponnese is home to the ancient Theater of Epidaurus, which has a capacity of 13,000 to 14,000 spectators. The theater puts on performances of ancient Greek plays and other plays every summer as part of the annual Athens and Epidaurus Festival. The acoustics in the theatre are perfect and every person in the theater has a clear view of the stage.

Nafplion, the first capital of Greece after Greece won its independence from the Ottoman Empire, is another must-see. It is a pretty city, close enough to the Theater of Epidaurus to stay overnight after the performance, or even longer. Wonderful attractions include the Palamidi Fortress with its almost 1,000 steps and the Bourtzi Fortress which is on a very small islet in the sea just off the shore of Nafplion.

Visitors might also want to see Sparta which, in ancient times, was the kingdom of Menelaus, husband of Helen and brother of Agamemnon. It was from Sparta that Paris of Troy stole Helen, who was said to be the most beautiful woman in the world, away from Menelaus thus beginning Greece's ten-year war with Troy.

And finally, anyone who is in the Peloponnese should find some time to visit Kalamata, one of my favorite cities in Greece. Kalamata is a fun place to visit any time of the year but especially in the summer, with its city beaches, fabulous food, and wonderful shopping.

The countryside is beautiful all over Greece, wherever you go. And Greece does exist north of the Peloponnese and north of Athens. One of the most popular areas in northern Greece is the Pelion. The Pelion combines the mountains and the sea, as elsewhere in Greece. The villages are filled with stone houses that have slate roofs rather than the ceramic tile roofs that are characteristic of the Peloponnese.

Stefan, Elias, and I went to a wedding in Portaria, a lovely village in the Pelion. The village was beautiful and so was the wedding. Destination weddings in Greece have become popular with the Greeks as well as with the tourists.

Another wedding that I went to was in Parga in northwestern Greece. Parga is on the Ionian Coast and combines, of course, the scenic duo of mountain and sea. The bride and groom were Dutch friends who had decided to get married in Greece because the bride had had her first job in Greece, in Parga. The wedding itself took place in a small church on a little island right off the coast of the town. We, the guests, got onto small boats to sail the short distance to the island. The church could not fit all the guests so the wedding took place outside. The wedding was lovely and, like all destination weddings, it was different. It was definitely something to remember.

One of the most impressive sites to visit in Central Greece is Meteora. Meteora, which literally means "suspended in the air", is a rock formation on top of which are several monasteries. The setting itself inspires awe and the monasteries atop the rock formation are worth the drive up a narrow road to get to the top. Inside the monasteries are beautiful icons, frescoes, and embroidered robes and tapestries.

Many years ago, the monks used a strong rope tied to

a basket to haul supplies to their monasteries. The rope and basket were also a mode of transportation for those (mostly monks and clergy but sometimes visitors, too) who wanted to go up and those who wanted to go down. The rope and basket haven't been in use for a long time but a rope and basket are on display in one of the monasteries in a small museum. My father, when he came to Greece several years ago, saw the rope and basket and asked one of the monks how often the rope was replaced. The monk's answer,

"Whenever it broke."

Now there are hundreds of stairs that lead to each of the monasteries, once the cars and buses have driven up as far as is permitted.

The monasteries perched on top of the rock formation look as though they could fall off at any moment. I cannot even begin to imagine how they were built or the effort it took to get all the materials to the top, although I have read that, for one of the monasteries, it took twenty-two years to get all the building supplies to the building site. It must have been a dizzying enterprise.

Meteora is both a holy place in Greece and a UNESCO World Heritage site.

In 2012, as Elias, Stefan, and I were driving to the wedding in Portaria, we drove by the memorial to King Leonidas of Sparta and his band of 300 Spartans. The memorial is near Thermopylae. We didn't stop because we were on our way to the wedding but I do want to go again, to pay my respects to these men who sacrificed their lives for their country. My eyes teared up as we drove by and my heart filled with pride for the heroes who held off Xerxes and his army of at least 100,000 men for three days, giving the Athenians the time that they needed to defend their city and repel the Persians. I want to see the plaque with the inscription:

"Ω ξειν', αγγέλλειν Λακεδαιμονίοις ότι τήδε κείμεθα, τοις κείνων ρήμασι πειθόμενοι."

"Stranger, tell Spartans that we lay here, staying faithful to Sparta's laws"

For a cosmopolitan and sophisticated atmosphere, another of my favorite cities in Greece is Thessaloniki, or Salonika. The first time I saw it, forty something years ago, I fell head over heels in love. I have been back only twice, but I have promised myself that I am going again, soon, for at least a week to shop and to eat, and to explore and enjoy.

Thessaloniki is on the sea and has a wonderful waterfront with impressive, and expensive, apartment buildings and a fantastic boulevard for walking, running, or bicycling. In good weather and on the weekends, the boulevard is filled with people enjoying the city and having fun. The boulevard is highlighted by the White Tower, the city's landmark.

The people of Thessaloniki love their city. They are all, men and women, excellent cooks and that is evident not only in their cooking but in the food served in restaurants. Some of the best meals that I have had in Greece have been in Thessaloniki. The shops are inviting and shopping is a happy pastime here and this is what I am looking forward to on my next trip there. The people are always well-dressed, appropriately for any occasion, and there is never even one hair out of place.

The last time that I was in Thessaloniki, I went to the Archaeological Museum. The major exhibit at the time was the collection of artifacts from several tombs in Vergina, but especially from the tomb of King Philip II, the father of Alexander the Great. The discovery of King Philip's tomb in 1977 in Vergina, in Northern Greece, was the most important archaeological discovery of the century. The exhibit confirmed this.

There was the gold jewelry. There were the tens of gold boxes. There were the mosaics, the wall paintings and artifacts. There was an elaborate gold wreath with perfect leaves and acorns. As I came to the end of the exhibit, I saw the shield and armor of King Philip II and then the bones of the king. The bones had been arranged so they looked like a skeleton. One leg was shorter than the other. It has been said that King Philip II was lame. If so, then the bones were proof of his lameness.

I was awestruck. All the gold had been beautifully and painstakingly crafted. The mosaics were striking. The wreath was otherworldly. But the shield and armor and bones of the king produced an emotional response in me that surprised me. I went through the exhibit a second time, from the beginning, and had the same emotional reaction when I came to the remains of King Philip II. I was still awestruck.

This exhibit is no longer at the Archaeological Museum

in Thessaloniki. A museum was built in Vergina, near the archaeological site where the tombs were discovered. All the items from the tombs are now housed in this museum.

One of my absolutely favorite places in Greece is Itea. It is a small town in the prefecture of Phocis (or Fokida), on the sea. It is down the mountain from Delphi and is near Arachova which has become a very popular ski resort for the Greeks and for Europeans.

This area is most well-known for the Delphic Oracle. In mythology, Zeus sent two eagles up to fly in the sky in opposite directions. The point where their paths crossed was to be the center of the world. That point, according to legend, was Delphi and, again according to legend, Zeus marked that spot as the navel, or bellybutton, of the world. There is a large stone in the Delphi Archaeological Museum that represents the navel.[xxvii] It has been part of Greek lore forever.

Elias' family was from two villages in this area – his father from Desfina and his mother from Chrisso. The area is filled with olive trees or what I call *green gold*. As one looks down

---

[xxvii] The bellybutton of the world was always a contentious issue in Greece. Prime Minister Constantine Karamanlis wanted to throw the stone that is in the museum into the sea so that the Greeks would stop thinking that they were the center of the world. Karamanlis did not destroy the stone. It is still in the museum.

from Delphi to the sea, the area in between is all olive trees.

While we were still married, I had talked to Elias about renting a house or even buying one in his father's village of Desfina so that we could go there in the summers with the boys. The boys could be outside all day and play with the children from the village. As you have probably guessed by now, I wanted us to buy a family home in the countryside. Elias didn't care for this idea so I campaigned for another village – Delphi or Chrisso. He didn't like the idea of these villages either.

I had saved my strongest card for last, for Itea, my favorite village in that whole area. Itea was by far more provincial when I first came to Greece in the 70s than it is now. But even then, there was something about it that I loved. It had wide streets, open spaces, a basketball court, and plenty of room for the kids to be outside, ride their bikes, and play safely. It was on the sea, with a simple but pretty waterfront with cafeterias and fish restaurants which have since become very sophisticated. But most of all, it had family. For me, the family, Elias' family, was the biggest attraction of all. But Elias was insistent. He did not want a summer house and so we did not go to Itea for the summers. Too bad.

In 2018, a group of us, about thirty people, went to Itea to attend the one-year memorial service for Elias who had passed away in 2017. I hadn't been back to Itea for years, but the area was still the same and familiar. I knew where I was. It was brighter and shinier and more touristy than it had been before, but it was still Itea. It was recognizable, just more modern.

Our group that weekend was made up of Elias'

relatives from Athens and from the towns and villages around Itea, two cousins from the States, and Elias' childhood friends. We began the day with a church service that started at 8 am. When the service was over, about two hours later, we all walked down to the waterfront where we sat at an outdoor café for coffee. Another two hours later, we moved next door, still on the waterfront and still outdoors, to a restaurant where we had lunch. And finally, the last thing that we had scheduled for that day was to scatter Elias' ashes in the sea. Stefan had hired a small yacht for anyone in the group who wanted to come with us. Everyone did. The skipper sailed out and when we were far enough away from shore, Stefan scattered his father's ashes. It was a beautiful and fitting ending to a lovely memorial service.

Greece is a beautiful country, as I have said so many times throughout this book, but we have to have our eyes open to see the beauty. As you drive to your destination or use some other means of ground transportation, train or bus, keep your eyes open. One of the best parts of seeing something spectacular is seeing something new and unexpected and simply breathtakingly beautiful.

Many books have been written about the sights to see in Greece. But the wonderful part about driving in Greece is discovering something new. When my children were young, their father would take them on road trips around Greece, together with their grandfather. Stefan and Costis have told me that they used to love these trips because they saw so much that they didn't know about or hadn't seen before. Discovery is definitely a key word, and a key goal, as well, in Greece.

One of the reasons that I love Leontari and decided to buy a house there is because I can drive there or take a bus. The islands are beautiful and magical but the majority of them are accessible by boat only. Some of them are large enough to have airports. The island of Crete has good-sized airports in its three major cities and a smaller airport in Sitia. The small islands, however, simply do not have the required space for an airport.

And if you fly to a destination in Greece, from any location, you really do not see anything. If you sail to your destination, it may seem that you do not see anything although you actually see a lot, if you look around. Even the expanse of the sea is a beautiful sight to behold.

But driving in Greece is a completely different experience altogether. It has its own set of challenges, such as bumper to bumper traffic on a winding mountain road, usually at Easter, or the car breaking down on a deserted street with no help in sight. But if everything goes well and smoothly, as it usually does, then the route provides scenic delights for the whole trip.

You will come across a stand on the side of the road selling freshly picked figs and you will stop to buy some. Or you will stop at a non-descript taverna and have a surprisingly delicious lunch. Or you will see a church that you just have to go into to light a candle. Or you will happen upon a shepherd herding his flocks of sheep and goats higher up the mountains to graze for the summer, or perhaps on their way down to the villages for the winter. Either way, you will be driving in their midst while they bump against your car.

About two years ago, a friend in Leontari asked me where I would have bought a house if I hadn't come to Leontari. I thought about it for a few minutes and then said that I would definitely have come to the Peloponnese but maybe I would have gone to Mani. Recently I have wondered if maybe I would have considered going to Itea. But then again, maybe not. My heart belongs in the Peloponnese. Whenever I leave Athens and cross the Corinth Canal, I know that I am home. And that includes Leontari, too.

- 15 -

The Church in Greece

"I'm jealous that you live in Greece because you all celebrate Easter together at the same time."

My mother

I never expected my mother to say she was jealous that I lived in Greece because she never wanted me to move to Greece in the first place. But I do understand why she said it. My mother grew up in Lynn, in the same suburb where I grew up. The church that she went to, as did the entire Greek-American community in Lynn, was a white wooden clapboard church that the Greek Diocese in Boston had purchased from the Russian Diocese.

Every Easter, Holy Week in that little white clapboard church, the Saint George Greek Orthodox Church, was a nightmare for the Lynn Fire Department. On Good Friday, all the parishioners would walk around the park in front of the church, accompanying the funeral bier of Christ, and everyone would hold a lighted candle. On Holy Saturday, the same parishioners would crowd into the small church and at midnight, when the priest would chant *Christ has Risen,* everyone would light their candles taking the light from the candle that the person in front of them was holding. That's how the light was passed through the entire congregation, and it still is. The priest would give the light to the people in front of him who in turn would pass on the light to others behind or beside them. And, as my mother never failed to tell us whenever she told this story, the Lynn Fire Department was parked outside the church for the entire midnight service, which finished at 3:30 am, just in case the church burned down.

The Catholics and the Protestants had celebrated their Easter one or two or even three weeks earlier and it didn't help that only the Orthodox faithful were celebrating Easter because the Greek Church stood out like a sore thumb. Therefore, I understood exactly what my mother meant because everyone does celebrate this very important holiday at the same time in Greece.

During 2020, because of the pandemic, Greece was in lockdown for the entire Easter period. The churches were closed to the public and all services, including all Holy Week services, were held behind locked doors. Many of the services were televised.

We all, or most of us anyway, adapted to the requirements of the times and watched the services on television. We got dressed up for church and then sat in front of the television to watch the service, and many of us watched two services on the same day. I would start with the service at the Patriarchate in Istanbul as Turkey is one hour ahead of Greece. When the service in the Patriarchate was over, I would switch to the service at the Metropolitan Cathedral in Athens, which was just beginning.

It sounds like a lot of church but it wasn't. Although I missed going to the services with everyone else in in my neighborhood, Easter in 2020 gave me the chance to listen to the hymns of each service twice. The Holy Week hymns are beautiful but, because of the crowds, especially on Good Friday evening and then at the midnight service on Holy Saturday, most of the people are outside and it is often not possible to hear the hymns because of the noise.

In 2020, as the Holy Saturday midnight service approached, we all heard, by word of mouth, that we should turn on our balcony lights on Holy Saturday evening and, at midnight, when the priest said the magic words *"Christos Anesti" (Christ has Risen)*, we should all go out onto our balconies with a lighted candle and sing the hymn with our neighbors, and then wish them a Happy Easter with the words *Christ has Risen.* That's what we did and it was beautiful. It was so different from anything we had done before, or at least in recent memory, and yet, in the middle of the pandemic, we celebrated the most important religious holiday in the Greek Orthodox Church with dignity and grace.

A few days later, I was talking to my friend Christina and we were discussing how we had celebrated Easter. I told her that I had enjoyed watching the services on television because I had been able to follow them in the quiet of my home and to hear what the priests were saying although I wouldn't want to do this every year. She agreed with me but added that she missed the people walking to and from church. She was right because this is part of any religious holiday in Greece and all over the world as well, I imagine. We missed that in 2020.

A few days after I talked with Christina, I called Father Emmanuel, one of the priests at my neighborhood church, to wish him a Happy Easter with the words *Christ has Risen.* I asked him how Easter had been for him this year and for the other priests. He said that they had performed all the services but the doors were locked so that people could not get in. From what he said, I understood that he had missed the people, too.

Easter in 2021 was a little different and a little more relaxed. People were in the streets and on Holy Saturday, many went to church to receive the Holy Light to light their candles.

Most years, the Catholics and the Protestants celebrate Easter earlier than the followers of the Eastern Orthodox religion. Sometimes, it happens that Easter for the Catholics and the Protestants is on the same day as the Orthodox Easter. The Catholic and Protestant religions calculate their Easter as the first Sunday after the first full moon after the vernal equinox. They do not take Passover into consideration. The Orthodox Easter, on the other hand, is on the first Sunday after the first full moon after the vernal equinox and after the Jewish Passover.

Holy Week in Greece, and in Orthodox churches all

over the world, begins on Palm Sunday and every service on the subsequent days is a service devoted to the various events that led up to the crucifixion of Christ and His resurrection. All these events, as they are described in the Bible, took place after Passover. Since the vernal equinox and Passover are not on fixed dates but vary every year, Easter, for all the Christian religions, is on a different date every year.

In the States, this led to some differences that, as children, we couldn't understand. The Catholics and Protestants observed Good Friday together, on the same day, and it was always a day off – no work, no school. If the Greek Orthodox Easter was later than the Catholic and Protestant Easter, there was no day off on Good Friday. Once, I asked my father if could stay home for Good Friday and not go to school. He asked me if I intended to be in church all day (and more about that later) and I said no.

"Then," he said, "you have to go to school."

Another reason for the difference in the way that the Orthodox, the Catholics and the Protestants calculate Easter is that the Greeks, who use the Gregorian calendar for everything else, use the Julian calendar to calculate the date for Easter. I read recently that after the year 2700, Easter for the different religions will never again share the same date. Apparently, there was a small discrepancy or error in the Julian calendar which will have accumulated for many centuries, and the full moon in the Julian calendar and the full moon in the Gregorian calendar will never again coincide in the same week.

In Greece, it's completely irrelevant how Easter is calculated from the point of view that it doesn't matter if our

Easter is later than the Catholic and Protestant Easter. It's Easter in Greece, and that's all there is to it. Good Friday is a non-work, non-school day as is the Monday after Easter.

Easter in Greece is the most important religious holiday. It is also the longest. There is a run-up of ten weeks from the beginning of Carnival to Easter Day and then, after Easter, there are forty days until the Ascension of Christ and then another ten days for Pentecost which is celebrated on the seventh Sunday after Easter. That is about four months in total, from beginning to end. It's a long time!

The Easter period formally begins with Carnival which lasts for three weeks. The largest Greek Carnival festival is in Patras with festivities and floats and treasure hunts and all-around revelry. Thousands of people go to Patras every year for Carnival to enjoy the partying and the Grand Parade on the last Sunday of the carnival and before the beginning of Lent. In 2021, Carnival began on Sunday, February 21 and Easter was on Sunday, May 2. Ten weeks.

Carnival lasts for three weeks and includes some milestones, the most famous of which is *Tsiknopempti* or Smoky Thursday in English. On *Tsiknopempti*, which takes place on the Thursday in the second week of Carnival, every single taverna and restaurant, and sometimes even cafés, light up their grills to grill or roast meat, filling the air with smoke. Almost everyone goes out in the evening to eat and to enjoy themselves before the strict Lenten fast begins. In 2020, nobody went out because everything was closed. But people could still grill or roast meat at home and celebrate this holiday.

The Monday after Carnival is *Kathara Deutera* or Clean Monday which marks the beginning of the second phase before Easter. The second phase is Lent, the major fasting period for Easter. Lent lasts for seven weeks and, if strictly and correctly observed, there is no meat or poultry or fish, no dairy and no oil until the fast is broken on Holy Saturday after midnight when *Christ has Risen.* There are many people who do observe the Great Fast, as it is also called, and many people who do not, although almost everybody does fast during Holy Week.

I observed the Great Fast in 2019. It was the first time that I had fasted for the entire seven weeks of Lent and when I broke the fast on Holy Saturday, after the priest had said *Christ has Risen,* I felt an enormous sense of accomplishment. I also felt clean. I was also very hungry, but it was a wonderful feeling.

I think that the only thing I truly missed during the Great Fast was the olive oil in food and in salads on Wednesdays and Friday. I did not abstain from olive oil during the entire Lenten season except for Holy Week although many of the faithful do abstain. I read that this tradition was established because, in ancient times, olive oil was stored in sheepskins or goatskins and therefore had become tainted from the blood of a part of an animal.

Otherwise, the food during Lent is delicious and plentiful. The menu can include octopus, squid, cuttlefish, and shellfish, (meat and fish are not allowed because they have blood in them but shellfish is allowed), vegetable dishes cooked in oil, beans and lentils, olives (yes, olives, but not olive oil), tahini and peanut butter (an American addition), fruits, and vegetables. Sweets are allowed if they are not made with butter, eggs, and / or milk.

Favorite dishes include octopus cooked with a short macaroni in olive oil and tomato, freshly shelled peas and potatoes cooked in olive oil, and fresh artichokes cooked in olive oil and lemon with carrots, potatoes, and dill. And although no one starves during Lent, the truth is that we miss some of the foods from which we abstain for forty days.

Fasting, however, serves another purpose. If we fast correctly and forego the pleasures of food on the days when we are strictly fasting, fasting then enhances our devotion to God. Most of these fasting rules, though, were defined for the monks and the monasteries. The laity, who are working and are not spending their days praying, may not have the strength to observe all these rules although, strictly speaking, the rules are not a menu from which we can pick and choose. They are the rules that the Church has set out because Lent is a deeply religious period.

There are many church services that are specific to Easter and are not celebrated at any other time of the year. During Lent, there are the *"Chairetismoi"* (Salutations) to the Most Holy Mother of God. The services take place during the first four Fridays of Lent. They begin at 7 pm and last for almost two hours. The service of the *Akathistos Hymnos* (following the service standing up) is on the fifth Friday of Lent. It is a combination of all the first four Friday services. The sixth week of Lent is silent week which means that there are no services at all. The last and seventh week of Lent is Holy Week and, during this week, almost all Greeks attend services every day and sometimes twice on the same day.

Holy Week begins with Palm Sunday, the day that Jesus entered Jerusalem on the back of a donkey and was hailed as the Messiah. For every day of this week, there are both morning and evening services. And each evening service tells the story of the Passion of Christ.

During the evening service of Holy Tuesday, the Hymn of Kassiani is chanted. This hymn, written and composed by the Byzantine Abbess Kassiani, is chanted only once a year and is considered to be one of the most important hymns of Holy Week. The hymn tells the story of the sinful woman who anointed the feet of Jesus with a very costly oil and then wiped His feet with her hair.

Easter is the holiday during which every Greek, or almost every Greek, takes communion. On Holy Thursday, most of the neighborhood and parish churches in Athens give communion to their parishioners and to the faithful. The early morning communion service is mostly for those who work although anyone who wants to can receive communion at this service.

And then, for the housewives, it's home again to continue Easter preparations - shopping, cooking, baking. Holy Thursday is also the day that we dye our eggs. This is the day that Christ was crucified and the red dye represents His blood.

The Holy Thursday evening service is one of the most emotional services during Holy Week. It is the service of the Twelve Gospel Readings and it lasts for four or sometimes five hours. I have a prayer book that I take to the Holy Week services. I need it especially for the Holy Thursday service to follow all the gospel readings.

It is during the fifth reading from the gospels that

Christ is crucified. Despite the fact that I attend this service every year, this gospel reading never fails to move me. My eyes fill up with tears and my throat has a lump.

The lights in the church are turned off. Everyone is holding a small lighted candle. We all turn to face the left where the priests come out of the nave, carrying the image of Christ over their heads. We all turn again to watch the priests as they walk up one aisle and then turn towards the Holy Altar and approach it to re-enact the crucifixion. They place the image of Christ on the cross at the front of the church and, with the lights still turned off, we can hear a tap *tap tap* from a hammer nailing Christ to the cross.

At about 11:30 pm, the service is over and most of the parishioners have kissed the cross and are going home. The streets are full of the faithful who have attended this solemn service. The next day is Good Friday on which there are two services in addition to the morning service, so it will be a busy day. This is what my father was referring to when I asked him if I could stay home from school on Orthodox Good Friday and he asked if I would be attending church all day.

Some women, young and older, have stayed behind, however. These women will decorate Christ's funeral bier with the flowers that the parishioners have brought to the Thursday evening service. Every church has a funeral bier and, in every church, the women, especially the younger women, decorate it with flowers.

On Good Friday morning, right after the morning service, a second service begins. This is the service where Christ is taken down from the cross and the nails are removed from his hands. It is, again, a service that inspires devotion and awe. During the service, the priests take the image of Christ and fold it in a white sheet and then, carrying the image over their heads, they go around the church. The faithful throw flower petals on the sheet as the priests take the image of Christ to His funeral bier.

Good Friday evening is when the funeral service takes place. It includes some of the most beautiful hymns in the Orthodox religion. The service is in the church and then some of the stronger men put the funeral bier on their shoulders and carry it around the neighborhood. The priests lead the procession, the faithful follow behind the funeral bier with their lighted candles, and the *psaltes* (chanters) chant those hauntingly memorable hymns. When the bier has been taken around the neighborhood, the crowd returns for the end of the service and then leaves their candles in the church.

One year, Stefan and I went to the center of Athens, near the Plaka, to the Aghia Irini (Saint Irene) Church for the Good Friday evening service. We went early and sat upstairs where usually the women sit but, on this evening, there were men and women. There was a very heavy influence from the Byzantine era and from the Russian Orthodox choir. The choir sang the hymns as they may have been chanted in Byzantine times. The veils on the head coverings that the many priests wore were draped differently than what we usually see in the Greek churches.

The funeral bier had been decorated professionally and was full of white and mauve orchids. At some point during the service, a net with flower petals opened from above and the petals floated down on the funeral bier. The bier was lifted by several men who took it outside and began the walk through the neighborhood.

Several years ago, Archbishop Christodoulos established a new Good Friday tradition. In the big cities, where there are many churches, four churches that are close to each other would meet with their biers, perform the service together for a few minutes, and then move on towards their own churches with their faithful following them. One year, Stefan and I were in the Saint George Church near Syntagma Square. We met three other churches, including the Metropolitan Cathedral of Athens, in the square where hundreds of people, most of them tourists, watched a beautiful service that they had never seen before.

Three or four years ago, Stefan and I were still on our quest for different experiences on Good Friday and had gone to the exquisite Church of Saint Catherine in the Plaka. As we expected, the church was mobbed. It was difficult but still possible to hear the hymns. But then the bier came out, carried by six men and led by several priests. As Stefan and I followed, trying our best to keep up, at least two other churches appeared with their biers and their faithful. The street was crowded. I turned to Stefan and asked,

"Are you sure that we're following the right bier?"

Stefan answered, "It's the right one. I saw it. It just turned left on the next street up from here."

In Athens, there is a saying, "Christmas in Athens, Easter in the village". I have spent many Easters in the village and, truly, there is a different atmosphere there. There are fewer people but the church in the village is still crowded, both inside and outside. The atmosphere is perhaps more intense because we all know each other and we are all celebrating together.

On Good Friday evening, the priest leads the funeral bier around the entire village. All the houses have their lights on, inside and outside, and their windows and doors open so that the blessing can reach the deepest recesses of the house. All the villagers follow the bier as it makes its way through the village and then to the church for the remainder of the service.

When cousin Janet and her daughter Jamie came to Greece to spend Easter with Stefan and me in 2014, we celebrated Easter in Leontari. Janet and Jamie arrived on Holy Thursday. They were exhausted from their trip, especially Janet, who had made the long trip from Boston and, then with Stefan, who had driven the three plus hours to the village. On Good Friday evening, Janet and I stayed home. I had candles for her and for myself. Jamie and Stefan followed the funeral bier around the village.

All the lights in my house were on, windows and doors were open. On the window sill outside the window, I was burning incense. My house is close to the church and is on the street that the procession takes back to the church so it took a while for the procession to reach my doorstep. When I saw them coming, Janet and I went outside with our lighted candles to wait for them. As the funeral procession approached, we crossed ourselves. The priest stopped to bless the house, swinging the thurible[xxviii] vigorously.

[xxviii] A thurible is a metal censer or dish suspended from chains, in which incense is burned during religious services.

Janet and I continued to cross ourselves as the priest showed no inclination to start moving forward again. Just then, I caught the eye of a woman who lives in the village. She gave a slight nod of her head, indicating her approval. I nodded my head slightly, too, thanking her.

On Holy Saturday, I went to church for the morning service and to take communion. Stefan, Janet, and Jamie went to Megalopolis, the town near us, to pick up the lamb that I had ordered. I spent the rest of the day cooking. On Saturday evening, after every priest has announced that *Christ has Risen,* all of Greece goes home a little past midnight to break the long fast. The service lasts until 2:30 or 3 am, but most Greeks go home shortly after midnight to have a small meal.

The menu is traditional. On Saturday night, the long Lenten fast is broken with a soup called *mayeiritsa* made of chopped lamb liver, the cooked and chopped intestines of the lamb, and green onions and dill, all finished off with an egg and lemon sauce. Some villages in the Peloponnese make the *mayeiritsa* as a stew in a tomato sauce. I make it with egg and lemon, just as my maternal grandmother did.

We also crack our first red eggs. The objective is to see whose egg is the strongest. A little bread, some feta cheese, some wine, and a couple of Greek Easter cookies and the fast has been broken. It's time to go to bed. Tomorrow is another day, and not just any day. It's Easter Sunday.

On Easter Sunday, we all had a leisurely breakfast. The lamb and potatoes were going into a slow oven and there was not much else to do – we were having the same foods that we ate on Saturday night, only in larger quantities, and complemented by the lamb.

But there was another tradition to follow. Once the lamb was in the oven, we all set out to take a walk around the village. Villages all over Greece on Easter Sunday are a sheer delight. In Leontari, people roast whole lambs in their yards, on a spit which is turned by hand, with all the guests taking a turn. In Itea, each little neighborhood prepares an area where the neighbors roast their lambs together. There can be up to twenty lambs in a row, turning slowly to roast evenly. There are also spits with *kokoretsi*, which is a long roll of liver wrapped in intestines – a delicacy.

In both Leontari and Itea, and in all other Greek villages, tradition requires that each person walking by is given a piece of lamb or *kokoretsi* that is roasting, to taste. A glass of wine, a sliced tomato, a piece of bread – all are offered. By the time that everyone goes home, they are full from all the tasting they have done as they walked around their village.

The walk that day in Leontari was delightful and Janet and Jamie had never experienced Easter that way before. We wished all our neighbors a Happy Easter, saying *Christ has Risen.* And we managed to eat our own meal, which I have to say was delicious.

We were going back to Athens on Monday, the next day, as Janet, Jamie and I were going to Crete for a few days. So, on Sunday afternoon, we decided to go to the villages where Janet's and my grandparents were born. We went first to Logganikos. Janet had been here before but Jamie had not and she was thrilled to see her roots. From there we drove to Alevrou, my grandmother's village, just twelve kilometers away. None of us had been there before.

On Easter Sunday, there is a service which more or less puts an end to Easter week. It is called the Service of Love and it is usually in the afternoon. Some people attend this service; many, however, do not because the fatigue has piled up over the week and they decide to rest instead.

When we drove into Alevrou, it was about 3 pm. Alevrou is a tiny village but there were signs that indicated that some of the villagers had spent time in the US. There was a pizza shop and something else that I do not remember now. There was also a parking lot so Stefan dropped Janet and me off in front of the church while he and Jamie went to park the car.

While Janet and I were waiting for Stefan and Jamie, Janet suggested that we go into the church. The village was empty so maybe some of the villagers were there, too. But when we went in, I was surprised that the priest was performing the service for himself, the *psaltis*, and the *neokoros*, the person who makes sure that everything is in order in the church. Janet and I each lit a candle and then sat down. The priest, the *psaltis*, and the *neokoros* (a woman) were just as surprised to see us as we were to see only them. The *neokoros* and the *psaltis* kept looking at us over their shoulders as if to say "who are these people?"

A few minutes later, Stefan and Jamie came in and sat down with us. I asked Stefan how he knew where to find us.

He looked at me and said, "We left you off in front of the church. Where else would you be?"

❧

988 AD is generally recognized as the year that the Russians converted to Christianity. This date, however, is not an absolute date but it has become the definitive date because Vladimir was baptized in 988. Prince Vladimir of Russia is the one who officially brought the Orthodox religion to Russia.

There are many stories about how the Russians converted to the Orthodox religion from their pagan religion, both in books and on the internet. One of those stories is in the book *The Orthodox Church* by Timothy Ware (later ordained as Bishop Kallistos Ware)[xxix] .

Vladimir's grandmother, the princess Olga of Kiev (Kiev was the most important city in Russia at the time) had already converted to Christianity in 955. Princess Olga had tried to persuade her son to convert to Christianity but he refused and it was Vladimir who, when he himself converted to Christianity, Christianized Kiev. Princess Olga was canonized after her death because of her conversion to Christianity, and became Saint Olga.

Before Vladimir converted, he thought carefully about which religion the Russians should adopt to replace their pagan worship. He sent envoys to various parts of the world to find the religion that would best suit the Russians' temperament. Many emissaries from other countries had visited Vladimir already to urge him to adopt their religion.

[xxix] Bishop Kallistos Ware (formerly Timothy Ware before his ordination), *The Orthodox Church*, Penguin Books. 1963.

But it was the reports that his envoys sent him that helped him make up his mind.

The envoys went to different countries to assess the major organized religions. They told Vladimir that they had found no joy or beauty in some religions and they were deterred by the dietary restrictions (no alcohol and no pork) in others. Even Prince Vladimir said that the Russians enjoyed drinking too much to give it up for religion.

When the envoys went to Constantinople, however, they came back singing the praises of the Orthodox religion. They had attended a Divine Liturgy at the Church of the Holy Wisdom, as they called it, and which we know as Aghia (or Hagia) Sofia. By all accounts, they told Vladimir that here, at last, they had discovered what they desired and what they thought was appropriate for the Russian people.

According to Bishop Kallistos' book, the envoys reported that "We knew not whether we were in Heaven or on Earth, for surely there is no such splendor or beauty anywhere upon earth. We cannot describe it to you. Only this we know – that God dwells here among men, and that their service surpasses the worship of all other places. For we cannot forget this beauty."

More than one thousand years later, this still holds true. Easter is a hyper-production everywhere in Greece but it is in my neighborhood church in Athens that I notice this the most. There are three priests in my church. Usually, one presides over the Sunday service, sometimes two. But during the Easter period, as well as at Christmas, all three are there at every service. There was a time when five priests officiated at this church but one has since passed away and the other retired.

During the Sunday services, there may be two or three altar boys and perhaps two or three *psaltes*. At Easter, from Palm Sunday to the Holy Saturday night service, and at Christmas, there are twelve altar boys and twelve, maybe more, *psaltes*. The priests are in their richest robes, especially at Christmas and on the Holy Saturday night service. In the other Holy Week services, the priests are in their black robes, with mauve or purple, the colors of mourning.

On the morning of Good Friday, during the service when Christ is taken down from the cross, the altar boys are dressed in richly brocaded robes and the young girls, who offer flower petals to the parishioners to throw onto the image of Christ, are dressed in white. Everything is beautiful. Attention has been paid to the tiniest detail.

The magnificence of the services underlines the awe, the reverence, and the veneration that we the parishioners have for what we are experiencing at the moment and the feeling that we are part of the service that is being held. The rituals, the hymns, the incense make it possible for us to feel that we ourselves are reliving the birth of Christ or His crucifixion and resurrection.

I love the rituals of the church and the services. I love hearing the bells on the thurible jangle and knowing that I must stand up. We all know when to stand up during the service, when to cross ourselves, when to bow our heads in reverence and respect as the priests walk by us with the Holy Bible held high over their heads or holding the vessels with the Holy Communion. I respect my fellow parishioners who feel the same reverence for the service as I have.

Sometimes, people of other religions come to our church to worship because there is no house of worship for their faith in the neighborhood. I have seen a Muslim woman kneel and touch her forehead to the floor to pray. I have seen Africans who stand quietly still, hands clasped in front of them and eyes straight ahead, and worship. The Church welcomes them and so do I. They show deep respect for the place where they are.

We all know why we are there. We are there to worship. We have our prayer books and follow along with the services during Easter Holy Week or during the Christmas – New Year - Epiphany season, or during the month of August for the Assumption of the Virgin Mary and for the Transfiguration of Christ. We listen to the hymns and participate when it is allowed. We take Holy Communion. Otherwise, we sit quietly, follow the service, and observe the rituals that guide us through the service. This is our house.

One of the things that I like best about the Greek Orthodox Church is that it *is* home for us. This is how I feel when I enter the church. I know the men and the women who are sitting where the candles are, as we first enter. They are on the church committees and ensure that everything works smoothly. Many of the young altar boys are their children. The women pass around trays during the services and the parishioners give whatever they can. The money collected is for the maintenance of the church and for food for the needy. The men manage the flow of traffic in the church. I know the *neokoros*, the woman who manages the cleaning of the church which is always spotless.

During one of the Friday evening services a few years ago, the priest asked us to bring non-perishable foods, such as rice, pasta, and dried beans, to the church so that the priests could distribute the food to families who were in need. On Saturday, I shopped at a supermarket a block from the church and then went into the church to leave the shopping bags with someone.

The church that morning was a beehive of activity. People were coming in with supermarket shopping bags, people were going out. Margarita, the *neokoros*, was with a team of women and men, cleaning the church from top to bottom. Rugs had been picked up, pews overturned to be dusted, candelabra had been burnished. There was an atmosphere of bonhomie and friendliness where everyone knew everyone and everyone talked to everyone and everyone mingled with everyone – priests, deacons, *neokoroi*, parishioners.

One of the loveliest images in my mind is from the Christmas service three or four years ago. On Christmas morning, I try to get to church by 6:45 am at the latest which is usually too late because by then the church is already full, not packed yet, but full. The service begins at 7 am. On this Christmas morning, I was standing in line to receive communion. The women line up on the left and the men, together with some women, on the right. It was about 9 am.

I noticed one of the *psaltes* sitting on the steps leading into the Holy Altar. He was sitting with his young son. The *psaltis'* robe was slightly opened. The top button of his shirt was undone. He had probably been in church since 6 am that morning and was most likely very tired and also very hungry since he had surely been fasting all week and because we do not eat before taking communion. The way he was sitting with his young son showed a familiarity with his surroundings but also respect. He was in his house and he was comfortable.

Another thing I love about the church in Greece is that every neighborhood has a parish church, sometimes two, and several smaller churches. Because there is almost always a church within walking distance, people are always in the streets walking to and from a church. This is what my friend Christina missed during Easter of 2020 – the people. This is what we all miss. We miss the gathering of people, the assembly of people, which is what the Greek word for church *(ekklisia)* meant in Ancient Greece.

The people are an important part of the church. They are the reason for the church. Yes, the priests continue to perform services behind locked doors because of the ongoing Covid pandemic. But the people are the ones who bring life to the church. Otherwise, we would continue to watch the services on television.

In the countryside, things are a little different. The church is more immediate there, closer, more accessible. There may be many small churches in every Athenian neighborhood, but even some of the smallest villages have one church and sometimes more than one. Leontari, for example, with a population of 350 to 400 permanent residents, has nineteen churches. They are not all active, but at least once a year, on the feast day of their saint, a service is performed in that church.

One of my favorite services is on August 6, the day of

the celebration of the Transfiguration of Christ. There is a very small church on the property of friends of mine, Christos and Voula. Every year, Christos clears out the overgrown grass on the property so people can walk to the church and then he and Voula clean the church.

I usually get to the service at around 8:30 am. I light my candle outside and then go inside to cross myself. Back outside, I sit on one of the wooden or plastic chairs that Christos and Voula have set up. And then I listen to the service. At the same time, I am also looking around at the magnificent setting – the mountains, the lush valley, and the villages that are just visible across the valley. One of the villages, Veligosti (or Samara), which is a short drive from Leontari, also has a church which celebrates on this feast day. We can hear snatches of their service and we know that we are all celebrating together.

During the service, Christos and Voula take the beautiful icon that is in the church and, together with the priest, walk around the church with the icon. After the service, during which many of us take Holy Communion, Christos and Voula bring out the sweet bread which has been blessed by the priest and serve something to drink and a small pastry, as well. It is a lovely service and one that I look forward to every year.

Greece uses the Gregorian calendar for its civil, official, and administrative purposes, as does much of the world, although not all countries. In Greece, for those of us who live in urban areas, the Gregorian calendar is the calendar we use most of the time and to keep up with the news worldwide. The people who live in the countryside, however, use two additional calendars. One is the agricultural calendar which tells them when to plant and when to harvest, when to fertilize and when to trim the trees.

The other calendar is the religious calendar which almost everyone in Greece uses for the feast days although most people know when the feast days are, even the more obscure ones. For those who are not quite sure, the calendars that are produced and printed in Greece include the names of the saints' days and important Greek holidays.

Anyone who lives in the countryside knows all the feast days. People in the urban centers who go to church frequently also know all the feast days. After living for fifty years in Greece, I know most of the feast days, but not all.

Life in the countryside revolves around these feast days. The villagers do not have the cafes and bars that we have in Athens, or the clubs, or the myriad stores where we can spend money without thinking. Social life in the countryside is the celebration of the feast days and drinking coffee either at the village café or at someone's home.

I would be remiss if I did not talk about the monasteries in Greece. The most famous site with monasteries in Greece is Mount Athos, more commonly known in Greece as the Holy Mountain or *Aghion Oros*. Mount Athos is in Halkidiki in Northern Greece and is the easternmost of three peninsulas in that area. Halkidiki is famous for its beautiful beaches but is perhaps more famous for Mount Athos which is a World

Heritage site. It is also a Holy Site and has twenty monasteries of which seventeen are Greek, one is Serbian, one is Bulgarian, and one is Russian. Two thousand monks live there.

No women are allowed to enter the Holy Mountain. Actually, there are no females of any of the species, except for cats, that reside on the Holy Mountain. All men, however, regardless of their religion, are welcome at Mount Athos although Orthodox men have priority. Many Orthodox men visit the Holy Mountain for a spiritual retreat at least once in their lifetime.

Why aren't women allowed to enter the Holy Mountain? Tradition says that the Virgin Mary[xxx] was sailing to Cyprus when she was blown off course and landed at Mount Athos. She liked it so much that She prayed to Her son that Mount Athos should be given to Her and He agreed. Since then, it has been known as the garden of the Holy Mother of God and, for that reason, no females are allowed on the Holy Mountain, except for female cats.

There are other monasteries, however, all over Greece which are accessible to women. Two monasteries, Boura and Ambelaki, are close to Leontari and are monasteries for nuns. I have been to both several times and they are lovely and well-kept. At the Boura monastery, a priest goes on Sundays to conduct the service. The nuns are the *psaltes* and sing the hymns.

[xxx] The Catholic and Protestant religions call the Mother of Christ the Virgin Mary. In the Orthodox religion, She is known as Panagia, the All Holy One, or the Theotokos, the Mother of God.

The Ambelaki monastery is in Lakonia, about a twenty-minute drive from Leontari. The Ambelaki monastery celebrates its feast day on September 8, which is the birthday of the Panagia or Theotokos. My friend Anna who was born and raised in Leontari but lives in Athens now (although her heart belongs to Leontari) has told me a lovely story about celebrating the monastery's feast day with her parents and her sister when she was a little girl.

Anna and her family, and all the villagers from miles around, would go to the monastery for the feast day, from the night before. The villagers took their donkeys and walked to the monastery, putting the children on the donkeys. From Leontari, this was about a two-hour trip. They also packed food and blankets because they would sleep over for one night. The food and the blankets were loaded onto the donkey.

Anna estimates that about three hundred people from Leontari and the neighboring villages would attend the service and the festival. On the night before the festival, everyone would spread out their food onto tablecloths that they had brought with them. People walked around to the different tablecloths, sharing food with their neighbors while the children played.

At night, they spread their blankets on the ground and slept under the stars. Early September is still warm in Greece, even in the mountains. Some people slept in the empty cells available in the monastery but most people slept on the ground. Anna told me that she was always a little wary about sleeping on the ground because of the bugs and whatever else might be crawling around.

For the children, the annual expedition to the

Ambelaki monastery was an adventure. For the adults, it was a mini-vacation and the chance to pay their respects to the monastery. But it was more than that. After the morning service, the traveling musicians would arrive, perhaps two or three groups, and there would be music and dancing. Families would feast on roast suckling pigs that butchers had roasted and on food that they had brought from home. When the festivities were over in late afternoon, everyone would begin the trek back to their villages.

My friend Poppy has told me a similar story about the annual festival at the Monastery of Boura. That festival took place every year on August 23, to celebrate the nine-day memorial service for Panagia.

Poppy remembers that the last time that she was at this festival at the monastery, she was about ten years old. Her brother Christos was about seven or eight years old, and the two of them had gone with their parents, on foot, to Boura with their donkey which was laden with food and blankets. It took about an hour to get to the monastery from Leontari. Two of Poppy's first cousins, Vassilis and Yannis, were also there with their parents so Poppy and Christos had company.

Poppy's father was a butcher and owned a taverna in Leontari. He and other butchers from neighboring villages brought suckling pigs to the monastery and set up spits to roast the pigs on the monastery grounds. Other merchants had come to the festival and had set up stands to sell drinks for the children and the adults.

Everyone went to the festival on the day before the celebration. About two hundred people would come from the surrounding villages. At night, they slept in the monastic cells in one of the buildings – Poppy called it a tower. There were enough beds for the adults but not for the children so the nuns would put straw mats on the floors of the cells so that the children could sleep with their parents.

But the children were not interested in sleeping. They wanted to play and they were also enlisted to turn the spits with the roasting pigs by hand. There was no electricity at the monastery – light was provided by lanterns and the spits were turned by hand all night so that the roast pigs would be ready the next day.

The nine-day memorial service took place the next morning. When the service was over, thoughts turned to food. The men bought servings of roast pork for their families and the families spread their blankets on the ground to eat and drink with their children and their neighbors, all together.

Two traveling musicians, one with a clarinet and the other with a guitar, would arrive and play music so that people could dance. After lunch, the villagers would clean up and begin the walk home with their children and their donkeys.

Poppy's memory is from 1965 or 1966. After that festival, the monastery, which was very old, closed down for two years for renovation. The nuns who had been there left and went to other monasteries. When the Boura monastery re-opened, new and younger nuns came to the monastery and they decided not to hold the festival on the monastery grounds because they did not consider it appropriate to roast the suckling pigs there. The festival was moved to a village close by, also called Boura. But the memorial service for the nine days following the funeral of Panagia continues to be held on the morning of August 23ʳᵈ at the monastery.

Poppy remembers this festival with affection. It was a time for all the children to play together, to have fun, and to be with friends and relatives.

Today, people still go to the monasteries to pay their respects and to celebrate the feast days but today they go with their cars, not with their donkeys, and it is doubtful that they sleep on the ground although some may sleep in the monastic cells if they can. But for those people who have lived this experience from many years ago, it is a memory that they always cherish.

In Chapter 10, The Glory of Greece, I mention that the Greeks maintained both their language and their religion during the almost 400 years of rule of the Ottoman Empire. Much has been said and written about the Hidden or Secret Schools and whether they are a myth or legend or whether they really existed. The romantic view, to which I ascribe, is that they existed. The historians' view is that they are a myth.

Whichever is true, and it is possible that the truth is a combination of both views, the fact remains that when the Greeks began their war for independence from the Turks in 1821, the Industrial Revolution and the Renaissance may have passed the Greeks by but the Greeks had retained both their language and their religion, no mean achievement for 400 years of occupation (plus several more years until the independence of Thessaloniki in 1912.)

And while the story may be only a myth, it was not by accident that both the religion and the language remained. Nor was it possible that the Greeks persisted on their own in maintaining their language and religion. They had to have had some support from somewhere. This support must have come from the church because it was the only organization that would have been able to provide it. Other religions and languages have survived difficult and compromising circumstances in the history of the world, but for much shorter time periods. But then again, as I have said before, where there is a will, there is a way. The Greeks certainly had the will and the church provided the way.

Whenever I look at Nikolaos Gyzis' painting of *The Secret School,* my romantic side wants to believe that this is what actually was, even if others disagree.

- 16 -

Gifts from Costis

"You must do the thing you think you cannot do."

Eleanor Roosevelt

In May 2011, while I was considering working until I was seventy years old, my younger son, Costis, passed away. Elias, Stefan, and I were devastated by his death. The three of us struggled for a long time to deal with the new reality of our lives and to learn to manage our loss and grief.

Costis was a good kid, a wonderful person – smart, funny, hard-working, low-key, and adventurous. He loved music, the theater, the movies, reading, travelling, running, and good but healthy food. He loved his family and his friends. He would have liked the idea of my writing this book although he would have shied away from any mention of himself. But I do mention him here so that you, the reader, can understand why you have read so little about him in recent events.

The truth of the matter is that the last ten years of my life have been heavily influenced by Costis' passing. I wonder sometimes what those ten years might have been otherwise but it is hard to imagine because emotions get in the way and I have worked so hard to maintain some semblance of balance.

The first major change in my life was that I did not work until I was seventy years old, as I had planned, but retired instead at the age of sixty-seven. I had been working since the age of sixteen, at summer jobs, with a social security number and, of course, had been paying taxes. I had thought that continuing to work would help to take my mind off Costis but nothing could take my mind off him so I retired to give myself time to grieve and mourn.

Not working or, rather, being retired, gave me time to focus on myself and on Costis and I began to heal. I joined a gym. I wrote a book about Costis for my family and friends. Costis had been a marathon runner and I ran a five K road race to honor him. I was joined in that race by friends who ran with me in Athens and in London and four who ran in Rochester, New York.

The second major change was that I became a volunteer in the library of the Athens University of Economics and Business, the same university from which both Stefan and Costis graduated, Stefan with a degree in Economics and Costis with a degree in Informatics or Computer Science. I volunteered there for eight years.

The library was a godsend for me. It gave me something

to do. It was part-time so I had time for my other projects. It brought me into the magical world of libraries and books. And most of all, it introduced me to a wonderful group of people who have since become my good friends.

All this came about as Elias, Stefan, and I were discussing what to do with the fifty computer science books on Costis' shelves. I suddenly had a thought and said that I would call the university library and ask if they accepted donations of books. The next day, the librarian that I spoke to said that they did accept donations and asked me to make a list of the books in a spreadsheet. Elias and I took the books to the library where I met the fabulous librarians who have now become such an important part of my life. And it was on that day that I expressed my desire to do volunteer work there.

The third major change happened in Leontari. I had been going to the village for several years and had spent my summer vacations there for about six years. I knew most of the people but not as well as I would know them after Costis died.

A day or so after Costis passed, I called my cousin George whose mother is my second cousin. I told him about Costis and asked him to tell his family but to be very careful with his Uncle Billy who had a heart condition. In addition to telling his family, George also told the man who was, at that time, the president of the Leontari Association of Athens. The president of the Association then told the publisher of a monthly newspaper with news from the villages. The next edition of the newspaper had an obituary about Costis.

At the end of June, George was in the village for the annual festival of the Church of the Holy Apostles in the village square. After the morning service, the women of the village had gathered for coffee in the bistro. They saw George and asked him if what they had read in the newspaper was true.

"Yes", George replied, "unfortunately it is true."

The women answered, "Tell Ioanna that we love her and that we are thinking of her".

At the beginning of July, Elias, Stefan, and I held the traditional forty-day memorial service for Costis at a church in Athens. It was not at my neighborhood church but in a small church in a lovely park near where we live. We had put an announcement in the newspaper although most people knew about the memorial service because we had made several telephone calls. George took care of informing the people in Leontari.

The service began early in the morning and the family was there by 8 am. At one point, I saw the priest who was performing the service glance up at the people in the church. He looked surprised. I turned around and saw that the church was full. One of the women who I knew from Leontari was there with her husband and son. They were leaving that evening for a holiday on one of the islands. Gina caught my eye and I mouthed the word for *thank you* in Greek, and then turned back to listen to the priest and the service.

More than two hundred people came to the service. Most were family and friends including many of Costis' friends. Some people came from Leontari and from the neighboring town, Megalopolis, driving two and a half hours to come to Athens, and another two and a half hours to get back to Leontari or Megalopolis. Those people who I had known up to then as my neighbors to say hello to, but didn't know that well, became my family with that one gesture, attending the memorial service for Costis. The outpouring of their support and compassion was overwhelming.

Three weeks later, I went to the village to spend some time there. I had not processed everything in my mind yet and I spent a lot of time by myself, crying. But every morning, at around 11 in the morning, I would go to the house of my friend Maria, sit in her yard, and cry. I would repeat the process in the afternoon. She would tell me not to cry but I couldn't stop. Nonetheless, my crying and Maria's love and concern were part of the healing process.

I was so absorbed in my grief that never once did it occur to me that maybe Maria was busy, that maybe she had something else to do. Often when I was there, some friends and neighbors would drop by but Maria never once said anything to me or asked me to leave. The entire village followed her example and circled the wagons around me. They protected me that summer and took care of me.

The Greeks who live in the countryside, especially in the Peloponnese, have a very practical way of looking at death. For them death is part of life. Despite that, they also understand the pain of losing a loved one. And in that summer of 2011, everyone in Leontari understood my pain.

There are times when I look back on that period of my life and wonder if I would have been able to heal without the support of the village and the support of the library. I have been blessed with the friendship of kind people who always welcome me with wide smiles and open arms.

❦

The Greeks have what I call a generosity of spirit. Patrick Leigh Fermor called it charity, but I prefer generosity of spirit. They are open and generous with what they have. They are hospitable. If you go to someone's house and that someone has only one tomato in the cupboard, he or she will cut the tomato in half and give you the bigger half.

The Greeks are also great storytellers as I have said in an earlier chapter. But the Greeks are in a special category – they tell wonderful stories even if they are not famous. And the villages are full of storytellers. They are the ones who bridge the past with the present and who pass on the history of their families and the places where they grew up and where they live now. My friend Anna, the same Anna who told me the story about going to the Ambelaki monastery with her family when she was a child, told me another story, a lovely story about her mother, Angeliki.

Angeliki had gone to Athens and was coming back to Leontari on the train. Angeliki was a nurse and she had been in Athens for training. It was night and the train was expected to arrive at the Leontari station in the very early morning. On the train, she struck up a conversation with a man who she did not know but who was also going to Leontari for some work that he was going to do there.

When the train reached Leontari, both Angeliki and the stranger got off. Angeliki asked the man where he would be staying. He said that he had nowhere to stay so she invited him to stay at her house with her husband and her two young daughters. It was 3 am, but they walked to her house from the train station, a twenty-minute walk in the deep and dark stillness of the night.

When they reached the house, Angeliki's husband welcomed his wife and the stranger and Angeliki prepared a bed for the stranger to spend the night. The next day, they all had a meal together and then the stranger left for his work. When Anna asked her mother why the man had stayed at their house the night before, Angeliki simply said,

"Because he was a stranger and he had nowhere to stay".

Another story I heard has the same theme of generosity and hospitality. This story is from my friend Voula. Voula grew up in the neighboring village of Tourkolekka which is high in the mountains but relatively close to Leontari. This story began in the late 40s when Voula's father, Mimis, and his sister Giannoula were walking home one late afternoon from the field where they kept their goats, an hour and a half walk from Tourkolekka.

While they were walking home that evening, the sun was setting. As they neared the village, they met a young boy, about twelve years old. The boy, whose name was Thanassis, asked Mimis and his sister if they could tell him how to get to Kalamata.

Mimis said, "Kalamata? You can't go to Kalamata now. It's getting dark and it will take two hours to get there. Come home with us and you can eat with us and spend the night and tomorrow morning we will take you to the road that leads to Kalamata."

They all went together to Tourkolekka where Mimis'

mother had prepared a simple meal. While they ate, Thanassis told his story. He was coming from Tripoli where he lived with his father and stepmother (his own mother had died). His stepmother had told him that it was time to leave the house and learn a trade to support himself. This was common practice in the countryside. Boys left home at about the age of twelve to learn a trade and to apprentice themselves to a master craftsman because other opportunities were not available to them. So Thanassis set out for Kalamata to find his aunt, his father's sister, and to find work to support himself.

Thanassis slept that night at Mimis' house and the next morning, he and Mimis and Giannoula set out. They reached the crossroads where their paths separated, and Mimis told Thanassis how to get to the village right before Kalamata where he could take a bus for the rest of the way to Kalamata.

Some thirty years later, Mimis had taken the bus from Tourkolekka to go to Megalopolis for the weekly farmers' market. After he had done his shopping, he got on the bus to go back to Tourkolekka. He was waiting for the bus to leave when another man boarded and sat in the seat next to him.

In the spirit of friendliness, Mimis turned to the man and asked him why he was going to Tourkolekka. The stranger told him that he was going there to see the man who had saved his life many years ago.

"And who is that man?" asked Mimis.

"Mimis Ziagos. Do you know him?" the man responded.

"No." Mimis said.

And the stranger proceeded to tell Mimis the story of how he had met Mimis and Mimis' sister by chance and how they didn't let him go to Kalamata but instead took him back to their house for a meal and to sleep that night.

It was then that Mimis revealed his identity and both men, Mimis and Thanassis, became emotional because they had, once again, met each other by chance. That night, they gathered around the table at Mimis' house for a meal that, this time, his wife had prepared. And, again, Thanassis told everyone his story.

He had gone to Kalamata and found his aunt. He stayed with her and went to school. When he finished school, he went back to Tripoli where he found a job at a hospital, got married, and started a family. To supplement his income, he sold lottery tickets. Thanassis and Mimis exchanged telephone numbers and spoke on the phone about once a month. When Voula's older brother went to Tripoli to do his military service, Mimis called Thanassis to tell him that he was coming to Tripoli with the family for his son's swearing in ceremony. Thanassis also went to the ceremony and then took all of Mimis' large family (ten people) to his house where his wife had prepared a feast for their guests.

The friendship continued for several years until Thanassis' son had an accident and died. A few years later, Thanassis died from sorrow and there the story ends. But the story remains indelibly etched in Voula's heart and mind.

These two stories are lovely. And there are so many more but there is neither enough time nor enough space to include them all. The stories describe a different era when everything was simpler and people were not afraid. They were realistic and practical, with a sweet innocence about them. They were also hospitable, kind, and generous. Villagers did not begin locking their doors until fifteen to twenty years ago. Instead, as these two stories illustrate, they looked after anyone who needed support or help or something to eat or a place to sleep. They still do.

For about eighty years, from 1900 to 1980, Leontari was the biggest and most important village in the area. But most of what my friends have told me about the village centers on a period of about fifteen years, from the mid-50s to the late 60s. This is the period that I will talk about here.

One friend, Ilias[xxxi], told me that Leontari had been the social and commercial center of a broader regional area for many years. His family owned a large tract of land across from the train station and he used to see all the traffic to and from the station. The trains, which were perhaps the most important means of transportation in Greece at that time, went as far as Kalamata. For Leontari, they were central to the village's economic prominence because both the customers and the merchandise arrived in Leontari by train.

My friend Poppy has told me that this fifteen-year period was when Leontari was at its peak. The population, at that time, was between seven or eight hundred. Poppy remembers that there was a vibrant market in the village.

[xxxi] Ilias is a Greek name that can be spelled in two different ways in English. My husband spelled it Elias. Many Greeks spell it Ilias.

The shops included meat stores with butchers to cut the meat to the customer's specifications. There were several stores with fruits and vegetables and a grocery store that also sold books. There were two bakeries that made fresh bread every day. Two stores sold small things like thread, needles, pencils and pens. There were also two tailors for men's clothing and several seamstresses who sewed dresses for the women, as well as two barber shops and a hairdresser, three stores which sold shoes and repaired them, and a pharmacy.

Public services included the Greek phone company, the post office, the police (or constables in the countryside), and a department for the administration of agricultural issues. There was a primary school and, in the 60s, a junior high school. Students who wanted to attend high school went to Megalopolis, Tripoli, or Athens. There was a small claims court to resolve disputes among the villagers and to keep the peace. The pharmacy, the small claims court, and the hairdresser functioned, at different times, in the house that I eventually bought and restored.

The village had two olive presses for the villagers to make their olive oil for the coming year. There was a blacksmith's shop to forge iron for the stores' needs and a cooper's shop that made barrels for wine and for cheeses. There were two traditional Greek coffee shops, for men only, and five tavernas. And there may have been other stores, as well, but they have escaped mention here. Once a week, every week, there was a farmer's market. People came from the nearby villages to buy their fruits and vegetables, to shop for their supplies, and to get their other chores done.

Leontari may have been an agricultural village then,

(and it still is), but it was not only an agricultural village. It was also the commercial center of the area and the Greek public services had a very strong presence in the village. Agriculture, commerce, and public services interacted with one another and the result had a pronounced influence on the way people dressed and behaved. They were cultivated and refined.

The women were known to be very careful about how they dressed. They wore their work clothes when they were in the fields – black dresses and a kerchief on their heads to protect themselves from the sun. But they also had fashionable clothes for church, for visiting friends, and for entertaining in their own homes. They always looked their best. In the summertime, they wore their lovely dresses when they went out and also wore gloves and carried parasols to protect themselves from the sun and the heat.

Many women didn't cook on Sundays, or at least they didn't cook every Sunday. The butchers roasted suckling pigs and the women would order some for their families and pick up their orders to take home. There are no butchers in Leontari today but villagers can go to either Megalopolis or to Potamia, a neighboring village, for that delicacy.

Life in the villages was not easy, however, or in the cities either, for that matter. Everyone worked hard, even the children. In Leontari, my friend Poppy, the oldest of three children, used to take care of her younger brother and younger sister while her mother went to work in the fields. When her mother was home, Poppy went to her father's meat store or to his coffee house. At the coffee house, she would wash the glasses and the coffee cups. She was ten years old and she had to stand on a chair to reach the faucet. But it was expected that the children would participate in the chores, at home, in the stores, and in the fields.

Poppy acquired a sophistication from working in her father's store and coffee shop. She was around people all the time – not just the people from Leontari but people from the neighboring villages as well, who would come to shop at the weekly farmers' market. The stores were exceptionally busy on farmers' market day. Poppy listened to the conversations that took place and learned to speak to everyone. Just being in the store at the age of ten was an educational experience for her.

The biggest event of the year in Leontari was the festival that took place in mid-September for three days. There are two important religious holidays in September – the first is the feast of the Holy Cross on September 14, a holiday celebrated all over Greece, and the second is the feast of Saint Gerasimos on September 15. Saint Gerasimos is a local saint who lived in the eighteenth century.

The festival would begin after the evening service on September 13 and would end on September 16. People would come from everywhere and there would be eating and dancing. Poppy told me that the tavernas in the village would compete with each other for the music. Each taverna would hire a musical group to play for them and their customers. Poppy called them orchestras although they were more likely a small group of musicians with one clarinet, one guitar, and one violin, and of course, a singer. The dancing would last all night.

The biggest attraction of all at the festival was the bazaar where merchants had come to sell their wares and their animals. What did the families buy? Parents would buy little plastic trinkets such as rings, bracelets, and necklaces for their young daughters and small toys such as tops and yo-yos for their young sons. The men bought tools to do their chores in the fields and at home. The women bought pots, pans, glasses, sheets, quilts, blankets, rag rugs, and yards of material to sew dresses.

Many families also purchased animals, mostly sheep and goats. The farmers who had brought their sheep and goats to sell were not allowed to bring the animals to the village square. They had to leave them tethered to trees near the entrance to the village. Poppy and her family lived there and her brother Christos remembers that it was almost impossible to leave the house during the festival because there were so many animals gathered there.

In the mid-60s, the population of Leontari began getting smaller. There were two major changes that affected the population of the village and the region.

The Public Power Corporation (PPC) built an electricity plant in Megalopolis in the mid-to-late 60s and the dynamic of the region began to shift. First, the public services left Leontari and went to Megalopolis. Then slowly, the commerce followed and eventually the farmers' market also left. Megalopolis began to grow and Leontari began to shrink.

Housing for the PPC employees and their families was built on a hill as we come into Leontari, on the same hill where the Saint Gerasimos Church stands. The village where Leontari had begun and where it had flourished for so long grew smaller and the population dwindled but the population in the housing on the hill grew larger quickly.

The second change was the advent of the automobile in the countryside. Slowly, the population began acquiring cars and pickup trucks. Farmers could now transport their crops and their animals by themselves and did not have to depend on the train. The train stopped being the major mode of transportation. It still operates but the Leontari station fell into disuse and is now abandoned because the train stops in Megalopolis. It's too bad because the station is such an iconic building.

I first went to Leontari in the mid-80s. I had gone to celebrate Easter with my second cousin, Makis, and his wife Georgia and their daughter Yiota. Several years before, my father's brother Peter had written to Makis about me and told him to find me and take me under his wing.

My uncle hadn't sent any pertinent details about me, such as address and telephone number, but Makis found me anyway. A few months later, Makis, his brother Billy and Billy's wife Katie, and Makis' sister Toula and her husband Panos all came to visit me. I still remember when they all came into the flat. Makis was tall and big and had a very impressive mustache. He opened his arms wide and gave me a bear hug. And in that instant, I knew that I had family of my own in Greece.

Some years passed by. Elias and I and the boys went to the

States for one year. Then Elias and I separated. I saw my cousins in Athens, sporadically. Then right before Easter in 1985, Makis called and invited me to Leontari.

I drove there with Toula's husband, Panos, and I remember that the trip was endless and tiring, almost seven hours. It was Holy Thursday and the traffic was bumper to bumper. The winding narrow mountain roads didn't help either.

But once I got there, I think that I fell in love. I was enchanted. It was then that I began to think about buying a house there and how nice it would be to be close to Makis and his family. Leontari was a pretty village and the people were friendly. Also, it was one of the few villages where the women were not confined to their houses or the fields. I made my decision to buy a house there and, one day, Makis called me to tell me to come to Leontari to see a house that was for sale. He had found that old stone house that had already been a courtroom and then a pharmacy. It had history and I was hooked.

Today, Leontari is where I go in the summer to regroup. Makis and Billy have since passed away but Toula is still there carrying on all the family traditions of generosity and hospitality. And I know everyone else now, too. They have become dear friends. Some live in the village permanently and others live in Athens but come back to the village every summer at least. I keep in touch with many of them, and look forward to seeing everyone in the summer at the bistro in the village square – in the morning, in the afternoon, in the evening, and at night.

The village square is our reference point, our meeting point. Instead of going to different houses every day, we all meet in the village square. We all love looking at the Byzantine church which has so much history of its own. It is lit up at night and the most fabulous sight of all is watching the children play and ride their bikes in front of the church.

The September 15 festival now lasts for only one day. And in that one day, or night actually, we eat, sing, and dance. And of course, everyone goes to vespers and to the liturgies for the two feast days.

Once a week, usually on Thursday evenings, the women gather at the bistro, to have something to eat and to chat, too. And, naturally, we all meet at church for the various services. August is the month of the Theotokos' Assumption and, for two weeks before August 15, there are services every evening with beautiful hymns. The whole village goes to those services.

It's a lovely way to spend the summer.

In the years that I have been in Leontari, I have observed the friendships among the Leontarians and the richness of those friendships – men and women who have been friends for sixty and seventy years and even longer. Their children and grandchildren, who go there for the summer, are also friends.

In 2020 and 2021, during the pandemic, those friendships became stronger. Some people, who live in Athens during the winter but are looking for any and every excuse to go to Leontari, decided to go to Leontari and wait out the restrictions there rather than in Athens. They joined their friends in the village who are permanent residents. They went on walks together in the fresh air every day. They went to each other's houses every day for coffee or for lunch and sometimes both on something like a rotation schedule. And everyone was included in the activities. No one was left out.

As in the days when life was simpler and people were more innocent, these friendships and bonds became stronger because everyone looked after everyone else during the pandemic just as they always had. The same hospitality, the same generosity, the same kindness.

And how fortunate I am to be a part of that community.

- 17 -

Migrations

"Humanity is fundamentally a story of migration."

Laila Lalami

In the 1950s and 1960s, the Greeks began setting down migration patterns that would change the demographics of their country, both in the countryside and in the urban centers. They were still reeling from the aftershocks of World War II and the Civil War. There was poverty and there were very few jobs. Those jobs paid very low salaries. But it was in this time period that Greece reorganized and redefined itself.

Many people left Greece to find work. They went everywhere – to North America, to Western Europe, to Australia, to Africa. Some went to South America; others went to the Middle East and some went to the Far East. The Peloponnese went mostly to the United States and Canada.

My father's village of Logganikos went mostly to Lynn. Leontari went mostly to Chicago. Northern Greece went to West Germany, and the islands went to Australia. These are very broad generalities but there definitely were patterns in the migrations.

Some people, but not all, who had left to work in various countries stayed in those countries, especially if their destinations were far from Greece such as Australia and the US. Many Greeks who went to the Western European countries found jobs, worked for several years, and then returned to Greece. Others stayed and came to Greece only to visit their families.

While a large segment of the population was leaving for parts unknown abroad, another large segment of the population was also leaving for parts unknown, but this time to Greece's urban centers. This huge domestic migration began in the 50s and continued into the 60s, tapering off by the beginning of the 70s.

When Elias and I moved to Greece at the end of 1972, the migration from the countryside to the cities, mainly to Athens, had just about finished. As a newcomer to Greece, it was impossible for me to distinguish between the Athenians and the non-Athenians. To the Athenians, however, the distinction was very visible and very obvious. The Athenians looked down their noses at their fellow Greeks who had come from the countryside. They thought of the new arrivals as country bumpkins who spoke dialects, dressed as if they were working in the fields, and talked loudly.

It wasn't easy for the families who came to Athens from

the countryside. They left behind their villages and their fields, their crops, their olive trees, and their fishing, to look for work wherever they could find it, in factories or in construction. They did, however, keep their homes in the villages to which they returned in the summers to see their families. It must have been difficult for them, adjusting to a culture which was unfamiliar to them. But as with all migrations, the generation that migrated faced the most difficulties. Their children fared much better. They went to schools in Athens, learned Athenian Greek, dropped the dialects that their parents spoke, and gained the sophistication that is acquired from living in a big city.

While the domestic migration was taking place, many of the Greeks who had gone to Western Europe, mostly to West Germany, began returning to Greece, mainly to the cities and especially to Athens. They had lived frugally while they were away and had saved their money. When they returned to Greece, they invested their savings in a small flat and to open a small business.

Added to this influx of Greeks from the countryside and from Western Europe were many Greeks in Egypt who were either expelled in 1956 and 1957 or left slowly on their own, with the migration from Egypt tapering off by 1972. Many Greeks were also expelled from Istanbul in Turkey in 1964 and 1965. All these newcomers moved into neighborhoods all over Athens, and in other cities, too, so every neighborhood was affected. The result was not only the urbanization of Greece but a sudden explosion in the population. This translated into an expansion of Athens, and elsewhere, with a corresponding construction boom.

At the same time that the migration patterns were developing, opportunities came up for many Greek students to go abroad to study. Universities in the US were opening up to students all over the world but especially to students from Europe. The American universities offered scholarships, fellowships and grants, making studies abroad more economically viable for the students, and for the Greek students, too. One of those Greek students was my ex-husband, Elias, who went to the United States in 1963 to get his PhD at a prestigious university in Washington DC.

Thirty and forty years ago, many Greek students began going to Italy or Bulgaria or Romania to study. Then they went to the UK, France, Belgium, the Netherlands and Germany. Many were going, and are still going, to the US. Greek students today are still traveling abroad to study, to expand their horizons and to get a broader educational experience.

I like this educational exchange. The students come back with new experiences and new ideas and some of them come back to teach in the universities. In the 70s, when Elias and I moved to Greece, people often resented those who had studied abroad. This is now more readily accepted because first of all, so many Greek students travel all over the world to study. And secondly, many foreign students come to Greece to have a six-month study-abroad experience as part of the EU ERASMUS program or to do a master's degree, in English.

The countryside was affected in a different way by the migrations than the cities were. As Makis, a friend from

Leontari, told me, the migration was defined as "those who left and those who stayed behind". And, as is usually the case, those who stayed behind resented those who had left.

Leontari was affected just as all the villages were in the Greek countryside. The common practice for boys to leave their villages at a young age for the big city to learn a trade was still very much prevalent. There were very few, if any, opportunities for the boys and young men in Leontari other than tilling the fields or working at the PPC so many of them went to Athens.

But it was not only the lack of other opportunities that motivated the young people to leave. They wanted to leave. They wanted to strike out on their own, maybe not at the age of twelve or thirteen, but they definitely wanted something different, something bigger. They wanted to spread their wings. And it was not only the boys who wanted to leave. It was the girls, too. The stories I have heard from some of my friends are astonishing.

My friend Poppy went to Athens when she was nineteen. She kept telling her parents that she wanted to leave Leontari. Her father's plan was to keep his daughter close by and rent a small flat for her in Megalopolis. Then Poppy would find a job to cover her expenses. But Poppy wasn't interested in Megalopolis. She wanted Athens. In order to go to Athens, however, she had to learn a skill so she did go to Megalopolis first. She became a seamstress.

When she went to Athens, she found a small flat and lived there on her own. I asked her if she had been lonely there, but she said no, that her two aunts, Lila and Soula, were there as well as her first cousins, Vassilis and Yannis. The cousins had grown up together in Leontari.

Poppy needed to work, however, to support herself. Her aunt Lila introduced her to a woman who ran a couturier dress studio where she and her staff sewed custom-made dresses for well-off women. The woman asked Poppy to come to her studio for a few days so she could see Poppy's work. She liked what she saw and hired her. Poppy stayed in Athens for four and a half years, sewing dresses for wealthy women. She learned to be independent, to work hard, and to do beautiful work.

She went back to Leontari to get married and, with her husband, moved to Megalopolis. There she opened a shop where she made and sold white goods such as curtains, sheets, and bedspreads. She was well-known in the town and many people shopped from her, not only the people from Megalopolis, but also the people from the surrounding villages who came to Megalopolis once a week for the farmers' market.

The little ten-year old girl who had had to stand on a chair to wash the glasses and coffee cups in her father's coffee shop had learned the art of made-to-order clothes and other sewing projects, the art of selling and talking to customers, and the art of supporting herself.

Ilias, the friend whose family had a tract of land across from the train station, left Leontari at the age of fourteen and went to Athens. His older brother and two older sisters were already there and he went to live with them. He was not lonely because he was with his siblings but it took some time to get used to being away from the village. He missed Leontari and not only because his parents were still there.

He went to school in Athens and finished high school there. He studied for four years at a vocational school where he learned everything about construction and construction projects. At the same time, however, he was working. The siblings were supporting themselves and everyone had to pitch in. Athens was in the middle of an intense building boom and Ilias found work at various construction sites. I asked him what he learned from working and studying. He replied,

"Everything I needed to know in order to start my own business in the construction industry."

Eventually, the siblings grew up. The two sisters married. One moved with her husband to the US and the other stayed with her husband in Athens. Ilias and his older brother Dimitris stayed in Athens. Once they had finished their studies, they started their own contracting company, specializing in construction projects. Their company became very successful. They married, started families and planted roots in Athens. But they go back to Leontari as often as they can.

Another friend, Makis, who had been at Costis' memorial service with his wife Gina, also followed the classic common practice for boys at the time and went to Athens when he was twelve years old to study and to work. Makis' mother, his older brother, and older sister were already in Athens. His grandmother, who had brought him up, and his father were in Leontari. His first year in Athens was difficult. He missed the village and he missed his grandmother. He was terribly homesick but despite being homesick, he didn't want to leave Athens and go back to Leontari.

I asked Makis if he had worked at all in Leontari before he went to Athens. He told me that he had always liked the idea of being in business so when the annual festival took place at the Boura Monastery, he would go to his Uncle Nikos' general store and get matches, candies, and other small items which he would then sell at the festival. What he really wanted to do was to set up a stand at the annual Leontari festival and sell his wares but he knew that he was still too young to do that. And by the way, whatever he hadn't sold, he would take back to his uncle's store.

He also cut wood for the winter and took it back to the village on the family's donkey. He collected the manure from the family's animals and took it to the fields for fertilizer. He would take the goat to graze and would help gather the olives every November. For a young boy, he was very busy and very hard-working.

Before Makis left Leontari to go to Athens, he went to Megalopolis to sit exams for high school. When he passed the exams, he went to Athens and did his schooling there. I asked him why he didn't stay in Megalopolis and he said that he wanted something bigger.

In Athens, he went to high school and worked at various odd jobs. When he finished high school, he sat exams for university and entered the school that today is known as the Athens University of Economics and Business. He studied there for three years and, at the same time, he got a job working in the office of a construction company. After three years at the university, he left. Makis had found what he wanted to do. He and a friend started their own construction company. They were both only twenty-one years old.

Makis is retired now. He maintains the roots that he created in Athens but, like all Leontarians who left the village, he hasn't really left. He goes back every chance he gets.

The young boys who went to Athens to study and work, and there were many of them, got together as they grew up and formed the Leontari Association of Athens. The purpose of the Association was to meet on a regular basis and talk about ways to contribute to the well-being of the village. They raised money to build a school and to build a guest-house where people, like myself, who didn't have their own house, could stay. Mostly the Association was a way for everyone who was from Leontari but lived in Athens to see each other and to stay in touch.

My cousin Billy took me to my first meeting right after I bought my beautiful stone house and became an official property owner in Leontari. It was the annual general meeting where the incumbent officers gave their summary for the year that had gone by, and new officers were elected and dues were collected. Billy introduced me to everyone who had come for the meeting and then proposed me as a candidate for the Board of Directors. Much to my surprise, and with many thanks to Billy, I was elected!

It has been my privilege to serve on the Association's Board. Makis has been on the board as have Ilias and his brother, Dimitris. Ilias has also been president of the Association. For me, being in the Association was the perfect opportunity to get to know everyone and to understand the needs of the village. I have also been fortunate to make wonderful friends because of my participation in the Association, both in Athens and in the village.

When I came to Greece with Elias to live here, I thought, for a while, that Greece had no real industry except for the agricultural industry. At least I wasn't aware of any heavy industry. For some reason, that bothered me. Why wouldn't the Greeks want heavy industry such as the automobile industries that Germany, France, Italy, and the UK had? Or any other industry for that matter?

It took me some time to realize and to understand that, actually, there was heavy industry in Greece including the oil refineries and the Public Power Corporation. When I got my first job in 1981 in a Greek multinational that was in the oil refining business, the deciding factor that convinced me to take the job was that this particular company had been listed in the International 500 in one of the US business magazines, either that year or the year before.

Greece had a strong shipping industry and it also had Olympic Airways. Now it has Aegean Airways. In the 60s and 70s, Greece manufactured kitchen appliances but the Greeks disdained the Greek products in favor of the kitchen appliances manufactured in Western Europe. We laugh about that now. Perhaps that was part of the reason that there was not a strong manufacturing base in Greece. Greeks may have thought that products manufactured elsewhere were superior to any that could be produced in Greece. Live and learn.

The fact remained, however, that Greece was more agricultural than industrial. Growing up in the States, I had always thought that industrialization was synonymous with the modern world. Instead, Greece had an agricultural economy and a large service economy in the form of a very swollen and mostly inefficient public sector. The tourist industry had not yet become the behemoth that it is now. It puzzled me. Until now.

The years passed, Greece became a European Union member, and the Greeks started traveling and working abroad. They moved to Athenian suburbs and acquired more than one car per family. Generally, they became more sophisticated, as the world defines sophistication in economic terms. But under the surface, Greece was percolating.

Many students were getting at least one university degree outside of Greece. They were learning Greek and English, and at least one other foreign language, maybe two. Sometimes, students stayed in the countries where they had studied and then returned to Greece with not only a degree and work experience, but with life experience as well. In other words, they had learned to live on their own, without their parents' support.

A Human Resources manager at a major foreign multinational corporation in Greece once told me that this last characteristic was critical when her company was hiring. If the company had two candidates with identical or similar education, work experience, and competencies, the tie-breaker was always the life experience. If one candidate had gone abroad to get a master's degree and had returned to Greece right away but the other candidate had found a job and supported himself or herself for a few years, then the company hired the candidate with the life experience because they considered that candidate more mature.

Others who were working in foreign multinationals in Greece were seconded by their companies to offices in the States, in Europe, or in the Middle or Far East. They took their families with them, giving their children the opportunity to go to foreign schools, to learn a foreign language, and to learn another culture. Their spouses often had opportunities to work, as well.

There has always been a fluidity of movement in Greece and there still is. From ancient times, the Greeks were moving around the world for commerce, for political reasons, and for military campaigns, with armies.

With that fluidity of movement, the pieces of the puzzle started to fit into place. First it was the young boys who left the familiarity of their villages to study and find opportunities in Athens and to spread their wings. It was their determination to improve their lives, to study, and to find work and to be successful that set the wheels of progress in motion. It took a while but it worked. The young boys who had come to Athens to improve their own lives brought up their children to become doctors and lawyers, scientists and computer programmers, businessmen and businesswomen, engineers, pharmacists, bankers, and teachers and professors.

The younger generation studied and worked hard, just as their parents had, and they traveled. And the economy began to grow and diversify.

Agriculture today still plays a huge role in Greece's economy but with a difference. Today, agricultural products from Greece are recognized everywhere for their outstanding quality and are exported all over the world. Food exports include olive oil, tomatoes and other vegetables, citrus fruits, feta and other cheeses, honey, yogurt, and the Greek wines which have begun to attract an international following.

The biggest industries in Greece are now the tourist industry (as in "Everyone wants to go to Greece."), agriculture, and shipping. Tobacco, mining, metals and oil refining, and transport are also major contributors to the Greek economy, with technology, finance, healthcare, and science coming close behind. The market has become sophisticated, diverse, and viable. And it happened almost without anyone noticing because people were moving around all over the map, learning from each other and exchanging ideas. It happened because it was time for it to happen.

There are similarities between much of what I have written about Greece and what other countries have experienced. The US went through the Great Depression. Europe was ravaged by two world wars. The Far East suffered through countless convulsive wars and upheavals. Wars changed the political landscape in the Middle East and most recently have been instrumental in creating another migration story. Africa suffered extreme poverty and famine for many years. And yet, most countries on those continents have managed to survive and prosper.

The Greek story has its own personality, however. The practice of sending off young boys to learn a trade and to more or less fend for themselves was a rite of passage. At the same time, that thirst for seeing and experiencing something new seems to be a universal need. The young men and women in Greece who had the opportunity to explore the world for themselves grew up to be resilient adults who take almost everything in their stride.

The exchange of ideas across the globe is always a two-way interaction. It's not only one country that benefits. All countries benefit, if they want to, of course. Several months ago, there was a brief news item on one of the Saturday morning shows that I watch once in a while. The item was about a man living in Japan. If I remember correctly, his father was Greek and his mother was Japanese. This man had been to Greece several times to visit his father's family and, on one of his trips, he fell in love with the bouzouki and learned to play.

In the news item that day, he was sitting in a coffee house in Tokyo with his Japanese friends. He was playing the bouzouki and singing old rebetika songs. And the best part? His Japanese friends were singing along with him – in Greek!

- 18 -

Gazing at my Feet

"I am not an Athenian or a Greek, but a citizen of the world"

Diogenes

The summer of 2014 was the summer that all Greeks were gazing at their feet. Were we descended from the ancient Greeks, or from the Romans, or from the Egyptians? No one considered any other options.

A burial site at Amphipolis in Greece had been discovered and it was one of the most magnificent archaeological sites to be uncovered. The BBC announced that "archaeologists in northern Greece have found a skeleton inside a tomb from the time of Alexander the Great, during a dig that has enthralled the public".

And indeed, the public was enthralled. The site at Amphipolis is a burial site and is one of the largest sites ever discovered in Greece. There was, and continues to be, speculation that the burial site belongs to a member of the family of Alexander the Great or to one of his military commanders.

In addition to a wooden coffin, some scattered bone fragments and scattered nails, the tomb also contains two sphinxes, two Caryatids, and a stunningly gorgeous "large mosaic showing a man with a laurel wreath driving a chariot drawn by horses and led by the god Hermes".

Despite the breathtaking beauty of the other finds, it was the Caryatids that caught every Greek's attention, the East Caryatid and the West Caryatid. They are two exceptionally beautiful carved maidens that are more than nine feet tall, including the base wall. When archaeologists discovered the tomb, they had to clear a barrier wall in front of the chamber where they eventually found the Caryatids. The archaeologists speculated that the wall had been built to protect the tomb from anyone who tried to enter it. As they dismantled the wall, the Caryatids were revealed. The archaeologists have described that moment of seeing them as wonderful. That is most likely an understatement.

What made the Caryatids so special and interesting to the Greeks was their feet. In the photographs of the Caryatids, we all saw that the second toe on their feet was slightly but definitely longer than their big toes. What did this mean for us? Clearly, the Caryatids were a representation of the classical ancient Greek woman[xxxii]. Being descended from the ancient Greeks, from the

---

[xxxii] The Caryatids at Amphipolis show the characteristic Greek Foot (the second toe is slightly longer than the big toe). As the excavations at Amphipolis are ongoing, I could not show the picture of the Caryatids.

BASED ON THIS
WHAT ARE YOUR ROOTS?

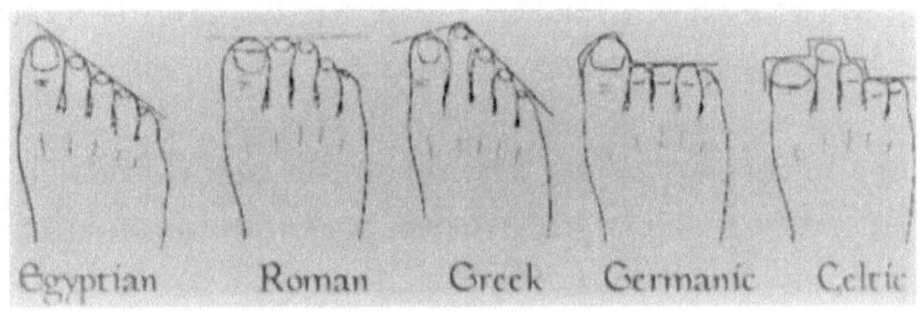

Romans, or from the Egyptians was most likely, given not only the proximity of the regions and countries to each other but also because there was so much interaction of the Greeks with the Romans and Egyptians in ancient times. Less likely was a Germanic or Celtic ancestor.

Judging from the picture above, I determined that my ancestry could possibly be mixed, maybe a combination of Greek and Roman. I want to believe that my ancestry is ancient Greek only but the toes don't lie. I have to straighten the crooked second toe on my right foot for it to be longer than the big toe. And when I do straighten it, it is longer, but only somewhat perceptibly. Most likely, I am a product of globalization, before the word became so popular. Who knows?

The idea of being descended from the ancient Greeks appeals to me enormously. It makes me feel as though my bloodline can be traced back through hundreds of centuries. It helps me to understand why I feel so peaceful when I am on the walkway around the Acropolis and the other ancient sites and why I feel that I am in a small part of ancient Greece. It also makes my Greek identity stronger because there is a straight line to the past. At least that is how I perceive it. And my own sense of identity is enhanced.

And yet, I still have a split root, and the Greek identity is only one part of the split root. The other split part is my American identity – also strong and sometimes dominant. But the identity that bridges the two parts of the split root and melds them together is my Greek-American identity. We, my brothers, my cousins, and I, were fortunate to have grown up in close-knit immigrant families that had one foot in the old country and one foot in the new. Although we didn't realize it at the time, it broadened our horizons. We learned two languages although some of us didn't learn Greek quite as well as we should have but it was good enough to understand and be understood. We learned to look at everything in our lives and everything around us, globally. We learned to keep the traditions in every aspect of our Greek-American lives, handing these traditions down to our own children.

I have lived in Greece for fifty years. It took a very long time for me to overcome the nostalgia I had for the first twenty-seven years of my life and for what would most likely never be again. It took perhaps ten years for me to stop complaining about Greece and to stop comparing Greece and the United States. It took me that long to understand that one cannot compare two countries with each other. I found that what I needed to do was to find the beauty in my surroundings and to find characteristics in the Greek people that I liked and found attractive.

Neither was easy. Maybe finding the beauty in my surroundings was easier. At the beginning, as I have said earlier in the book, every day I would look for one thing that made me smile. After a while, I started looking for two things that were beautiful or made me smile, every day. After that, I got used to my surroundings and everything seemed familiar to me. Which I guess was the point.

Finding characteristics that I liked in the Greek people was harder. They were loud and they talked too fast. They were more than a little pushy and didn't know how to form a queue. They still don't know how to form a queue although they are a little better at it now than they were then. Their favorite, and sometimes only, topic of conversation was politics. And within the framework of politics, their second favorite topic was how much they disliked America and the Americans. Once any Greek realized that I was American, I became the whipping post for their anti-Americanism. More than once, I wanted to ask, "So just exactly what do you expect me to do about that?"

But slowly, I got used to that, too, and I stopped reacting. That's when I started to see the positive all around me. And that's when I stopped complaining and comparing.

What do I love about Greece? I love the scenery, the mountains and the sea together, and the rocks, too. I love the summers – they are long and hot. I love Greece's magnificent history and its heroes and heroines. I love the ancient monuments. I love the Greek religion and the Greek language and the Greek music. I love the unbelievably beautiful body of art that the Byzantine Greeks left – the icons and the art of iconography.

I love the villages and the cleanliness of those villages. Three years ago, I went to my father-in-law's village and was invited into a house. I was stunned by how clean the outside stairs leading to the house were. I could have eaten off them.

I love the old movies – I learned how to speak Greek while watching them. I love the food. I love the islands. I love Greece's public transportation system. The trains could use a little upgrading but at least they exist. I love the public health system which is available to most of the population. I love the public school system, especially the public universities which are affordable. Because they are affordable, a majority of Greeks have a college education.

And the Greeks? I love their sense of humor – I have laughed out loud, spontaneously, numerous times, because they are so funny. I love the way that everyone knows and talks to everyone else. When I walk down my street to shop, I do exactly the same thing. It takes forever to do my errands. I love the Greeks' generosity and their hospitality. I love their friendliness and their kindness.

Most of all, I love the Greeks' sense of survival and their dignity, their persistence and their unity when they face adversity. Given how much they have lived through over thousands of years - the wars and the multiple invasions, the IMF and the financial crises - it's remarkable that they survived. The Greeks never gave up and even now, they don't give up. Ever. They keep going, confident that they will get through whatever it is that they are going through.

The Greeks lived through almost four hundred years of Ottoman Empire rule and occupation, yet they kept both their religion and their language alive. They lived through the brutal Nazi occupation for three and a half years but resisted quietly, and sometimes not so quietly.

Then came the financial crisis in the early 2000s. Everyone was frightened, terrified even, that Greece would be declared bankrupt and then be thrown out of the EU. Many people had lost their jobs and most Greeks had very little money, if any at all, to spend on frills. Yet every day everyone would go to their favorite cafes, order one cup of coffee for which they paid one Euro, and sit for hours and hours nursing that one cup of coffee. The Europeans were pulling their hair out, strand by strand. It was almost worth the pain just to see them react that way. Of course, the rest of the world took that as a green light to call the Greeks lazy tax-evaders. However, the Greeks not only survived the crisis and the clumsy, mean-spirited attempts at humiliation, they recovered, with their dignity intact.

My favorite Greek heroine is Lela Karagianni. I love the stories of all the heroes and heroines, ancient and modern, for what they achieved, for what they represent, and for the history they made. But Lela Karagianni is my favorite. She was smart and she was determined and she had character. Her role in World War II required her to take risks that many of us today would consider unthinkable and unimaginable. But she loved her country and she took those risks anyway. She had unstoppable courage and bravery.

Lela Karagianni lived in my neighborhood. The street

where she lived was renamed to Lela Karagianni Street several years ago right around the time that I moved into my new flat.

This neighborhood was also home to one of the heroes of Greece's War for Independence in 1821, Konstantinos Kanaris, one of the team of fierce revolutionaries who blew up the Turkish fleet in Spetses. He later became an admiral and a politician. Kanaris also owned a large tract of property in Kypseli which was countryside two hundred years ago. He built a small church on his property and, for several years, before I moved to my current flat, I lived across the street from that church.

Konstantinos Kanaris and Lela Karagianni were two of the many heroes and heroines who made it possible for Greeks to be free and to live free, to be proud and to hold their heads up high. It makes me happy to know that I walk on the same ground on which they walked. I wonder sometimes if just a tiny bit of the bravery and courage that distinguished them might have rubbed off on me.

In 2020, many restrictions were imposed on the Greeks because of the pandemic. The restrictions kept changing but their purpose was to contain contagion. I'm not complaining because I think that Greece has done an admirable job of dealing with this crisis.

With the newest set of restrictions in 2021, my son Stefan found some time to walk around Athens when most people preferred to go down to the sea to walk. Twice now, he has gone for walks on Philopappos Hill.

Philopappos Hill could be considered prime real estate in Athens. It's near the Acropolis. The National Observatory of Athens, with its magnificent library, is there. Pnyka Hill is there. This is where the parliament of ancient Athens functioned, which means that this is where the Athenian men congregated and voted. The cave where Socrates was jailed is there. The cave was carved into the rock on the hill and, during World War II, the Greek authorities used it to store the antiquities from the National Archaeological Museum to protect them from the Nazis.

Philopappou, as the Greeks call it, is not developed but instead is a small but beautiful park, or what I might call a nature reserve, with many species of wildflowers and trees and trails that allow hikers to explore the hill. A lovely church on the hill, Saint Demetrios Loumbardiares, was, for a few years, the church of choice for many couples to marry and to baptize their children.

But the main feature of Philopappou is the amazing views it offers of Athens, the Acropolis and the Parthenon. It is right across the street from the Acropolis. I have seen the Acropolis only once from Philopappou and, truly, the view is beautiful.

Stefan had never been to Philopappou before and now he has walked the trails twice. Both times that he has gone there, he has described, with unbridled enthusiasm, what he has seen. What impresses him most is how the Parthenon changes from different points on the hill.

I enjoy Stefan's enthusiasm. He is now forty-eight years old. He was born in Athens, he went to school and university in Athens, and he works and lives in Athens. And yet he is neither jaded nor indifferent to the symbol of what man can achieve. He still appreciates the beauty and the significance of the Acropolis and the Parthenon which are beacons not only for Greece but for the entire world.

So, I ask myself if it really matters what the toes say. Perhaps not. Being Greek is a feeling, a feeling that is not measured by how long our toes are. It's a feeling of deep appreciation and love for the country, for the beauty of the landscape, for the kindness and generosity of the people. I still like to imagine, however, that if the second toe on my right foot were just one tiny millimeter longer, I could very well be descended from the ancient Greeks. But I'm fine, even I'm not a direct descendant.

Epilogue

*"It takes a lifetime to discover Greece, but it only takes an
instant to fall in love with her."*

Henry Miller

About twenty years ago, I read an article in one of the
women's magazines that we women were all reading. I think
it was *Cosmopolitan* but I'm not sure. Apparently, according
to that article, exciting things happen to women who polish
their toenails red. I read the article with some puzzlement
and then said to one of my friends,

"Katia, I've been polishing my toenails red for as
long as I can remember and I'm still waiting for something
exciting to happen to me."

Katia looked at me and said, "What are you talking
about? Your whole life has been exciting."

I have never given much thought as to whether my life is exciting or not and I'm not quite sure what exciting means or entails. My life has been full of the mundane and the routine just like everyone else's lives. But I have lived through exciting times and exciting events. I have seen things that I may never have seen or thought much about if I hadn't moved to Greece and if I hadn't lived here for so long. Life may not have been exciting according to the conventional definition of exciting but it has never been boring. And it still isn't.

The book is filled with my observations as well as with my feelings and my opinions. I wanted the reader to see Greece through my eyes. Because Greece is an intrinsically beautiful country, many people, including myself when I first moved here, think of it in travel-catalogue terms. But Greece is not a travel catalogue, or it is not only a travel-catalogue. Greece is multi-dimensional and cannot be characterized with one word only or one theme only. There is so much to appreciate, admire, and love in Greece.

In discussions with friends and acquaintances that I have had in the past, I know that a lot of people will not agree with some of what I have written. However, I would not have been true to myself if I had not written what I myself think. Last year, when I was in Leontari, I was discussing the book with my friends Makis and Gina. Makis said that I not only should write what I see but also what I think about what I see. He was right, and this is what I have done.

A couple of years ago, I met a young woman at a conference in Athens. We struck up a conversation and she asked me how it happened that I came to Greece to live. I looked at her and smiled. She reminded me of myself when I was a young and impressionable twenty-something, always looking at the world through rose-colored glasses. I answered her question and told her the reason but I gave her the fairy-tale version. It was true, just a little embellished.

I told her that a Greek student had gone to the States to get his PhD and, completely by chance, our paths crossed when he came to Boston to do his post-doctoral research. He saw me, he was smitten immediately and made a plan to steal me away from my family and friends and take me to Greece with him.

Her reaction was predictable although I was surprised by the vehemence of her response,

"That is so romantic!"

And it probably was romantic. And it was brave. And it was foolhardy. My brother Tom has always contended that there is a fine line between bravery and foolhardiness. Perhaps it was a combination of all three. It was brave because I had to start at the beginning to build a life in Greece although I didn't know at the time that I would have to do that. It was foolhardy because I didn't think about moving or not moving here. I just did it because if I had thought about it, I probably would have backed out. As for being romantic, it was romantic just because it was.

And here I am fifty years later. I live in a geopolitical region of the world that, at the best of times, is tense. But it has taught us all to prepare for the worst and not to expect very much in terms of support from anyone. It's a region where, despite the intense hatreds, entrenched prejudices, and bitter rivalries, there are also unlikely alliances. There are wars and there are invasions but, when trouble starts, usually the powers that be know when to stop before things get out of hand. Usually. Not always.

I have no idea what my life would have been like if I had stayed in the States. Maybe Elias would have rebelled against the idea of not returning to Greece and we would not have married. And then we would not have had the two fabulous sons that we had. Then again, that is only speculation and I truly have no idea what my life would have been like if I had stayed in the States. And then again, maybe this was simply my fate.

I built my life in Greece. I gave birth to my children and brought them up here. I have family and a large circle of wonderful friends. I have had several interesting jobs and a successful career. I traveled around the world. And slowly but surely, contrary to Henry Miller's statement, I fell in love with a country that accepted me just as I am, a country where I feel safe and secure.

Over the period of fifty years, Greece and I made the journey to change and realign together. I changed and so did Greece. And we met somewhere in the middle.

When I first arrived, and even as recently as twenty years ago, if I let a word of English slip into my sentences because I didn't know the Greek word, someone would inevitably turn to me and say that this is Greece and in Greece we speak Greek. Today, things are different. Today if I realize that someone is speaking to me in English, probably because they have picked up on my accent, I might gently say that I speak and understand Greek so it's okay if they talk to me in Greek. Today that person will tell me,

"Oh, I'm sorry. This is such a great opportunity for me to practice my English. But I'll speak Greek if you prefer."

Times have indeed changed.

I learned how to cook real Greek food as my mother urged me to do when Elias and I left the States to move to Greece. I raised two children who became cosmopolitan in an era when that was not common. The boys learned to speak two languages fluently and traveled every year to the US, on their own, to spend time with my family. I live in an exciting and vibrant European capital where there is always something to do. And I am a resident and citizen of the European Union. It might not always be easy living in the EU but I would rather be part of it than not.

Do I miss the US? Yes, of course I do. I miss my family and the way they still get together as much as they can just like we did when we, the cousins, were growing up. But I don't miss it the same way that I used to miss it. I used to crave the US. I couldn't wait to go there and see my parents and brothers and my friends and relatives. I couldn't wait to go shopping.

But Greece is home now. I will always be grateful to the US for everything that I learned and experienced over the twenty-seven years that I lived there. I taught Stefan and Costis to love and respect the US, too, and I am glad that I did. We are enormously fortunate that we have two homelands. I truly believe that because of this, not only have our lives been enriched but we have also shown the world that this can be done. Most of all, I enjoy each and every day of my life in Greece and I can't ask for more than that.

Acknowledgements

Writing a book "takes a village", to bring back a phrase from the 60s and 70s. There are so many people who supported my efforts and to whom I am grateful. I hope that I remember everyone, even if you are grouped together.

First of all, thank you to G. C. Eleftheroudakis and to the team for their graciousness, their professionalism, and their savvy ideas for doing what needed to be done to get the book to the printer. The team's attention to every detail is impressive.

Thank you to my editor, Jenny Saranti, who walked me through each stage of the book. Jenny pulled the book together with her insightful comments and her strict editing. She encouraged me to continue writing even when I was ready to give up. She would always tell me that "this is a story that needs to be told". She still tells me that.

To Nikos Gazetas, a huge thank you for converting the manuscript of the book to an electronic book. Nikos and I discussed the various issues and obstacles that come with an e book and we resolved them all. An added benefit of working with Nikos is that I always felt calm after my discussions with him. Thank you, Niko.

To Tasso Nikitakis, thank you for navigating me through the intricacies of on-line self-publishing and for removing all the stress out of the process. Once we started working together, I would tell Tasso what I wanted to do and then Tasso would get everything done. Tasso also introduced me to the millennials' world of technology and communication. Completely new to me but, thank you, Tasso.

My thanks also go to Christina Delioglou, the Director of the Library at the Athens University of Economics and Business. My last day at the library was the day before the first Covid lockdown in Greece began in March 2020. On that day, I told Christina about my book and that I needed an editor to guide me through the writing process. I asked her if she could recommend someone. After giving my request some thought, she referred me to Jenny.

Thank you to my lawyer, Dorina Koraka, for her patience, her knowledge, her advice, and her consistently calm demeanor and disposition. I can bounce ideas off her at any time, and the advice she comes back with is always rock solid.

To all my friends and family who are part of the book, thank you. Your stories made the book real.

To my friends in the Library of the Athens University of Economics and Business - it took only a few weeks of volunteering at the library for me to start smiling again. Thank you for welcoming me into your group.

To Leontari and the Leontarians, thank you. The village is my safe haven because of you. We have laughed together and we have cried together. You taught me so much about the village and about Greece with your stories. You taught me about the church. You taught me how to recycle and to repurpose everything. Most of all, you were there when I really needed you. Your friendship is precious.

To Elias' family, thank you for making me part of your tribe.

To all my cousins, first, second, and otherwise, thank you for being part of the story. It would not have been the same without you or without all the memories and laughter that we have shared forever.

I am grateful to my brothers Tom, Greg, and Paul, and my sisters-in-law Debbie and Joan, for the love, support, and encouragement they have given me. My brothers know the whole backstory so they can confirm that what I have written is what actually was. Tom probably remembers more than Greg and Paul because Tom is just two years younger than me. Thank you all for being part of that story. And a special thank you to Greg who pushed me to keep going when he told me to "finish the damn book so we can read it."

Thank you to my son Stefan who listened to me patiently whenever I told him that "I'm writing". He was, and is, my biggest supporter. He was also the inspiration for the ending of the book. I had wanted to end the book with a reference to the Parthenon and the Acropolis and Stefan gave me the idea when he told me about his walks on Philopappos Hill.

Finally, and posthumously, thank you to my parents, Charlie and Betty Demakis, and to my son Costis. For everything.

ABOUT JOAN DEMAKIS

In early 2020, a new pandemic reared its ugly head and took the world by surprise. Everyone's lives were upended. Many of us, myself included, used the lockdown time to look at what we had accomplished pre-pandemic and what we could and would do going forward. Several of us wanted to tell our stories.

Pre-pandemic, I had done everything I was supposed to do. I got married, settled down (in Greece), and had two children. I worked for three multinational companies in Greece and volunteered at the 2004 Athens Olympic Games and at an international library and librarian conference in 2019. I retired in 2012 and then volunteered at the Library of the Athens University of Business and Economics for eight years.
When I moved to Greece with my Greek husband, I saw so much history unfold in front of my eyes. I thought that I had a story to tell and, slowly, starting in 2016, I began to write it. The pandemic gave me the chance to finish my story and I completed *Gazing at My Feet* while we were in lockdown.

The telephone was my link to the outside world as it was for so many people. Reading was my comfort zone, a place to retreat to. Now, however, that the post-pandemic era is cautiously emerging, I am enjoying my friends and my family, going to the gym, and going out for coffee, dinner, the theater, and the movies. And like everyone else, I have become more appreciative of all the good things around me.

I spend some of my happiest days in my village in the Peloponnese with friends and family. We have coffee together in the morning, have lunch together, and go out in the evenings and eat, talk and laugh together until midnight. Life doesn't get any better than this.

•